Becoming the Husband
Your Wife Thought
She Married

Becoming the Husband Your Wife Thought She Married

It's Your Life, Too, Man

JAMES A. SCHALLER, M.D.

BLUE DOLPHIN PUBLISHING

Published by Blue Dolphin Publishing, Inc.
P.O. Box 8, Nevada City, CA 95959
Orders: 1-800-643-0765
Web: http://www.bluedolphinpublishing.com

ISBN: 1-57733-059-5

Library of Congress Cataloging-in-Publication Data

Schaller, James A.
    Becoming the husband your wife thought she married : it's
your life, too, man / James A. Schaller
        p.   cm.
    Includes bibliographical references and index.
    ISBN 1-57733-059-5
    1. Marriage. 2. Husbands—Psychology. 3. Husbands—Conduct
of life. 4. Wives—Psychology. I. Title.

HQ734.S3768 2000
306.81—dc21   99-087696

Printed in the United States of America

10   9   8   7   6   5   4   3   2

Dedication

To each "lost" husband whose relationship is not what he expected or wanted, and who desperately wants something better, and

To Marianne, my beloved wife, who hasn't given up hope, and therefore still works with me daily on the most important project in our lives.

For those men who fail to see the problem, the possibilities, the grievances, and the lost opportunities, **I pray.**

For those men who got it right from the beginning or eventually, and whose wives did the same, **I thank God.**

Contents

Preface

> "The goal is not to be the person your spouse hoped you would be.
> That sort of servitude is a common, and dangerous, solution
> to marital discord. The task is not accommodating so much as
> appreciating what . . . [is] true of your spouse. . . .
> You don't have to compromise your values."
> —Peter Kramer

This book's *title* was chosen before one word of text was written. My sampling of family, friends, and patients showed a definite interest in any book advising men how to become better husbands. After all, isn't this what women are about from day one of every marriage? While virtually every wife has specific ideas for marital improvement, the husband in each case probably hasn't given that subject much thought, proving once again that men and women are different in more ways than anatomically.

My previous book, *It's _Your_ Life: A Gynecologist Challenges You to Take Control*, was written out of my reverence and deep regard for women. A fascination for the opposite sex, which borders on awe, has always been part of my psyche. Thus, it was inevitable that women's relationships would be a major concern in my writings.

Recognition, early in my career, that most wives were unhappy, or at least very disappointed, in their marriage, prompted my ongoing research of the best ideas for making marriage more fulfilling.[1] By adding my own observations as a doctor, husband, and father, to the literary research for *It's Your Life*, I reached the conclusion, put forth in that book, that American husbands needed to be **reconnected to their buried feelings** so that their wives might relate to the person they really were, not the insensitive, macho guy they were pretending to be. Thus, I had the hope, that now seems wistful (and a sign that I suffer serious delusions, periodically), that husbands, too, would read my book. Only a few gave it a try, perhaps because I am a gynecologist and listed many chapters on female physiology. Whatever the reasons, many a wife whose husband rejected the suggestion that he "at least read the few chapters on **creating love**," ended up proclaiming her spouse an "unspeakable" something or other, who wouldn't read *anything* that she suggested, especially if she implied that the book might "help him!"

The central thesis of this book is that **men desperately need help in recovering, as husbands and fathers, the warm and wonderful qualities that our culture does not allow** *real boys/men* **to retain, develop or demonstrate.** Men must be convinced that it takes more courage to hold onto, or to seek, the ideal that this book presents for all husbands and fathers, than is being required to forsake or to abandon it.

The **challenge to men** issued in these pages is again prompted by my gynecological experiences. Nonetheless, the gauntlet I place before husbands demands more energy, perseverance, honesty and courage than any other manly quest I know, including a tour of duty in the Marines or Navy Seals. Indeed, no achievement in life (none, not any) can be more praiseworthy than being a great spouse. The most common request written by my patients on the questionnaires I asked them to complete for me (anonymously) during the past year was that their husbands "be nice to them." Obviously, what this country needs is not a **few good men but millions of nice ones.**

Success in marriage requires that the boundaries around each of the three entities involved—the **he, she, and us**—be preserved. Thus, a separate **Part** of this book will be devoted to precisely what that statement means in the practical terms of a couple's day-to-day living.

Part One outlines the **Boy Code**, that is, the rigid blueprint for **masculinizing** boys so that they will grow up to be **real men.**[2]

Because the highest value in the Boy Code is success, not a relationship with one person, very few husbands give their highest priority
to becoming a great mate. Even though sharing feelings is vitally
important to women, and virtually always a "safe" approach to
women for men, the Boy Code prohibits a boy/man from exhibiting
emotions or even admitting to himself that he has feelings. As a
result, it is virtually impossible for him to share any feelings, especially those feelings variously described as **soft, weak, or feminine**—
sadness, weakness, fear, anxiety, doubt, and pain.

   Part Two concerns the "she" who eventually signs the marriage
contract. Even more than adolescence or the birth of a first child,
marriage has the power to change forever a woman's goals and
priorities, feelings, emotions, reaction patterns, and behavior.[3] Subsequent to her decision to marry, a typical "wife" soon senses that
her performance is being judged according to norms or guidelines
that are, in fact, cultural imperatives extant and operating for the
past three-hundred years. Thus, the soon-to-be, or the new wife—
like a gymnast or figure skater beginning her routine who is keenly
aware that the judges evaluations are eminently important—quickly
discovers that she must prove herself to be a "good wife," or suffer
society's disapproval.

   Despite their vastly **different cultures**, or sets of priorities, men
and women enter marriage sharing the **same foolish expectation**—
that their mutual (and generally unmerited) acceptance and affirmation of each other will last forever. The fact that, in most marriages,
the **stroking**, that is, the pats on the back or the mutual admiration
doesn't continue, provides the starting point of **Part Three's** consideration of the **couple**. The efforts to get the good strokes back
provoke the best and worst of both participants in a marriage. Of
course, it is the elegant provisions of the marriage **bond,** that is, the
life-time contract, that guarantees each husband and wife a good
sparring partner. No other friend or associate would stay around
long enough to tolerate the level of abuse that spouses routinely
heap on each other. Tragically, the truth is often proven in marriage
that no one can hurt a person as efficiently and as deeply as the
person who holds the key to that person's heart—the one who has
seen what is hidden in the deepest recesses.

The mutual need to love and be loved by someone of the opposite sex, plus the sometimes desperate desire to be privately and publicly affirmed, has led one-hundred-eleven million present-day American men and women to live together under a marriage contract, even though the statistical odds for success are stacked against them.[4] The partners exude confidence that **their** marriage will be different. Each bride and groom is convinced that he/she is getting a **good deal**, that is, that the other's good qualities are worth affirming. The mutual affirmations remove his and her concerns about being seen as inadequate. But, when the honeymoon phase of marriage, eventually, is only memories, the search for another way to again feel good about themselves begins in earnest.

Unfortunately, most couples never come to realize that a **great marriage** or even consistently **great sex** requires that both partners **grow up.** Showing what "growing up," "becoming mature" or "achieving the goal of intimacy" means in the practical events of day-to-day married life, and motivating men (and women) to go for it, is **what this book is all about.**[5]

Is the ideal of **intimacy** the **only** standard of a successful marriage or a successful life? Of course not! A man can derive contentment from being a good provider and a loyal husband, filling up his free time with an endless array of diversions. A woman can use being a good wife, being a good mother, or even achieving career success, as her measure of a fulfilling life. Even those married women who choose to concentrate the bulk of their energies on simply being good mothers, and who consequently give as little effort and attention to their husbands as their husbands give to them, cannot be faulted.[6]

Because the marriage **ideal** proposed in this book involves achieving the ability to be **intimate, new marriage vows** are proposed in **Part Four** that focus precisely on the goal of intimacy, and the reasons one should desire that talent and skill. The proposed vows retain the essential elements of the marriage contract: the decision to love each other is made freely; and, the commitment is for life. But, because few men and women would make vows to love each other unconditionally unless they had **compelling reasons**, several are provided in the final four chapters of the book.

Before Proceeding . . .

"It takes more courage to reveal insecurities than to hide them, more strength to relate to people than to dominate them. . . ."
—Alex Karras

Depressed? Not Me!

Our culture covers up depression in men. "Men are too fragile" to be confronted with their own defects, especially a "woman's defect" like depression. After all, depression is a "wimp" disease. Studies of college men, for example, revealed that anyone who admitted being depressed, subsequently encountered social isolation or downright hostility.

In socializing our boys, we make assertiveness an ideal, while discouraging emotional expression. A male's increased likelihood for exposure to physical abuse and neglect, plus the modeling provided by TV, movies, and society-at-large, of stoic or "macho" ideals, as a substitute for any signs of human feelings, not only prevents him from developing intimacy skills, but also often makes him dangerous to others.

It is common to hear teachers, coaches, mentors—even physicians—cover up our society's biased attitude toward depression in boys (or men) with euphemisms like "trouble coping," "immaturity," "bad attitude," "lacks motivation," or "just looking for attention." These assessments should prompt this logical question: "If attention is what a boy is searching for, why not give it to him, for God's sake?"[1]

Am I Somebody?

A depressed person always lacks a sense of personal worth. Whether the lack of self-regard is the cause or the result of the depression makes little difference in what happens as a result. The man who is depressed will resort to just about anything to get rid of his **one-down** feelings. Work, success, control, exercise, sports, alcohol, gambling, drugs, and domestic abuse are ways for a man (or woman) to escape or deny the reality of his (or her) shame or guilt for being inadequate. Depressed men are almost always filled with guilt or shame. They simply deny those feelings. They "stuff" them, to use an AA term.[2] Unfortunately, stuffed or suppressed feelings can explode at any time, in violence to self or to others. No one, no matter how strong he (or she) is, can permanently endure the emotional isolation that results when he runs from **all** his feelings, even from feelings of anxiety. Even those who do achieve a big bank account, sexual conquests, power, or status do not achieve a sense of adequacy because of their inability to find anything **within themselves** they can accept and love. The only thing they see is unworthiness and incompetence.[3]

Fear, doubt, anxiety are very much a part of everyone's life. But, the denial or suppression of these feelings can consume all the psychic energy or resources a person has. That is why **feelings must be shared**. Any man (or woman) will eventually crumble if he is not "connected" to another human being on some level of love and concern, and share or express his anxiety, his pain, his doubts or his fears.[4]

Shedding Depression by Opening Our Heart

When a man (or woman) disowns a part of himself by repressions and other denials, he is not **"whole," and his heart is not open**, that is, he shares nothing of himself or his vulnerabilities. Indeed, he must close his heart so completely, and defend so forcefully that part

of himself which he disowns, that eventually **he** cannot see it anymore. The subsequent **unfeeling** results in the emotional numbness
that accompanies a closed heart. Instead of intimacy, shared feelings,
openness, and healing, such a man is isolated, lonely, and in pain.[5]

A man must face and accept **whatever** he finds in his own mind
and heart. Otherwise he can never keep his heart open and begin to
live . . . or to love anyone. A person might value himself (or herself)
because he recognizes correctly that self-esteem or self-regard is the
birthright of every human being, that is, every person ever born is
worthy of reverence. Or, he might simply regard himself as an
interesting and worthwhile human being. In either case, he will
consequently avoid practices that would bring harm and pain to his
body or to his relationships. Such a man (or woman) has the potential to be a great spouse and a great lover precisely because he
recognizes the value of his gifts.[6]

Understanding the Message: A New Ideal for Men

"Each man's a bridge, spanning in his lifetime all the images and traditions about masculinity inherited from past generations and bestowing— or inflicting—his own retelling of the tale on those who ensue."
—Terence Real

What I Am *Not* Proposing

Trying to guide boys/men to the **feminist model of intimacy** is not only foolhardy, but also dangerous. The fashionable definition of intimacy would require the husband to develop those qualities generally associated with women, especially a willingness to talk or listen at any time about anything. He would also be expected, of course, to share readily his most private thoughts and feelings.

❖ Mary's new project is to get her husband Dave to stop the pretext of being perfect and become vulnerable. I tell Dave that is not necessary and that I staunchly reject this notion for the precise reason that the first prerequisite for intimacy is that men and women **accept and nurture** their own, and each other's differences, avoiding demands and conditions. In virtually all the problems between a man and his wife, their natural differences will play a role. But never will I propose that those differences be eliminated—only understood and appreciated. Any woman— Mary included—who insists that her husband share his feelings, may experience his further withdrawal into silence.

My advice to Mary was to send her husband vibes of "acceptance" whenever she honestly could, and in the meantime put into practice in her own life the self-improvement suggestions (that I am going to explain throughout this book) that could eventually lead to wonderful changes in him and in the relationship.

While ignorance of the natural differences between men and women continues to be a source of much marital discord, it is wrong to attempt to deny or to squash such differences, for example, male aggressiveness or the female proclivity for building relationships. On the other hand, a wise husband encourages his wife to be assertive whenever she sees a need or a problem requiring her "manly" talents. Similarly, the woman who responds affirmatively, though gently, to her husband's attempt to share or express his feelings, or to connect emotionally, has her priorities well-ordered.

Understanding the unchangeable differences between the sexes and how they impact the marriage relationship is often very helpful in heading off trouble before it gets too far.

❖ One quick illustration—taken this week from the anonymous responses to the "questionnaires about your husband" that I have been giving to my patients the past year: three different wives criticized their husband's "tone of voice" or "attitude when speaking to them."

This judgment of husbands as "pompous asses" would be made less frequently if wives understood that **most men** "pontificate" or give concise, bottom-line "reports," preferring never to ramble or to waste words in "rapport" talk.

Of course, individuals of either gender can manifest any human quality— many men are naturally gentle peacemakers, and many women are naturally forthright or assertive. But, generally, as the next example and many others to be given throughout this book will illustrate, the interaction of boys/men with girls/women is remarkably predictable.

If You Can't Lick 'em, Join 'em

❖ Pam felt that she could never "connect" with Tom. "He connects with the TV set more than me," she told me. "What am I to do?" she half-asked, since she had already given up hope. Perhaps, she should have given up hope in her failed strategy of making him feel guilty for watching the game (and of then concluding that his desire to watch the game was meant to be a rejection of her), but not give up hope in her self. She needed to be steadfast in her belief that she was a wonderful woman to be around. But, she had to figure out why *Tom was not experiencing that.*

"She resents the football games I relax with," Tom sighed. "As if I don't work hard enough. Now, unless I spend my precious leisure time doing emotional work with her, I am a loser. I feel that way enough, as it is."

My suggestion to Pam was that football is intensely relational, but in a way that doesn't threaten Tom's boundaries or his limited willingness to talk about feelings. The feelings she wants between herself and Tom are there in the drama of the players and teams.

Pam decided to sit through several football games, paying attention only to the feelings and emotions, even those feelings and emotions in the "stupid commercials" that, admittedly, were so clearly aimed at the little boy/adolescent in every man. Whether due more to desperation or to insight, Pam's view of the power struggle involving sports changed radically. "Sports can be a cut above the minutia of life," she confessed later. "I see some of the passion and feelings these sports people have—their intense caring and loyalty to the team is amazing."

On rare occasions, she started switching from her favorite music to listen to **sports radio**, certainly not for the stats, but for a very brief taste of that other world, that taste of her male's heaven, that appreciation of the little boy stuff which seemed to be still very much a part of her husband's psyche. She felt empowered and "sneaky" when she said, "I guess the coach will get fired today. I think he tried. The talent just wasn't there. I feel sorry that he seems so bummed out. I really think he had the heart, at least, to do a good job."

"Heart, but not the skill." Tom chimes in. But later he comes out to visit her, as she is gardening. He is not even sure why. "To check in on her," he says, but even he knows that makes no sense in their relationship—she knows how to garden and no one is going to kidnap her. She now shares some of his world, with apparent interest and appreciation. I am not at all surprised to observe that he is making small steps—incomplete, but real—to enter hers.

As Escapes Go, Television's Pretty Good, But *Growing Up* Is a Better Choice

Any spouse's withdrawal or "escape" to the tube may be in self-defense of the way his mate **leans too heavily** on him (or her). Obviously, a man (or woman) who spends so much time watching TV, or at the home computer, or pursuing anything so much that it interferes with his work or his marriage duties, may be using that addiction as his defense **against any emotional connection**. At least "television wives" know where their husbands are. They see them. The wife whose husband uses work as his ticket to success, his addiction, or his escape, may rarely see him, except as a worn out grouch.[1]

The *Boy Code* Promises Success, Not Happiness

This book rejects the notion that a boy/man's esteem or success is based on performance or achievement, whether he ever achieves a good relationship with another person or not. That notion is precisely the message of the **Boy Code,** the rigid set of rules for guiding boys to manhood. **Part One** spotlights this Code. The **new ideal of success** being proposed gives the highest priority to **growing up and achieving relationship** (these concepts will be explained throughout this book, but especially in **Chapters Thirteen and Fourteen).** Translated into practical language for this book on marriage, an adequate level of maturity will have been achieved when **each marriage partner** can **honestly and accurately** answer the question, *"what is it like being married to me?"* by saying "it's a wonderful experience."[2]

If a man **assumes responsibility** and reaches out in friendship and reverence to his wife and family, a **proud legacy is assured.** In the meantime, he will discover a thrilling secret. Nothing, including the thrill of seeing his team win "the championship," the pride and satisfaction of meeting the celebrity he most admires, or **anything else,** will bring him greater joy and satisfaction than making his wife the number one priority in his life. Because two people are needed to maintain the status quo in any relationship, or to keep the relationship conflicted, tense, or boring, but only one person is needed to change it (simply by deciding he or she will "grow up"), it is possible for any man to change his home for the better, even in those instances where his wife has been embittered by years of neglect.[3]

Because the Boy Code models **performance-based esteem,** those who don't succeed and continue to succeed, have no right to feel good about themselves. We must reject this model because it's emphasis on achieving independence above everything else has been leading our men and our society to an unprecedented level of violence, and destroying our marriages. Our recognition and emphasis should be given to the **heroism** and **commitment** required for boys/men to **reject** the present ideal, that is, reject the "gender straight jacketing . . . that they face every day . . . the double standards and the toxic view about the male gender . . . blaze a path for a far more expansive, far less oppressive set of guidelines and expectations—a New Boy Code that respects what today's boys and men are really about—one that will be based upon honesty rather than fear, communication rather than depression, [and] connection rather than disconnection."[4]

Because almost one-half of America's children go to bed at night unable to say good night to their own fathers, the **new ideal for American men** has two parts: first, that husbands give higher priority to their wives than to anyone or any**thing** else in their lives; and second, that they give full attention to the legitimate needs of their children.[5] I will suggest that a husband's re-connection with the family through the simple, ordinary, day-to-day gestures of love and caring, could finally make marriage what it should always have been—the **best** path to health[6] and happiness on this planet.

Part 1
The Perilous Path
to Manhood

"The use of shame to 'control' boys is pervasive. . . . The idea is that
a boy needs to be disciplined, toughened up, made to act like 'a real
man,' be independent, keep the emotions in check. . . . The second
reason we lose sight of the real boy behind a mask of masculinity,
and ultimately lose the boy himself, is the premature [and traumatic]
separation of a boy from his mother and all things maternal at the
beginning of school. . . . Boys often suffer a second separation
trauma when they reach sexual maturity. . . . Parents—
encouraged by the society around them—may once again
push the boy away from the family and, in particular,
the nurturing female realm."
—William Pollack

". . . [B]eing a man means not being a woman. . . ."
—Nancy Chodorow

What Can You Expect from "Snakes and Snails and Puppydog Tails . . ."?

"While it may seem as if we live in a 'man's world,' at least in relation to power and wealth in adult society, we do not live in a 'boy's world.'"
—William Pollack

The Chain of Disconnection

American men are trained to worship the god of independence above all other gods. Our ideal is the man who is unaffected by anyone or anything around him, who sticks to his goals and does not falter, providing for spouse and children, and being loyal to his job, church, community, and country—the transcendent hero glorified by Emerson and innumerable movie heroes from John Wayne in *Stagecoach* or Gary Cooper in *High Noon* to the next generation's "James Bond" or "Dirty Harry." Brave, stoic, or unemotional, any relationships these silent heroes might have had were clearly secondary to getting the job done. Take your own survey, if you like, and you will find that the loner is "a man's man."

When Walt Whitman, who has been proclaimed *the* American poet, the writer who best expressed the unique American spirit,

3

wrote the words "I Sing of Myself," in his most famous work, *Leaves of Grass*, he was echoing two centuries of male idealization of non-attachment. Carl Rogers, the man of the twentieth century who, along with John Dewey, his mentor at Teacher's College of Columbia University, most influenced our educational system and our view of human development, never included marriage or "affiliation" on his pathway to human maturity.[1]

Precisely because this male ideal of independence does not give priority to **affiliation**, that is, the creation of loving relationships, the domestic and social violence in America greatly exceeds the level of violence in any other developed nation in the world, and contrasts sharply with our natural riches and blessings. Besides leading the world in the speed in which a divorce can be accomplished, no industrialized nation comes close to our statistics for violence. In the words of Mother Teresa, we are "the loneliest, the most disconnected, and the most unhappy nation on earth."

"Give My Wife and Family My Best Efforts? Who Are You Trying to Kid?"

The Feminists, specifically the most radical ones, ascribe the blame for America's woes (and the world's) to **the innate qualities of men**. Certainly, these women have a point, especially when they assert that men, not women, possess the **penis envy** (translation: excessive competitiveness), which fuels the need of American men to dominate. However, most experts would say it is the way boys are raised, not their nature, or innate qualities, that produces the violence in our country. Nancy Chodorow, for example, insists that masculine gender role training is much more rigid than the feminine. A boy is forced to repress all those qualities he takes to be feminine which he discovers inside himself. [2]

My book, *It's Your Life!*, responded in detail to the assertion that men are violent by nature. It is granted that those of male gender are biologically wired to be aggressive, to need plenty of space, to constantly compete, to measure all relationships in terms of status, but all this does not make them thereby violent, or sadistic. Indeed, the large number of diverse "male movements," for example, the

"Promise Keepers" and the "New Warriors," whose meetings are supported by lay and church groups alike, reflect a change in consensus, namely, that the root cause of violence is the way boys are guided to manhood. The idea is finally being accepted that too many men are living our country's misguided male ideal.

When boys/men are constantly reminded that "bonding" and "community" are for women, many eventually attain a level of autonomy or isolation at which their only major human "connection" is a competitive one (for survival of the fittest) with other men. Led away by economic, political, and social realities five hundred years in the making, from any idea that a deep and abiding love for a woman should be their life's highest priority, American men are wasting their opportunities, betraying their true calling, and hurting themselves and others.

Breaking the Link to Violence

It is not too much of a stretch to connect a man, whose life is devoid of love or human consolation, to violence. Destructive behavior is simply the final link in the chain of disconnection. Violence is now our number one killer of males under thirty-five, replacing war. Suicide is next. Over 1000 times more people are killed with firearms alone, than in any other industrialized nation. The year in which there were forty thousand people killed with guns in America, there were thirty-three deaths from guns in Great Britain and sixteen in Japan!

This country seems to excel in producing more and more violent, isolated, and angry men. What can be done to reverse the trend? Certainly, nothing will be achieved by arrogantly deciding, as some feminists have suggested, that we should raise boys in the same way we raise girls. Nor would I suggest that we accept violence, often mislabeled as "bullying," as a normal part of a boy's (or girl's) socialization. To label any form of violence—even verbal abuse or intimidation—as "normal male aggression" is a serious mistake. Any violation of one person's free choice by the use of force (exception: in the proper exercise of authority) is wrong, whether we are talking about girls/women or boys/men or any combination of these.

Everyone Has a Bias in Dealing with Boys, Fueled by Natural Differences

Boys have always "played harder," and this will probably never change in our lifetimes. But, again, the strong should not, in any circumstance, be allowed to intimidate the weak, and certainly should never be praised for such actions. In socializing our children we need to guide both genders to an awareness and acceptance of their separate ways of thinking, feeling, and doing things, and provide each gender with an understanding of the other's differences. Abundant scientific data exists proving that boys are different from girls in every part of their body, brain, and mind—a fact that most parents of both sexes would affirm. My wife, Marianne, mother of our three sons and three daughters, correctly predicted the sex of each baby before birth, presumably on the basis of how often and how hard they kicked, while the incredible difference quickly became apparent to me in the first few weeks after delivery.

There is plenty of scientific and anecdotal data that shows clearly that even those parents who claim to treat their infant sons and daughters in the same way, typically do not do so. [3] When I was revising parts of this chapter during a vacation in Disney World, an article appeared in the *Orlando Sentinel* written by a feature editor about her two-year effort to raise her son—she "wanted a girl"—like a girl. Unfortunately, all her son cared about were trucks, both **real** ones like the trash truck, whose coming made his day, as well as any kind of toy truck.

The "gleam" in the parents' eyes—the "unconditional positive regard" as defined by the child psychologists—that makes a child feel treasured, worthy, and affirmed, is much more likely to be bestowed on a daughter than a son, even in infancy. Consistently, boys are talked to less, held less, stroked less, and kissed less. Experiments have shown that, when an infant girl cries, her parents tend to judge that she is afraid, and hold and soothe her, but when a little boy cries, they often judge him to be angry, and leave him alone! The **trauma** of infancy and childhood that is the most common cause of an adult's feelings of "unworthiness," or of not being lovable, is the trauma of **neglect.** This **passive** trauma is three times more likely than the **active** trauma of physical abuse. Both traumas are much more likely in boys, as explained below.[4]

Boy Babies Are Very Feminine

Male infants and young toddlers are proven consistently to be **more sensitive** from birth to injury and deprivation than their female counterparts. Their heightened sensitivity also causes them to be more emotionally expressive than girls in the first two or three years of life. This increased sensitivity remains for life, and accounts for their heightened biological responsiveness, specifically those bodily responses described in any medical text or dictionary under "fight or flight reactions."

Those old enough to have watched and enjoyed the Lawrence Welk "Family Christmas Show" over the course of many years might recall that it was invariably the little boys who refused to perform or to say anything. In fact, most of them seemed to be an embarrassment to their parents, typically preferring to cry or to hide.

Ironically, the **masculinization process**[5] becomes even more powerful after boys reach the age of three, and have completed the first, and most important stages of psychological development, namely the **attachment,** or bonding stage in the first year-and-a-half and the **exploratory** stage that follows and lasts the same period of eighteen months. In the **emotional-affiliative** years from three to adolescence, the increased adult pressure and influence drastically changes the outward reaction patterns of boys. By adulthood the average man exhibits **no feminine qualities**, and has effectively, but at great personal cost, buried his feelings and emotions.

Narcissus, from Greek mythology, though only an adolescent, was so far removed from innate feeling and authentic internal emotion, that he never connected the changes in the expressions of his image reflected in the water with the changes in the expressions he was making in his own face. He fell in love with the "person" in the water—ignorant of the fact that it was his own reflected image—and starved to death pining for a "love" he could never capture.[6]

While American husbands have often been described similarly, and accused of being totally oblivious to what their wives are asking, saying or feeling, the reality in most instances is that they **are** aware, but that they are unable, or unwilling, to frame a visible or audible response that is comfortable for them. Perhaps a few men are without a clue as to the effect their frowns and sneers and grimaces and other visual signs of scorn, annoyance, anger, or uncaring are having on other members of the family, but I think that that level of insensitivity is not common. Thus, a husband does not typically "speak," or express any emotion other than his **anger**. This emotion is acceptable according to the **Boy Code**, that is, the set of rules for raising boys. Weakness, sadness, fear, anxiety, doubt, pain or desperation are **women's emotions**, never to be seen in a real man. Even though anger is allowed, men will more often employ **silence**, or coldness, to **express** anger and resentment. The sad result: "more families and marriages are dying from silence than from violence."[7]

Refuting Other Myths

Besides the "myth" of the sameness of both sexes, there are several other equally false patriarchal and gender myths. For example, anyone claiming that "boys have it easier than girls" in this generation has had to ignore the much higher incidence in boys of neurological and psychological problems, abuse, infant deaths, and suicide. [8] Just as understanding adolescence is key to understanding women, so also is acknowledging that boys are **hard-wired from birth** to be vastly different. If the term hard-wired turns you off, as it does a lot of practitioners, please substitute **markedly different brain anatomy and physiology**.

All boys don't **have to** act differently than girls, but their different anatomy and physiology results in **proclivities**, that is, tendencies, that generally result in differences. Demonstrable differences in their language, verbal skills, and the ways they connect with others, their perceptions of spatial relationships and their resultant need for more space, makes the nurturing of boys a formidable challenge, one guaranteed to make an honest woman of their mother. I have never met a woman who had raised at least three sons whom I didn't like and admire almost immediately. Such mothers are invariably open and honest in their relating to males.

The increased incidence of neurological problems and learning disabilities in boys, their problems with language and social interactions, reflects the different sequence in brain development, physiology, and final anatomy in boys. Anatomy and physiology also underlie the normal male propensity for aggression and striving for more space.[9]

The little girl's natural desire for close quarters and affiliation has also been shown to have a basis in anatomy and physiology. For example, because the male hormone, testosterone, is not continuously available to the developing female brain, certain areas of the brain "trigger," or send out impulses, to the rest of the body, in an intermittent, rather than continuous fashion throughout life. Those same systems in males send out continuous impulses because testosterone was continuously available as these areas of the brain developed.[10]

Unquestionably, both **nature** and **nurture** generally make a boy's development to emotional maturity follow a path that is different than a girl's. But not always. That is why parents, teachers, and mentors need to stay tuned to the exceptions, that is, to affirm those boys who wish to be more relational and emotionally expressive, and to affirm those girls who wish to be assertive. Often, we evoke in young people responses **we** think are most appropriate for their gender, but which are, in fact, not responses they might have chosen without our interference.

Both Parental Modeling and Bias Can Create a Self-fulfilling Prophecy

Many of the so-called **gender roles** are just that—imposed and coercive instructions for thinking, feeling, and acting "like a boy" or "like a girl." Most of the time, the gender roles are simply copied from the parent models. Children are born with a fantastic talent to "mime"—thus, they can imitate and reproduce exactly an amazing number of parental attitudes, expressions, mannerisms, and gestures.

❖   When John R., M.D., comes home from eight straight hours in the office, having made sure all his patients' problems have been addressed well, he is too tired to help anyone else. Understandable? Of course. Tired, John sits silently throughout the family's dinner. He rebuts all his wife's attempts to discuss the children or any of their problems, though she is very respectful and cheerful and tries in every nice way she can. Not once does dad say "honey," or "I'm just too tired now," or "I want to talk about the children, but not now." He simply gives a grunt of dismissal, with eyes that flash clear annoyance.

What lessons have the children been taught during that dinner? To name a few: it is normal for men to put women down (boys/girls? boys/mothers?); a father's involvement in family problems is totally discretionary; and, father doesn't care about his family.[11]

No Child Should Be *Molded*

Those experts who assert that it is as easy to mold boys into men as it is to mold girls into women should be reminded that we should **raise** our children, **not mold** them, trying to preserve and affirm their natural qualities and tendencies. We certainly do not want to try to model or encourage a boy to emulate the "rugged loner," or the "Dirty Harry." Rather, the goal is to inspire and guide enough boys to try to stay connected on a feeling or emotional level, at least with their peers, and to stop all the "suffering in silence" that saps most of their social energy. Allowing our little boys to **connect with their feelings**, rather than being **shamed,** that is, humiliated or embarrassed by them, should help them learn to "live for others." [12]

Please note that I have never suggested that we do an excellent job at raising our daughters. My previous book discussed the rigid and confusing "cultural imperatives" to which girls are subjected from birth. **Part Two** includes some of the most obvious problems that girls must deal with as they grow from children to adults. Our daughters have been assailed over the last forty years with the absurd notion that modesty, mystery, romance, and sexual vulnerability are "constructs" from a repressive past. So-called feminine "hang-ups"—like adolescent embarrassment over sexual feelings, "rejection hypersensitivity" when a love affair is abruptly terminated, and the whole notion of virginity or nudity or any other "concern about our bodies"—supposedly keep women from being accorded equal status with men. [13]

Parents Need Wisdom . . . and Plenty of Help

No one seriously disputes the notion that it takes a **village** to raise a little girl to womanhood. However, because a boy naturally seeks "space," he will explore beyond the village limits, one way or another, as soon as he is able. Thus, it would be more accurate to say that a boy needs a **tribe** that extends over several villages, and which will provide a consistent sense of belonging.[14]

Clearly, it is a **minority opinion** that boys are easier than girls to guide into maturity. Some of those who hold the minority view even dismiss fathers as not absolutely necessary for the successful raising of boys. I think they miss the point: **patriarchy still reigns**. Does it ever! In the patriarchal system, one unspoken reality is that "Boys damn well better act like boys, (translation: men), or they are going to have one hell of a social problem." A father is needed not only to discipline and to model virtue, but also to shield his sons from the "macho" nonsense that fills the TV and movie screens, permeates our schools, especially the sports program, and makes many of our neighborhoods dangerous places to live.

Boys of all ages especially need protection from the violence that is much more an everyday part of their life than it is for little girls. Around every new corner—and, since boys often wander great distances, in every new neighborhood—lies a perpetrator of violence, one who has probably been schooled in the training ground of his own physical abuse. Too often, that abuse has been inflicted at home. Surely, a father who is actively abusive, physically or sexually, is **worse than no father at all**.[15]

Very importantly, boys definitely need love or affirmation along with the discipline, however macho and independent they may pretend to be. Because the Boy Code dictates that they should suppress all emotions except anger or rage, boys must cover up the gentle, caring, vulnerable sides of themselves. For example, when boys are frightened, they believe they can't confess this feeling to anyone. Most of the time they are wise to be silent. The experts confess that the injunctions of the Boy Code are so pervasive that even **they often forget** that, when a boy proclaims "everything is fine," he may not be telling the truth.

More Tips for Boy-Raising

Reaching out with **a project** that tests his skills is often a better way to reach a troubled boy than trying to talk to him. Especially since most boys, even those considered quite "normal," prefer "wrap around" care from a large, informal group setting, where they can pick the time, place, duration, and person for any verbal exchange, rather than being forced into specific one-on-one conversations, which always have the potential to become intrusive or personal. Boys definitely prefer "one-way talk" anyway, or even no talk at all, since the mask of silence gives them safety. If they do not say anything, no one can find out that they are in pain, lonely, afraid, anxious, or desperate. Husbands who don't "listen" may be simply continuing a tradition **of tuning out** the spoken word. One can almost always reach the boy/man better by putting it in writing. When a boy feels threatened, anxious, or confused, he is much more likely than a girl to resort to a "fight" reaction in order to avoid ending up **one-down** to anyone. Therefore, it is always wise before suggesting any activity or project to let a boy know the objective, what the rules are, and who's in charge. Most boys will not pay attention to, or believe, adults who can't understand where they are coming from in these matters of purpose, rules, and goals.

Because of a boy's abhorrence of anything feminine in himself, no parent, teacher, or mentor should ever try to force a boy to act or to think like a girl (or vice-versa). He/she might try to get revenge or become more aggressive or more anti-socially dangerous. But, "letting boys be boys" **never** means letting them be violent or physically abusive to anyone; nor does it mean allowing them to engage in unstructured and unsupervised group competition. When a large group of boys are left to themselves, the bullies invariably take over.

It might be well to remember that, however deep a boy (or a man) has buried his yearning for connection as a result of having been shamed in the past for admitting weakness, he still retains the human longing to be close to parents, coaches, friends, or family. It is to this hidden yearning that those responsible for boys should be sensitive and responsive. Environments must be provided that are supervised and structured, where boys can aggressively test and measure themselves against their peers. Otherwise, boys will seek to "prove themselves" in much more dangerous circumstances. When close supervision is not provided, boys placed in a group of their peers, will typically feel restless and inadequate until they can get **one-up** on at least some of the others in the group.

In American culture, manliness is still equated with rugged individualism. Unfortunately, our society also still insists that **manhood** is something that is **earned and conferred** and that a boy/man must prove his courage, bravery, or lack of fear, over and over and over. Thus a **mentor**, in the interim between childhood and adulthood, can have tremendous power—conferring or withholding the affirmation of "manhood" which the adolescent boy desperately needs for his sense of adequacy.

Gangs Are Not the Answer

Boys join **gangs** partly because such large peer groups promise a chance for affirmation. Gangs provide the "boy culture" he must have: a place to relax, compete, have tasks, cooperate in projects, and feel group power. Most gangs provide options or opportunities for getting affirmation without intrusive emotional stimulation and without the intensely personal demands that boys dread.

A boy probably would define heaven as a quest requiring cooperation and sacrifice, but where his personal feelings were not going to be probed or monitored. When a child's character is formed by a gang of his peers, rather than by loving adults, the child will probably still learn cooperation with others, especially how to serve the group's interests. Unfortunately, boys (and girls), who are placed in a large group without adult guidance and values, often also develop a tolerance for violence. Because projects and priorities are invariably determined by the leaders of the gang, a boy will be unlikely to learn in the gang setting how to develop his own independence and sense of purpose. Sadly, blind loyalty to the typically dubious goals of the group also make it unlikely that the members will learn how to love.

❖   It was peer pressure that induced me, at age seven, to begin smoking. If you didn't smoke (and inhale), you were not "man enough" to hang out at the store around the corner, where the older guys hung out. It required thirty-six years of trying before the habit that caused paroxysms of coughing, and sometimes an overwhelming sense of fatigue, was permanently licked.

(Now, of course, the "rite of passage" is more likely to be a 9 millimeter pistol and a vial of crack.)

The only "gang" in my childhood existed only briefly, but it provided me with a sense of belonging, and closeness to my peers, which I remember warmly to this day.

Fortunately, the wooden knives, swords, spears and whips, which I and Pee Wee and Porky, and twenty other boys from just one single city block spent one entire summer making in Chubby's basement, were discovered and confiscated before anyone was seriously hurt.

Forging the First Link in the Chain toward Violence

Boys/men accept **physical vulnerability** routinely. Rough or dangerous sports, and military service have been part of male culture since the beginning of recorded history. **Emotional vulnerability** is another matter entirely. The pressures on boys begin soon after birth to narrow and control their emotional expressiveness. Studies have repeatedly shown that male infants startle, cry, fuss, and excite more than their sisters. Most mothers handle this "problem" with boys with methods of control decidedly different than those employed with daughters, even applying the Boy Code in the first few months of life.[16] By the time a boy reaches five or six he is well aware that staying close to mother is something shameful or somehow not a sign of "healthy" masculinity. The message gets stronger as he gets older, being especially enforced, by virtually everyone, when a boy reaches puberty.

To avoid the shame that would come with feelings of weakness, fear, vulnerability, or despair, many or most boys/men bury and deny such feelings with great intensity throughout their lives. By rejecting the **soft emotions** just delineated, that cause shame, they are left with only the **harsh emotions,** that is, the alienating disgust, resentment, or anger by which they close their hearts to any meaningful connection.

People who open their hearts to us, by being emotionally vulnerable, invite us closer to them. When we accept them as they reveal what they are feeling at that moment, we experience more of our own humanity, that is, our own vulnerabilities. As a result, we are more fully alive emotionally, ourselves. Thus, when a man cannot allow himself to be vulnerable, to admit depression, sadness, fear, weakness, or even anxiety, he invariably becomes isolated and sad. Typically, such a person resorts either to addictions, which are a form of violence to **himself,** or resorts to violence or uncharitable actions **toward others** as a "sick" way to connect with someone. These violent or addicted men seem unable to see the profound truth in the concept that ". . . [I]t isn't our perfection which allows us to fulfill our potential, but our vulnerability that allows us to become fulfilled [through friendships]."[17]

The blueprint for survival in this different "male" world is continued in the next four chapters. Hopefully, when men have seen how the blueprint is drawn, and then in **Part Three** see how adherence to the Boy Code can impact a marriage relationship, they will be motivated to find the **courage** necessary to shed the straitjacket of gender. Without the **narrow ideals of the Boy Code**, our boys/men can stop suffering in silence and isolation, reconnect with their deepest feelings, and eventually share something, at least, of what they think and feel.

Summarizing . . .

Boys and girls are different **by nature,** that is, they are born with many anatomical and physiological differences that result in **proclivities,** or tendencies to act or relate differently. But **the nurturing process,** that is, the signals they get from day one from their caregivers (and, in fact, from everyone else) sets boys and girls on an entirely different approach to those of their own sex and to those of the opposite sex.

2

"No More Tears" . . .
"Everything Is Just Fine" . . .

"The young man who has not wept is a savage,
and the old man who will not laugh is a fool."
—George Santayana

Learning the Boy Code

Before any adult makes it explicit, even the very young male child seems to sense that **showing tears** would be wrong for him. Even before "outside" influences forbid it, the little boy senses "the lose of something vital to his being, to his self-regard, when he cries."[1] A few pages earlier, we alluded to evidence, both scientific and empiric, which suggests that it is more natural for little boys to cry than for little girls, since from birth, boys are believed to be more sensitive and emotionally expressive. Whether it is due to a boy's own awareness of increased vulnerability, or society's mandate that it is totally "unmanly" to cry, it remains a fact that soon after the age of two, the boy's tearfulness is seen less and less.

Undeniably, a boy/man would be well advised to hide his tears in public if he doesn't want to be ridiculed. Just one generation ago, a famous New England senator's run for the presidency was aborted by his exhibition of tears on national TV. The next day the media was discussing whether or not "Americans would want such a 'weak man' as President."

In the pre-school years, most boys learn how to suppress the feelings that would cause a girl to cry. Boys substitute action or problem-solving; or, they displace the feeling of sadness with a feeling that seems more acceptable.

❖   A few times in my childhood and adolescence I permitted myself to cry, but, God forbid, I never let anyone see me. When I was being humiliated and intimidated by the neighborhood bully, who was able to pick me up and throw me almost like a sack of potatoes, I did not cry. My only thoughts were to return the favor when I was big enough to do so. Fortunately, by the time I was big enough, such things were unimportant to me.

A "Dear John" letter at age 24, from my second love, brought tears to my eyes for weeks. But **every** tear was shed in private.

Approaches to Avoid with Boys

Because the indoctrination of a boy starts before he attains the ability to explicitly **remember** anything, trying to force any boy to be "more open" about his long-buried feelings may violate his present sense of what is right or good for him. Thus, your efforts to "help" him may boomerang. He may take your approach as a personal criticism of who and what he has become, and he may angrily flee from you.

It is surely a mistake to think society can impose **feminist-inspired changes** in our "boy culture." This thinking represents not only an unnatural approach, but also an arrogant one, and is doomed for failure. Clearly, the solution to reversing the violent trends in our society does not lie in unnaturally molding our sons into adopting a " 'female culture in transition' . . . an approach to life that would rob the world of the future of their . . . indomitable spirit, humble hopes, courageous love, and unflagging energy. . . . If we do not teach boys how to be brave, truthful, and good, they will not feel real—that is, alive, complete, loving, wise, and powerful."[2]

❖   There seemed to be no quick solution to the sense of inadequacy that I "lived" in my late teens, even though I was a high school "success." I still remember daily a nun, now deceased, who would spend several hours on Saturday morning, nearly every month for two years, helping me handle the difficult transition from high school glory to the challenge of college pre-med.

It didn't help me at all, when, on my first day at college in Philadelphia, the professor in charge of my dorm warned me, "one 'C' on your record could keep you out of medical school."

Because the competitive pressures—some of them necessary for finding the best qualified students, and some manufactured by a sometimes-sadistic system of discipline—never lessened, I could never say enough good things about the nun who let me cry on her shoulder. I owe Sister Rita Gertrude my career, if not my life.

❖   Playing golf with my nine-year old grandson and his buddy from school, I was not at all surprised when he reported our final scores: "he and his friend had the same score and I had won by a stroke." I would have been surprised if he had claimed victory. First, because we were playing "best ball," and my ball was the one played most of the time.

The second reason I would have been surprised is that, from the time my grandson, Matthew, and I started competing from age four or so—in *Monopoly, Parcheesi*, and the like—he has invariably played down the final results, even at those times when he trounced me badly.

❖   The strong aversion of even young boys to being "one down", or, to witnessing anyone except the "bad guys" being "one down" to their peers, is carried into marriage. This is a fact of male culture to which my last patient yesterday would attest. Her husband planned and embarked on a "fishing trip" with a "despicable drinking buddy of no account" within three hours from the time that she had "dared" contrast his lack of neatness to George next door, whose "grooming is beyond reproach."

The wife's criticism prompted his "flight reaction"—a response to criticism that is built right into human physiology.

Through the years, I have exploded a fair number of times at criticism, which in retrospect, was often justified. In a few cases, my own over-reaction to criticism betrayed a deep sense of **guilt.** Someone had noted a fault that even I couldn't stand. (Of course, I didn't realize this at the time the criticism was rendered.)

The Terrible Power of *Scorn*

Criticism is bad enough and rarely produces change, but mockery or scorn is a despicable form of sadism that not only speaks volumes about the mocker's lack of self-regard but can also produce deadly consequences. [3] This extreme form of criticism—being belittled and ridiculed—is a dark fact of life, but in childhood and adolescence, the wound can go so deeply that the mind and heart is forever after infected with an ugly and bitter resentment that frequently breeds violence. How many more school massacres have to occur before we learn this lesson?

❖ Since I did well in high school, I had my share of jealous friends. Their most effective weapon was to joke about my pathetic physique. At six feet, one and a half inches and 149 lbs., I well deserved my nickname "Bones." Since it was evident that I was quite sensitive about this, those wishing to taunt me would sing my name, to the melody of the tune "them bones, them bones, them dried bones."

I still have no "use" for any of the students who "abused" me in that way, which perhaps only proves the clergy's insistence that "being willing to forgive" is the most difficult commandment of all.[4]

❖ Five minutes before my college Baccalaureate ceremony was to begin, a classmate, whom I had never met and do not now remember, informed me that the program revealed that I was to receive most of the medals. His method of giving me this happy news was to shout in my face, "Even though you got the medals, Jim Dorney is a much better man than you'll ever be!" Whatever truth there may have been to this classmate's appraisal—and, I agree that the Jim to whom he was referring was a nifty guy—I believe those who resort to such tactics are still arrested in the same adolescent phase of development as some fans of the NFL. When the home crowd cheers an opposing player's serious injury it is painfully apparent that their identification with their heroes has supplanted their sense of fairness and decency.

Simple **thoughtlessness**, too, can sometimes be permanently traumatic to those who are victims. Boys/men are frequently thoughtless, usually as part of their tough approach to peers.

I cannot claim that I was always above thoughtlessness. One instance nearly cost me my life, or at least serious injury.

❖   A schoolmate from elementary and secondary school, whom I hadn't seen for several years, called to invite me to visit a new mall that was some distance away, and I accepted. Though we were both now of college age, I used the name I had always used in addressing him, "Pee Wee." His hatred of that name became apparent only after his reckless driving nearly wrapped us around a tree. When we finally arrived at the mall, he turned to me and said, "If I had killed us both, good riddance."

Modeling Love, Not Stoicism

Obviously, those entrusted with guiding boys need to be watchful for ridicule and thoughtlessness, if those boys are to grow up without serious emotional scars. What the "Promise-Keepers" and "The New Warriors" have recognized as the answer **is** indeed the answer: that violence is simply the inevitable final link in the chain that begins with the disconnection produced by our misguided Boy Code. By relentlessly forcing a young boy to deny or separate himself from feelings of weakness, sadness, doubt, fear, or anxiety, and to "tough it out" alone, not only when he first goes to school, but also at adolescence, the boy is separated from the family before he is ready and able, and, at the same time, separated from his own feelings, often permanently.

Certainly a boy's natural differences, and unique talents, must be appropriately parented, mentored and educated, but his parents, mentors, and educators must model an **ideal of manliness that gives priority to nurturing or to creating love.**

As long as any part of the present Boy Code remains, the role of the father remains crucial. When a boy is not "fathered," whether by a father present and active in his life and/or by an extended family and tribe—especially if he is not shielded from the influences of the present repressive culture that is, at once, shamefully ignorant of gender differences, and at war with many of them—the boy grows into manhood following an incomplete and mistaken ideal, which gives little priority to love. Worst of all, a child guided to the present narrow ideal of "rugged individualism"—modeled by the movie heroes who show no emotion except anger, and whose relationships are always secondary to their job—is unlikely to ever recognize that what he has buried is much of his own humanity.[5]

Summarizing . . .

By the time a boy reaches adolescence, the natural differences between him and his "sisters" have been magnified many times over as a result of all the contacts to which he has been exposed at home, at school, and with his peers outside the school environment.

3

Is Mom Really a Problem? Who Else Cares about Us?

"Authority without wisdom is like a heavy axe without an edge,
fitter to bruise than to polish."
—Anne Bradstreet

The present socialization of boys places little or no emphasis on reverence and respect for women. Equally damaging to our society, the prevailing consensus places a high priority on getting a boy away from his **mother's influence**.[1] The implication is that adoption of her approach to people will ruin a son's chances for success in the "real" world—that is, a society still pretty much controlled by men. To most fathers, that approach makes a lot of sense, even today. This separation from mother includes separation from mom's unique approach to relating. The clear message is: the son must get rid of any hint of emotionalism. Unfortunately, the adolescent's determination to "stand on his own two feet" (translation: being independent of mom) also moves him farther along the path toward final **emotional isolation**.

Reconnecting Boys/Men to Their Feelings

The single most important idea in the **Men's Movement** is that boys/men must be re-taught how to contact their own deepest feelings, and then they must be shown how to **share them** with someone. By identifying and accepting their feelings after acknowledging their need to be **connected to themselves**, men can then begin to reconnect to their families.[2]

Only Russia has more men in jails and prisons than America has, demonstrating that men who are emotionally isolated, who have not experienced love, or who have rejected love, will seek destructive ways to "connect" or to relate to others. The destructive solutions that men use as a substitute for human relationships are not only filling our prisons, and producing the world's most violent society, but these same attitudes and priorities are also **wrecking marriages.**

A boy/man's repression of feelings, and his refusal to attach much importance to affiliation or intimacy, brings him to marriage with little appreciation of a need vitally important to his wife (and to him). The result greatly reduces her chances for happiness. It also diminishes the rewards of marriage for him. Admittedly, husbands might be more likely to let their wives share their thoughts, and see their true emotions, if they didn't think the risk was too great. Harville Hendrix has written that, "When there are future arguments, what [men] have shared in their closest moments has been used against them." A man's perception, that his wife is discussing his personal assets and liabilities with her closest friend, is a common one among husbands. As a consequence of this perceived chumminess among women, a husband tends to keep the blanket of secrecy over his private thoughts and feelings, even with his wife.

Thoughts Versus Feelings

In Chapter Twenty-One, the important distinction is made between sharing **feelings**, which is almost invariably safe (at least in the present), and sharing **thoughts**. When a man shares his honest opinions or evaluations of the relationship, it is typically seen as criticism by his wife, and resented. Women admit that they can be enraged by the same spoken criticism from their mate that they would accept, even appreciate, from their closest female friend. Their claim is that **his** criticism seems more often to proceed from arrogance, and makes them feel "one-down."

Boys/men, with rare exceptions, do not share their feelings with other boys/men. Despite their protests to the contrary, some mothers and wives either "enable," that is, make possible, or actually encourage their sons or husbands to hide fear or weakness from other people. Wives can set limits for what is appropriate for a man to share, without any conscious awareness that they are being censors. John Gray teaches that women definitely "abhor" weakness in a man, and most men easily get that message. He adds that rarely does a woman want to know the whole truth about a man's failings and problems, even when she claims otherwise. I agree.

The (Limited) Role of a Focus Group.

Focus Groups can be helpful in getting a man (or woman) in contact with his feelings. For millions of Americans, a focus group provides the "safe haven" where they can be themselves, and allow themselves to be **seen** without "fighting or fleeing." The meetings with persons like themselves enables men or women to become vulnerable, at least to people with the same problems or weaknesses. The personal identification and admission of what each is feeling creates connections. The open hearts that are created by the focus techniques can reduce or, in some cases, even eliminate a man (or woman's) emotional isolation and destructive loneliness.

Getting a grown man into an encounter or focus group for the purpose of teaching him to contact his own feelings, so that he can share them with you, may be successful. You may get a mate with a more open heart, or at least one who can show some of his feelings.[3]

❖   My wife and I joined the Marriage Encounter Movement in 1973, and along with eight other couples, have been meeting nine times a year ever since. None of us see any further need to share much that is personal, but we do share the weddings, funerals, burdens of illness, and disappointments or problems with our children and grandchildren. The nine men in the group now have little trouble showing emotion, or admitting doubts and fears, even to each other.

Unfortunately, there is a potential danger in any **group therapy** approach. A person with deep-rooted emotional problems, or one who is psychotically depressed, may react to the encounter with others by "flight," that is, a withdrawal even farther into emotional isolation. Or, he (or she) may "fight" back or get revenge against the person who pushed him/her into the group situation. To use the psychological term, persons who are harmed are designated as **casualties** of the group therapy technique. Persons who enter focus-group therapy can also become casualties by personal disclosures that are later regretted, by the actions of participants who try to solve everyone's problems and thereby sabotage the exchange of feelings, and, by violations of the pact of secrecy. Sharing another's personal information with people outside the group can be especially damaging. Finally, a person can become a casualty if anyone insinuates, in a group situation, that he/she is **inadequate.** The accused will generally fight such a judgment with a frightening intensity, even if that means destroying the group. Even the most mature among us can be undone by personal criticism and try to get even. Unfortunately, it is men whose ideal is to be **one-up.** As a result, they are the gender most allergic to criticism, which they see as putting them **one-down.**

In Chapter Five, a wife's success in getting her husband into "marriage encounter" has a surprising ending.

Summarizing . . .

The **biggest single change** produced by America's system of nurturing boys is that they are afraid to show any feelings except anger. One hopeful sign is provided by the **Men's Movements,** which are giving their greatest emphasis to convincing men that it is "OK" to show fear, anxiety, doubt, sadness, regrets, or pain.

4

Man's Futile Search for Sports Glory

*"It's by being in touch with our feelings and feeling loved
that we are able to heal ourselves."*
—John Gray

A Boy/Man's Relentless Struggle to Be
One-Up Often and Never *One-Down*

Does a man judge himself inadequate because he does not measure up to the narrow and misguided ideals of manliness he sees on TV, in bestsellers, or at the movies? I believe the answer, in most cases, is **"yes, he does."** Because he does not see the ideals as misguided, he adheres to them. Then, he must **hide** the guilt and shame he feels when he inevitably fails to reach the unreachable standards. To admit his guilt or shame, or to "own" them, would be "unmanly." That, as we have seen, is **the message** of the Boy Code. There is a very practical reason for being stoic: most men are involved in a relentless competition for advancement with other men. To show weakness might provide encouragement to a man's competitors to be even more ruthless and use his weakness as an opportunity to go directly for the jugular.

From early childhood, a boy devotes a great deal of his time fantasizing about heroes and victories, and invariably connects bravery, much effort, and honor to the men who win, who save the day, or who receive the acclaim. A boy's **imaginary** heroes reflect a large part of what he has decided a good man should be. The **real-life heroes** for American boys are almost always **athletes. No activity inculcates the traditional male values more powerfully than competitive sports.** Sports can be a form of intimacy, where a boy may be honest and express many of the emotions and feelings the Boy Code forbids. But competitive sports often push boys and men deeper into shame and loneliness and when the competition gets ruthless, boys can become violent to each other. **When sports can remain play**, it allows a boy to regain connection with his feelings and experience the joy of performing high energy, spirited activity without constraints. Thus, he can discover new competencies, gain or strengthen his self-regard, express a variety of deep emotions buried within his heart, and widen his circle of personal connections. With the right attitude and the right coach, sports can be a boy's salvation from loneliness and isolation. Sports can be "transforming ...opening a boy up, giving him a new *elan*, a new authenticity . . . [and] simply make many boys into far happier, far more fulfilled human beings."[1]

Sports: The Modern Day Dragons

In most of our schools, sports success is the undisputed "gold standard" in the quest for glory. The "jocks" are envied by nearly all their peers, which is why, I imagine, they get all the girls. Unfortunately, all the dragons have been slain, and, the **spiritual values** that inspired the knights of old to heroism have been replaced by **material** values like good looks, money, prestige, and winning. Sadly, there are coaches who **link manliness** and **prestige solely with winning.** In their efforts to win or even to dominate the competition, such coaches use and teach **shame** as their primary motivator. Yet, only a very small number of men among the millions who have been subjected to this attitude toward sports ever get the brass ring that fulfills their male ideal. Most men never even "make the team." Nearly all those who do, achieve only shallow and temporary relief from anxiety about their status, relative to other men. Even if they are not permanently injured physically (and many thousands are), many athletes have disturbing memories—of failures, of finishing second or of being "second string," of the dropped pass or key fumble or missed kick, or, the inevitable failure to reach the next level of competition.[2]

In the very obvious one-up/one-down world of competitive sports, the sense of personal failure is a frequent, and sometimes permanent reality. I am convinced that the scars from being repeatedly one-down in high school as a result of competitive sports are never truly erased from a boy/man's psyche. This needn't be, and wouldn't be, if the **emphasis** in American sports competition was not the notion that "winning is everything" or the "only thing." Unfortunately, winning is what parents (mainly fathers, of course), coaches, athletic boards, alumni, and fans want the most. The famous basketball coach, who won more NCAA titles than anyone, declares in his TV ad for an investment firm, that **winners** are always the ones who **have made the most mistakes** in their quest for perfection. My reaction to such "wisdom" is to agree, since the battle to be **number-one** in anything requires a willingness to persevere, to accept defeat and to come back from mistakes. But, the coach is probably being even more accurate than he might realize: **making winning the number one priority is probably the greatest mistake of all!** Until the day comes when American men get their priorities in better order, add **sports** to sex, power, alcohol, and drugs, to the **things** men love, as a substitute for loving or connecting to **persons**.[3]

In the next chapter, I will provide a few case histories that show clearly how a man or (woman's) inability or unwillingness to even examine his priorities, much less put those priorities in reasonable order can easily lead to marital disaster.

5

Coping with Inadequacy in a Boy/Man's Way

"In the middle of life's way, I found myself in a dark woods where the right way was lost."
—Dante, *Inferno*

In **Part Three**, the actions—even violent ones—that a man uses to remove his sense of inadequacy is placed in the marriage context. Several male techniques for dealing with self-worth problems will be previewed now.

❖ When a dear friend, Dottie, came home to a house that was suddenly without furniture or a husband, she was stunned. She and Joe had a "perfect" marriage.

For seven years, they had been giving the "couple" talks—the ones explaining how normal married people might get along better—at the marriage encounter weekends. Their **love letters,** that is, the short ten-minute letters to each other that are an integral part of the marriage-encounter technique, had been exchanged at least four times a week for ten years.

Slowly, over a few very tearful years that followed Joe's abrupt disappearance, Dottie came to realize that, while Joe learned to be very open about his feelings, and could even cry as well as any man, he hated sharing his feelings and couldn't wait to find someone who wouldn't ask that of him. Dottie has since remarried, and it has become quite evident in the first decade of this marriage that she will not make the same miscalculation again.

A Legacy of Control

If the dominant feature in a **man's** family of origin was "to control or be controlled," he will be inclined to bring into a marriage the same sado-masochistic techniques of relating. This transfer is especially likely if he has not achieved independence from his parents. However, unlike the woman who enters marriage still letting her mother tell her what to do, and consequently transfers that subservience to her husband as quickly as she can, a previously-controlled man will be much more likely to become an angry, resentful, and **controlling husband.**

The next two cases feature controlling men. While both certainly exceed the national average for husbands, they each illustrate just one of the many reasons a spouse might resort to control.

❖   George was described at the divorce proceedings as a "hard man to live with." His wife, Sherri, testified in court that she had "incurred his wrath" for seven years, especially every time there was a "control" issue. Whether it was the temperature in the car or the house temperature, George was clearly in charge. The list of "rules" that George enforced by loveless intimidation went literally from "soup to nuts"—the kind of soup he wanted for lunch and the type of nuts they would include in any party cocktail hour.

George's "family of origin" would have been a family therapist's delight, but the family had never sought counseling. His father was definitely a controller. In fact, he was a compulsive controller. His mother's defense was "avoidance." Although she was a **withholder**, that is, a woman who wouldn't allow anyone to know her thoughts or feelings, George's mother still managed to skillfully manipulate her husband by her selective "weaknesses." For example, she never learned to drive a car, thus forcing her husband to do the grocery shopping and all the family chauffeuring.

As a result of George's unrelenting control, Sherri eventually did what all their friends expected, which was to file for divorce. The settlement awarded her a substantial part of his assets.

COPING WITH INADEQUACY IN A BOY/MAN'S WAY

George apparently didn't take the divorce very well. He spent the three years immediately following the divorce acting very bitter about it all, and had even tried suicide.

Because I had known George since we were eight years old, I couldn't forget him or ignore what had happened to him. Especially mystifying to me was his wife's seemingly uncontrolled anger. The George that I knew was a kind, even considerate boy, though very shy and frightened most of the time. During the summer, we could play and swim for hours and have more healthy fun than most inner city kids would have in a lifetime of summers. If I had to fault him for anything, I would have had to admit George worried a lot about his parents. He confessed as much to me, once.[1]

I did not know Sherri as well as I knew George, of course, but I did see her from time to time in high school, and for a few years after that.

After the divorce, I made discreet inquiries (which is not like me at all, though I have been writing about the family and marriage since 1948). I was amazed to discover that, after the divorce was final, George disclosed to three different acquaintances that he was a **homosexual.**

Apparently, George had endured and used his marriage as a form of **denial,** destroying two lives in the process.[2] I did not seek to know if Sherri knew about it or not. I do know that, in the environment in which we grew up, an admission like that would have been disastrous. Despite the failure of our public schools to teach values (seeing them as repressive and invariably biased) adolescents, both then and now, have consistently evidenced a ruthless intolerance of homosexuals. In my younger days, virtually all of society shared that view. While the changes in our laws on homosexuality reflect society's present more enlightened view, that view seems not to be shared by our adolescents. The rate of suicide for adolescent homosexuals is four times the general adolescent rate.

My friend eventually left town and went to another large city looking for work. His meager savings, after the divorce settlement, had been quickly depleted. George is now one of the pitiful homeless that 54 percent of those Americans who live in our cities see as part of their daily routine. George is a **typical** member of that unhealthy fraternity. Like seventy percent of the nearly one million homeless (on any given night) he is now a male adult without any present family connection.[3]

The second example of **controlling husband** I would like to describe is a **misogynist,** that is, a **man who hates women.** Surprisingly, these misguided individuals are rarely "Don Juan's," which means that they do not try to exploit or dominate **many** women. Just their wives. In fact, misogynists give control their highest priority. They strongly support the "institution" of marriage as a permanent arrangement, as I pointed out in another book, making them difficult people to divorce without a bitter fight.[4]

❖ The "role" of Tobias Jonathan from birth was to provide his mother with the love, respect, and affirmation her husband wouldn't or couldn't give her. Toby and his mom did everything together. Their exchange of affection was mutual, until the son reached puberty. Mom's unwavering love and protection made Toby's childhood a peaceful and contented time in his life. But Toby was a keen and perceptive child and his mother's devotion started slowly, but clearly, to make Toby feel different than his peers.

Sports, camping out, even movies with a friend, were subtly discouraged, yet what his mother suggested as replacements always struck Toby as "sissified" stuff. Toby gave so much of his time to his mother that his classmates dropped him from their social calendar. He became a "loner" at school. Several times he tried to explain his isolation at school to his mother, but he sensed that she wouldn't care very much about how many friends he had there. Toby suffered his lack of friends in silence, but began to withdraw from his mother's control. From age 14, he gave his mother as little regard and affirmation as he could get away with.

In the four years following his seventeenth birthday (there was no party, then, or at any other of his previous birthdays) the feelings of affection and concern for his mother were totally lost, replaced by stirrings of anger and resentment, which Toby scrupulously kept in check. When his mother died of breast cancer, at the age of fifty-two, Toby was twenty-one. Toby was "too sick" to go to her funeral. His father thought his son was too overcome with grief to go, but Toby was afraid that someone would see that he didn't even care.[5]

When Toby eventually got married—eight years later—not even Toby himself was aware that his **anger toward his mother** would affect his relationship with his wife. Toby, the "favored son," had unconsciously become Toby, the **misogynist**, that is, the woman hater. He proceeded on a path that threatened to destroy the sanity, and nearly the life of his wife, Marie. Using only psychological intimidation to control his wife's decisions, Toby changed his wife, in the space of just four years, from a confident lady of decision into a frightened and obedient child.

Yet this "sick" and damaged husband saw himself as an attentive and devoted spouse. To everyone else, he, in fact, appeared a model mate, who "involved" himself in all the domestic activities and decisions. His wife, Marie, even though she was very unhappy and confused, blamed herself, and her "inattention" and "carelessness," for her husband's anger!

Miraculously, the family doctor, a wily and wise octogenarian, diagnosed Marie's "illness," and issued this frightened woman, who was then thirty, a wake-up call in the form of a short course in "misogyny." Though the doctor nearly got herself sued for her intervention, by Marie's husband, the facts at issue were so clear and unassailable that Toby "broke down," and agreed to counseling.

The couple went weekly to counseling for only eleven months, which is a remarkably short time considering Toby's need to be "one up, not one-down" to a woman, and Marie's apparent need to have someone control her. But, the path from hate to love is much shorter than from indifference to love. Anyone willing to confront his/her issues and feelings, and acknowledge past sins (and sometimes change his/her perceptions) can literally put a relationship back on course. The decision to love, if a person is truly in control of his life, is as easy, or easier in some cases, than the decision to control. Great anger proves that the person **cares.** Such anger constitutes a strong bond, or connection, in a relationship.[6]

Hate or anger are feelings and emotions that can, and often do come unbidden, in anyone's search for intimacy. I will discuss this point more fully, and how we can sometimes hate the one we love, in Chapter Seventeen.

Soon, the marriage of Marie and T. Jonathan (as he now signs his name) "blossomed" as though they were newlyweds. Despite all the past pain and cruelties, this couple managed to turn the marriage completely around, doing most of the healing on their own.

T. Jonathan was certainly capable of loving. He had been showered with love (admittedly, a controlling and sacrificial love) for most of his life. It was this **potential** for empathy and caring that Marie must have sensed in him, and which probably attracted her to him in the first place. The "Toby" of before is never mentioned. That child/boy has been replaced by a man who loves and respects himself enough to reverence and appreciate the fine wife that he has.

Toby's case is not presented to discourage any mother from "mothering" her adolescent son. The mother in this case was surely not typical.

Boys Are *Damaged* by a Flawed Perception of the Mother's Role

Freud was wrong when he said the son's relationship with his mother must be "destroyed." That tact, or approach, may speed a son on the path to independence, but it will guide him away from relationships with meaning.

Still, any boy in this society who flaunts the rules of gender, whether it be a boy who cries in front of his peers, or an adolescent who allows his mother to make decisions he should be making for himself, must be prepared to pay the price. Society's vilification of a "mommy's boy" continues, with the same tragic results as all the other misguided attempts to strip boys of their emotions, feelings, and connection to others. All these narrow-minded cultural directives often leave the boy forever disconnected from himself—like Narcissus, unaware of any of his own emotions or feelings.[7]

The so-called **castrating mother**, like the **emasculating wife**, is a erroneous judgment based on ignorance of where the mother (or wife) is coming from, that is, a lack of understanding of the reasons she relates to her son (or husband) the way she does. Few, if any, mothers want to dominate, or **unman**, their sons. Their sacrifices for the sake of the son's success usually match, or even exceed, the father's. And, whether our patriarchal society likes it or not, a mother has the same rights as the father to assert parental authority. For the same reasons, few wives wish to dominate their husbands. Weak men are not appealing to either gender.

For the sake of their sons (and husbands) women should insist on the right to **assert their equality**, and to impart their wisdom. Many do exercise that right, even though such assertions of equality can make some spouses even harder to live with.

The Formula for Creating Violent Men

Tragically, American men, who are **violent** to a degree and in numbers unmatched by any civilized, industrial nation on earth, have tremendous problems with **intimacy**. How can anyone seriously dispute the obvious fact that violence is but the final link in the chain that begins with the boy's disconnection, first from his own feelings and then from his family relationships, as a consequence of following a narrow ideal of maturity. Our misguided ideal doesn't allow **real** men to be "sensitive" or to feel or admit to (much less share) negative emotions of fear, weakness, doubt, anxiety or pain. Even mothers can have their own unresolved conflicts about what "masculinity" should mean, and can promote toughness and athleticism in their sons. Many mothers frown on too much sensitivity, thereby aiding and abetting the "rugged individualism" which leads only to isolation, loneliness and the hardness of heart that will commit or allow violence.

Intergenerational Violence—Violation of Boundaries, Misuse of Power

Another common source of resentment and an obstacle to a son's escape from "smothering" parental control that is part of a larger problem labeled "intergenerational violence," is his continuing financial dependence on them.

❖ Jerry was a "very good son" by everyone's standards. But, because no one can serve two masters, he was not a good husband, at least by the standards of his wife, Anne. As long as Jerry continued working for his father, giving him first priority on his time and energy, and for much less money than he could have made elsewhere, the marriage of Jerry and Anne was "on hold," at least as far as Anne was concerned. By his "slavish" obedience to his father, Jerry repeatedly sent his wife the signal that her interests were secondary, earning her passionate resentment, and justifying her refusal to have a child. Ironically, Jerry was almost as unhappy with his dependence on his parents as was his wife. But, as he expressed it, "What could they do?"

Jerry's parents were not mature enough to "see" the justification for Anne's position. Certainly, they were guilty of the same kind of intergenerational interference that was present in Toby's case, that is, one generation taking advantage of age, status, power, or money to force other family members to violate their own responsibilities.

The common element in all the cases presented so far, was the refusal, or inability, of the husband, the wife, the parents, or the children to confront, to deal with, or to step aside from, an obviously abnormal situation. **No one**, in these examples, evidenced the **sense of personal responsibility,** which is required in order to deal with **any** problem in relationships. Little evidence was seen to indicate that any of the other partners had a **sense of self-worth**, either, that might have motivated them to protect their own interests.

Fortunately for Toby and Marie, in the case described earlier, a family doctor was able to awaken in Marie a sense of personal responsibility that eventually solved everything.

The *Solution* to Troubled Relationships

To stay on a path to personal maturity and intimacy, each spouse has to develop a **sense of personal worth** and a **sense of personal responsibility** for all that is happening in his or her own life. These are the **two legs** upon which all of us make our life's journey. In marriage, each spouse must do his/her own walking because no spouse can carry the other for long. Because most of us have been infected with a "consumer mentality" (translation: fulfillment is something outside us that we can buy or get from someone else), we have a difficult time appreciating that our **peace and healing occurs**

within us, and that achieving what should be the most important goals in our life depends almost entirely on what we do.

The Process of Growing up Starts with Awareness

Obviously, a boy/man must be aware of his fear and vulnerability before he can reasonably **accept, or admit it.** If anyone wishes to gain this **self-awareness**, he (or she) should start with an examination of how he spends his day, especially the free time. Does he get his kicks from people, or from things? If it's from people, he's on the right path. If it's sports, booze, power, prestige, or wealth (in the fable, King Midas turned all his friends into gold), then he is **not** on the right path, because he is not aware of the damage he is doing to himself and those closest to him. A boy/man who pretends everything is all right, when it isn't all right is living a lie that will always prevent those close to him from getting to know him. How could anyone know him, if he remains a mystery to himself?

An **in-depth look** at any of the **major news stories**, that is, about war, destruction, mass violence, crashes of commercial or private planes, train wrecks at crossings, deaths from recklessness on the ski slopes, or calamities like the *Titanic* or the *Hindenberg*, invariably **reveals one common, and quite startling fact**: the tragic event was the result of a supposedly-mature man or men being more macho than wise, that is, a man or men who obviously lacked any clue as to how foolish he/they were acting. There is a plethora of men who do not know who they are or what they are about. One recent National Public Radio (NPR) debate on the role of "faith" in healing, uncovered an "expert," who was also an avowed atheist, who asserted by way of an aside, that there have been "plenty of atheists in the foxholes." There wasn't time for me to call in and ask him if he had ever personally interviewed such an atheist while he was **still in** the foxhole, or had ever known someone who had. Perhaps such an interview had been conducted and the atheist's assertion accurately reported. That still wouldn't remove my skepticism. Before I would believe any man who proclaimed that he wasn't wary or afraid of the possibility of facing imminent judgment for the harmful things he had done, or the good that he had failed to do, he would have to admit that there were some things in **this life** that he did fear. If he was indeed fearless (there are certainly such men), I would inform him that he was in denial, not only of any fear but also of any pain or anxiety. He was clearly **disconnected from himself**. And, I would bet the ranch that he had never achieved a committed and intimate relationship with anyone.

Summarizing Part One

Until the Boy Code, which prepares boys for future success primarily by removing their sensitivities, has been eliminated, ways must be found to get the adult men in our country to **grow up** to the extent that they **can be** good husbands, fathers, and friends. The point has been made: no one can grow-up until he has completed an honest search for his own assets and liabilities, and their effects on those who share his life. Admittedly, a man must follow his **awareness** of precisely who he is with **acceptance** of who he is. No one can establish a sound long-lasting relationship until he (or she) has accepted, admitted, **owned** (translation: taken responsibility for) **everything** he has discovered by his search within, including his negative feelings, like fear, weakness, anxiety, doubt, and shame. These feelings may have been buried or denied as part of his adherence to a misguided code for manhood. He must somehow find the courage to admit to and accept his fears and weaknesses and imperfections. To hide behind pride, arrogance, control, and bluster, is to remain a little boy whistling in the dark, using action to hide his fear. Violence often results when a boy/man acts out his fear. But violence wouldn't be necessary if this boy/man would simply turn on the lights, that is, **admit** his fear and vulnerability.

Dean Ornish writes that "this **simple idea**—taking responsibility and examining my own issues—was the foundation of a powerful motivational shift that began transforming my life." [8] This **motivational shift**, this **personal commitment** to assume full responsibility for **all** that you think, feel, or do in your closest relationships, and to also accept responsibility for the consequences of the same, is the essential **first step** on the path to **healing marriages** and to achieving marital **intimacy**.

Boys/men are not alone in their immaturity. A typical woman will reject, bury, deny, or compensate for feelings of unworthiness, too, especially if she does not feel loved. However, only in the rarest cases will she resort to violence as her **first** *solution*. Most often, she will "fix" her feelings of inadequacy by building, renewing, strengthening a bond of friendship with whomever is available at the time. Ironically, women's task for becoming alive and in touch with their deepest and true selves often means manifesting their strength, asserting their intelligence, following their heart. Intimacy will forever be impossible to the woman who accepts bondage and subservience, just as it is impossible to the man who would impose it. In **Part Two**, we will consider the unique problems a **woman** brings with her to the marriage. In addition I promise to provide some thoughts and opinions on the very contentious question: **What is the nature of a woman?**

Part 2
The Different Nature
of a Woman

FACT OR FICTION, MYSTERY OR MYTH

"I didn't value myself enough . . . to reflect even privately on whether
my existence had . . . any meaning. I took it for granted that
like most of the billions of people who are born and die on this planet
I was just an accident. There was no reason for me."
—Nuala O'Faolain, in *Are You Somebody?*

"'How did a guy like [that] win a glorious creature like yourself?'
'He swept me off my knees.' In one remark,
the history of the Western World."
—Dalma Heyn, in *Marriage Shock*

6

When "Sugar and Spice and Everything Nice . . ." Becomes Something Else

"The pubertal brain is so aware of the world that it throbs, it aches, it wants to find the paths to calm it down and make sense of the world. It is an exposed brain, as tender as a molted crab, and it can be seared deeply. Who can forget adolescence? And who has ever recovered from it?"
—Natalie Tangier

No One Has Ever Claimed It's a Women's World

My previous book summarized my knowledge of what women want.[1] Most women have a lifetime of reasons to have anger toward men, and the world that male-power has always controlled. That reality must be noted, accepted, and taken into account, as boys relate to girls, and as any man begins serious negotiations with a woman. A man who wants to better understand his wife (and his daughters) should note the "hurricane" of female **adolescence**, when a young girl-woman first experiences the full power and control of the male-directed culture. Several recent books vividly describe the cruel and confusing world of our teenage daughters.[2]

The "thinness envy" that permeates our culture is not simply a matter of health and beauty, but of female "obedience."[3] The emo-

43

tional and psychological stresses of adolescence, much more than
the physical changes, can adversely affect the whole course of a
woman's life, especially since the gains of the feminist movement
have yet to provide girls adequate protection from an ever more
dangerous, more sexually pre-occupied, and more hedonistic environment.[4] To make matters worse, as the physical changes of adolescence begin, the young lady is often thoroughly confused by mixed
cultural messages. Naomi Wolf refers to the **messages** prevalent
before her generation of teenagers rebelled against them in the
sixties. Before that decade when the "sexual liberation" of women
began, virtually every "young lady" was sent the message: whatever
a teenage girl "feels" or "experiences" of a sensual or sexual nature
must be ignored and denied as not happening; or, that all such
happenings are perverse.[5] Wolf refers to the judgment prevailing
before the sexual revolution as the "great forgetting" of women's
more passionate nature. She claims that such ideas resulted from an
exercise in mass male "denial" that began with the **industrial revolution,** a few hundred years ago. When wealth became tantamount to
nobility, the men who had acquired it re-wrote the rules for the
women who would be their wives.

Wendy Shalit supplies ample documentation to support Wolf's
view that female desire "was not actually discovered for the first time
in the 1960s."[6] Tragically for adolescents (and, ultimately for women
generally), the other and **stronger message** that has been taught
since the 1960s is that of sexual liberation—men and women are the
same, and any so-called "femininity" was always a social construct,
defined and imposed by men."[7]

Both messages, added to other evidence to come, demonstrate
convincingly that men (and thus society *officially*) have persisted in
a wish to control and to deny women's sexuality. Men clearly do not
understand the "eroticism" that has always been part of women's
nature. [8] More importantly, men (and many feminists) no longer
acknowledge a woman's special vulnerability, reflected in her **modesty**. An adolescent who is assailed in the schools to stop acting as if
she's different from everybody else, and ordered to "drop her
hangups about sex and sexual feelings" is eventually injured much
more than was her mother or grandmother who was trained to

either repudiate what she felt in her body as she was becoming a woman, or, to deny that anything was happening. Wendy Shalit writes that "a society that has lost its respect for female modesty is not just one which no longer teaches men to be protective of women, it is a society which treats its women as a kind of joke."[9] "It is no accident that harassment, stalking, and rape increased when we decided to let everything hang out. A society that has declared war on embarrassment is one that is hostile to women."[10]

"Today we are taught that this 'every woman's a lady' idea was sexist, that it made women into property, but sometimes it seems that abandoning it has made women all the more into property." [11] Shalit argues convincingly that the sexual revolution is "trying to cure womanhood," that is, to strip women of the natural defense that their modesty provides, thereby eliminating the challenge to an honorable response that such a virtue presents to men.[12]

Neither Chivalry nor Modesty Will Ever Die

Vive la difference! The French admirably delight in all the ways boys and girls differ. So do I. Even after American society's forty-year effort to eliminate gender differences and to prove that even the obvious sexual differences are "no big deal," most of us hold fast to the traditional notions of manhood and womanhood. The male desire to be chivalrous, that is, a gentleman who is not only courteous, but gallant and generous, is undeniable. The woman who reject's a gentleman's actions, such as, giving up his seat, letting her off the elevator first, taking her hand as she descends from a bus or (very rarely) even tipping his hat, may see his courtesies as an insult, or a carry-over from an age when women were deemed weak **and inferior**, but most men and women would say that such a woman doesn't have a clue about what **both** genders prefer.

Without question, when a society denies gender differences, a woman's **modesty** or embarrassment or sexual vulnerability is viewed as simply a **hang-up** from a repressive past culture. For example, a modern woman is supposed to reject any notion that a failed love affair should be **any more traumatic for her than it is for him**. But it often is precisely that.

Admittedly, most of us born before the sexual revolution just lived or carried on many of the gender differences. We seldom discussed them seriously. In fact, little or no effort was made to understand them, let alone trying to profit from any understanding. Now that so many persons getting married have been convinced that no important gender differences exist, marriage keeps becoming for them more and more of an eye-opening experience. Ironically, it is only in the area of sexuality, that men will acknowledge very real gender differences. In fact, most men will insist that women are **different, less sexual, but certainly more dangerous.**

The Argument Over Women's Sexual Equality

Camille Paglia, in her controversial work *Sexual Personnae,* asserts that women have always had to hide their sexuality because men's ego, or sense of adequacy, is threatened by women's sexual assertiveness. She maintains (and provides many examples) that men have tried to escape not only by embracing other men but that men have also used the creative arts to express their avoidance of any confrontation with women. Paglia challenges us to find an alternative explanation if we can't blame a man's pride—specifically his fear of failure, or of being found inadequate—for his reluctance to accept his wife as his equal.[13]

Terence Real, in an opposing view, claims that a man does not reject equality because he fears either women or intimacy. Rather, a man **fears subjugation,** that is, being one down or controlled. "Vulnerability, openness, yielding to another's wishes—many of the requisite skills for healthy relationships—can be experienced by most men as invitations to be attacked. . . . Men's fear of entrapment, of female engulfment . . . is a transposition of the male model of interaction to the living room and the bedroom. . . . [T]hey fear that women will act like men."[14]

It is ironic that a man who, for whatever reason, refuses to treat his wife as an equal in the bedroom is usually the same man who will reject the notion that a woman can be more vulnerable to sexual, emotional, or psychological exploitation. In the first instance, the wife is subject to him, and in the second instance she is not entitled to any extra protection. What does he think he's doing, but wanting to have his cake and eat it too. In this matter of vulnerability, I am definitely on the woman's side.

It is precisely in the bedroom where the challenge to allow full equality demands **manliness**—not in any narrow sense, but in the best sense of that term—holding on to those strengths uniquely male, and allowing his wife to **own**—to keep, to exhibit, to experience—**her eroticism**, and do it on her terms.[15]

A Woman's Open Heart Can Get Her into Trouble

I subscribe to women's special vulnerability, especially in matters of the heart. How much of this susceptibility to psychological injury is due to nature and how much to the way girls are raised from birth, should not be the point. Rather, the fact that this difference exists must be remembered, and always taken into account.

Studies have found that about forty percent of husbands admit to erectile or ejaculatory problems at least occasionally, and sixty-three percent of women experience orgasmic difficulties. Despite these figures, from a practical point of view, most marriages should **not** be described as **sexually dysfunctional**, that is, requiring the services of a professional counselor or sex therapist. Sexual **adequacy** exists in most American marriages even though husbands bring selfish motives to the marriage bed. For their part, wives have generally acknowledged that they do not object to being **used** for a man's pleasure as long as he pays attention to their desires as well. Any wife may object to, and resent, being **used poorly** (translation: insensitively.) Again, in practice, aggression that reflects desire is great (don't we all want to be desired or admired?), but aggression reflecting demand or impatience is almost invariably resisted. Note that I said "being desired" or being **wanted**. Being **needed** introduces much different dynamics. Being too needy—in this instance, a man needing his wife for sex—can create a potential "inequality," since she can use his need to manipulate him. Equally true, a wife who needs to have her husband close during most of his free time, may frighten him or smother him. **Neediness,** the habitual stance of dependent people, is what frequently generates a man's complaint

that "marriage sucks." Undeniably, too many men and women **do
neediness well.** Of course, needy or dependent people are rarely
perceived as appealing or sexy. Thus neediness, or any act of dependency, is always a step away **from intimacy**, since that is defined as
a **skill** exercised between independent equals, who maintain their
freedom to choose.[16]

Maturity: Wanting to Be Wanted, but Not Needing to Be Needed

Unlike a man, a woman tends to be quite open about her **needs.**
However, she typically presents them, not as **desires**, which a man
would welcome (recall that men love to please women and provide
service), but rather as assertions or confessions of dependency. This
is unfortunate, because the expression of need represents a flight
from intimacy. Naomi Wolf writes that even strong and assertive
women typically adopt a meek and passive approach with a new
romance ". . . The certain attractiveness to dependency, something
we are so used to, that it's almost synonymous with being female."[17]
So, as a woman, whether you simply want to save your marriage, or,
you long to join the ranks of the "select few" who achieve the skill of
intimacy, the path is the same: the more strengths and assets **you**
bring to, or develop in the relationship, the better your chances for
success.

On the other hand, **a man who cannot admit to any need should
be avoided at all costs**. Any woman married to such a man, knows
first-hand that he is incapable of passion, as a consequence of his
denial of his own feelings. The first five chapters should have provided some understanding of the processes that could make the
most sensitive male child the most **insensitive** of husbands. But,
while these nurturing excuses may **explain** why a husband isn't
romantic, they **cannot solve** his insensitivity problem, or provide his
wife the romance she desires.

Why do twenty million American women spend nearly a billion
dollars a year on **romantic novels? Erotic** is now a more accurate
description of these books, in my judgment, even if they are still not
placed in the Erotica section of the book stores among the other

Women's Studies. Most of these novels are written by women for women, and all strongly suggest that a "real" woman does not submit sexually from a sense of obligation, in gratitude, to keep the peace, or to keep her mate.[18] In these mass-marketed women's novels, you invariably discover men who are strong and brave, but sensitive; and, you also see women who are equally strong and assertive, but wise. You rarely find a woman using a man's desire for sex as a way to control him, or as an opportunity to sadistically deny him. Even though these books are presented as fantasies, their popularity would suggest that at least twenty million women want not only equality with their consorts, but also something more in their life that is specifically sexual. Since the equality women seek includes both their bodies and their minds, and because they cannot find that **equality** (better translation: **reverence**) in real-life, they obviously use these novels as a surrogate. Why else would wives need to fantasize about sexual partners, if not because their own husbands do not allow equality or show enough respect, especially in their sexual approach?[19]

Summarizing . . .

If husbands were up to equality and respect—and if men did not feel it necessary to keep women in their **place**—maybe men wouldn't have to spend so many weekends, in groups, going back to nature to reassert their manhood, to beat drums and to shout of their power and comradeship. Also, perhaps, if women were accorded in the home the equality the law has prescribed, the **Women's Movement** wouldn't have to spend so much effort protecting women from exploitation and other abuse. If both these changes came to pass, the feminists could even cooperate with, and wholeheartedly support the **Men's Movement**. Each wife might even be willing to buy her husband his own set of drums, and/or, to pack him enough food to last his entire "escape" weekend!

Unfortunately, in this matter of equality a lot of husbands just "don't get it."

Keeping Women
in Their Place

> . . . *[T]he world needs more girl drummers.*
> *The world needs your wild, pounding, dreaming hearts."*
> —Natalie Tangier

The More Things Change,
the More They Remain the Same

The industrial revolution created an entirely new class, namely, persons without royal blood but with power derived from wealth. Men with acquired or inherited wealth used their power to demand mates who were "worthy," "fitting," or "classy." The result was an abrupt cultural change in the "use" or "role" of young women and their preparation for a satisfactory marriage. Sexual attraction was officially treated as if it didn't exist. Under the rules of that system, any display, public or private, of sexual desire was fraught with dangerous consequences. Heyn insists that these repressions were still operating as recently as 1993. As evidence, she points to the ban on the sale of *The Erotic Silence of the American Wife*, in all K-Mart stores, solely because the title contained the word **erotic**.[1]

By the end of the nineteenth century, a woman's "place" had become precisely defined. The **conduct books**, which first appeared at the end of the seventeenth century as detailed instructions on cooking, cleaning, sewing, and every other duty of a wife, evolved into books which unequivocally insisted that, besides a strong back and a constant cheerfulness, a wife must have the patience, humility, kindness, appreciativeness, thriftiness, simplicity, and the "purity" of a saint.[2]

In her role as "light of the home"[3] a wife had to exercise great care to avoid even a suspicion that she was not, everywhere and at all times, a "lady." The very long list of what a "lady" did, and did not do, was powerfully enforced. The "rules and regulations" spelled out so clearly in the conduct books of the Victorian era marked the zenith of women's subjection in marriage. The unfeeling **and unloved** husband and father in James Barrie's *Peter Pan*, written a century ago, was undoubtedly representative of the husband's role in the dynamics of that era.[4]

However, those historians of the Victorian era who insist that a considerable amount of fun was being had under the sheets, including pre- and extra-marital sex, are probably correct. As pointed out in the previous chapter (especially in the Notes), women are at least as passionate and sexual as men, and both men and women delight in doing "naughty," or forbidden, things, as Eve demonstrated. Neither conclusion contradicts the preponderance of data confirming women's total subjection within the home during most of the seventeenth and all of the eighteenth and nineteenth centuries. Under the system of oppression extant in those centuries, most women, most of their lives, were little more than indentured servants. Admittedly, conditions for women in the home and society did improve in the twentieth century, especially after Betty Friedan jump-started the feminist movement in 1963 with *The Feminine Mystique*.

The question, now, is "Have the inequalities in the home been corrected?" As far as **most** women are concerned, no amount of skepticism or bluster— "Women never had it so good," "Who takes all the risks?," or "Who gets killed in the fighting?" (all the comments could well be true)—can change the bottom line: **male control remains now, as it was then, the primary reason for women's frustration, depression, anger, and rage.**[5] Very happily, women **have** come a long way, and they remain optimistic that marriage is the best route to happiness and fulfillment. Ninety percent still get married before they reach fifty, ignoring their own instincts and past experiences with men, the advice of friends, and the depressing statistics.[6]

Unfortunately, a majority of women eventually decide that they are giving up too much by getting married and that they are not getting what they want. Wives rightly maintain that they are not accorded equal rights in their own homes. Two-thirds to three-quarters of present-day divorces are initiated by women, even though a divorced woman's income goes down an average of seventy-three percent, while a man's goes up an average of forty-two percent after he sheds his wife. Since the Census Bureau's figures in 1993, for example, showed that divorce is twice as likely for couples living below the poverty line, it should not be surprising to learn that the majority of women who are single parents are impoverished, at least temporarily.[7] Men can deny that women have a valid grievance against the present marital system, but no good jury, that is, one that weighed all the evidence, would agree. Wives rightly maintain that they are not accorded equal rights in their homes.

8

Oppressor and Oppressed: Still a Core Marriage Dynamic?[1]

"We are not going to stop wars by politics or aggression.
We are going to stop it at the basic level of healing the individual."
—Joan Borysenko

When Will Men Be Up to Equality?

In the three years of intensive research for my book on women and their relationships, I was stunned by the extent to which American women have been enslaved/subordinated /undervalued/deprived/and abused. In President Clinton's 1999 State of the Union address, the strongest applause was for his plea for equal pay for equal work—there being a twenty-five to thirty-three percent shortfall for women, depending upon whether the job is on a lower level, or one that is closer to the glass ceiling.

But, it has been in the privacy of the home that many of the most horrific tales of abuse have occurred. Although now much less frequent, atrocities continue to occur despite the passage of specific laws protecting women (and children) from domestic violence or abuse. In my practice, physical abuse seems no longer to be a problem (if the answers to abuse found on my questionnaires can be believed). On the other hand, countless patients have characterized their husbands as **tyrants,** which I would define as a person who coerces another person to act against their wishes. Husbands seem to decide in most families what everyone else in the family will do or must do. Although incredible progress has been made in bringing **equality into the home,** my patients, for nearly four decades, have insisted that they are not considered an equal very often, especially in matters that "count." One obvious example: even though both parents work in fifty-eight percent of two-parent families with children, seventy-four to ninety-two percent of the housework and child care tasks are done by mom. Management of all the social obligations appear to be *shared* in the same proportions. Not surprisingly, even those women who are reasonably happy and content (and this still represents a minority) give little credit to their husbands. A majority of wives, in fact, still feel their husbands are a *negative* influence in their families.

Many marriages function well because one partner (usually the wife) sacrifices for the sake of the other, or to preserve the "marriage." Even though such **arrangements** will work, that is not what marriage is all about. They are **not intimate marriages,** as such marriages will be defined in **Part Three.**

The traditional religious view of marriage can be credited with preventing society's shameful treatment of women from being totally duplicated in the home. Despite this protection, most often religion has been silent about, and even resistant to, the concept of a **wife having equal rights.** This failure of nearly all organized religious bodies to move more quickly in recognizing women's absolute equality is inexcusable. If we ever hope to improve our marriages, we must stop denying women **all the rights that men have.**[2]

Women—Equal but Vulnerable

The issue of "rights" is so vitally important to married women for the simple reason that the socialization of American men gives little recognition to the concept of **womanhood**—a concept that asserts that a woman's natural differences make her more vulnerable and in need of society's special protection.

Whether you consider her God's greatest gift to humanity or not, it is now the law that a woman is in every way equal to a man, and deserving of the same reverence that he demands for himself. Distinct from the issue of **equality** is the issue of **safety**. If girls/women could also be reverenced as "special"—if only because of their unique vulnerability—American women and wives would not have to live in so much fear.

Of course, it doesn't help that "essentialists"—those of us who believe in the natural differences, especially women's vulnerability—are ridiculed by sexual libertarians and the immoderate feminists.

(The political and social aspects of control and equality, and those goals of feminism that I wholeheartedly endorse, were covered at length in my book *It's Your Life!*, so they will not be repeated now. Undeniably, the concept that a husband should be **in control** of the family, dies hard.)

The myriad of issues involving control in a marriage are most often "played out" in subtle ways—ways is which the domination is not obvious, though the wife often sees **selfishness** being demonstrated on a routine basis. Her husband may disagree strongly with her assessment, but the bottom line, if a **short list** was compiled, favors the woman's view of the subject:

❖   A man generally prefers to devote his time and attention to projects outside the home, or to diversions for his own amusement, rather than spend valuable free time **rapport talking,** or sharing thoughts or opinions on any subject not vital to his own interests. **Sharing feelings** is simply not part of the repertoire for most men. **Just listening** to his wife's domestic aggravations is demanding a lot from any man, in his opinion. Or listening with **compassion?** That's really pushing him to the limit of his abilities. Even **hugs, kisses,** or a **bright smile** seem often to sap too much of his energy. Doing **any domestic chore,** for some men, is unthinkable. Even in families with both parents working, no study seems to turn up husbands willing to do more than one-quarter of the work in the home. The number one reason given by a woman who is divorcing her husband is the guy's refusal to share the housework. The number one quality for tuning him out of her life, even if she never files for divorce, is his **stinginess.**

Men—Saving Precious Energy to Compete

Perhaps, a man's unwillingness to be generous with his time and energy at home is simply a reflection of an overall stinginess. Then again, he may have made the judgment that his energies are needed for other goals, ranging from success in his job or profession to winning at handball, tennis or golf. Whatever the reason, wives' dissatisfaction with the way marriage chores are shared (rather, **not** shared) is widespread. There are of course other relational "downers" for the wife in a marriage, especially those that directly proceed from her husband's competitive style of relating. Even those persons without children of their own know that a **superiority** complex, manifested by bragging and haughtiness, is characteristic of boys, even from infancy. Their one-up approach toward their peers could accurately be described as grandiose, haughty, or condescending. Some children, on the other hand, adopt an **avoidance**, or no-risk approach. Their apparent **inferiority** complex is used to hide the truth that they are too proud to risk losing. Both complexes represent a boy's effort to counter his self-perception of inadequacy, or of being "one down." Neither approach to relationship works because neither is **authentic**, that is, honest.

This **concern with status**, and the ever-present threat of being **discovered** to be inadequate, which concern is so obvious in little boys, is **carried along into manhood, and into marriage.** Boys/ men see virtually every transaction with the opposite sex as a potential battle for supremacy. Wives report consistently, and correctly, that their husbands bristle, or become openly hostile, when corrected or approached in any way that would threaten their status of being adequate, correct, or competent in everything. Most women, by contrast, generally have no desire to get one-up, and consistently avoid even an appearance of superiority. They are thereby more inclined to negotiate cooperation and consensus. As Deborah Tannen explains, they seem to have a natural talent for developing complex networks of friendship with little effort. Ironically, despite a woman's great talent for getting to know **other people**, she can still adopt an approach to her husband that would suggest that she was wearing "blinders" that prevent her from understanding his differences. A man and his wife can celebrate many years of sharing the same bed, and still remain **total strangers** in matters of the heart.

In **Part Three**, we will look closely at these strangers and observe how gender differences, misguided goals, unrealistic expectations, pressures from antiquated or faulty sociological theories (for example, "a woman's place is in the home"), and, a motley assortment of human frailties can sabotage the best-laid plans of even the most highly motivated and educated bride and groom.

Part 3
A Most Worthy Challenge: Getting Marriage Right

"Love and intimacy are at the root of what makes us sick and what makes us well, what causes sadness and what brings happiness, what makes us suffer and what leads to healing."
—Dean Ornish

"Millions and millions of people besides me have thought that another person is what you need to complete yourself and to offer completion—that together you can unlock the best in the world and the best of yourself. . . . It is not about sex, the desire to share with another person. But it is about creation."
—Nuala O'Faolain

9

Brides and Grooms Rarely Get What They Expect

"You have to kiss a lot of frogs to find a prince."
—Unknown (but printed on Princess Diana's pillowcase)

"You train people how to treat you by how you treat yourself."
—Martin Rutte

Henry James wrote twenty outstanding novels of love and relationships, but none with a "they lived happily ever after" ending. His explanation was, "I am a realist." Natalie Tangier advises that "if you want consummation, read Jane Austen."[1]

G.K. Chesterton wrote that a man is judged by his good works, and a woman by what she is. That may still be a valid observation, even though the words were written nearly a century ago. But that doesn't mean it isn't a reflection of a double standard, and of male oppression. It is. [2] Hopefully, a man and woman will be judged equally from now on. She for what she accomplishes, even in the ways of worldly success, and he by what kind of a man he is, and what kind of a husband, and father, he has become. Even the most beautiful and talented women of our culture, who have been assured that a controlled body and a beautiful face guarantee them a powerful womanhood, cannot deny that the beautiful face and body will not guarantee them a happy marriage, or reverence in their old age.

Obviously, for us to understand marriage, we will have to keep focused on the two players who are so utterly different in their approach, yet so alike in their expectations.

The Problem of Unrealistic Expectations

Marriages would not be so stormy and traumatic if all the expectations were **realistic**. Each bride and groom should realistically expect caring, fairness, respect, support, cooperation, commitment, affection and monogamous sex. Resigning oneself to anything less is not recommended if one wishes to build a successful marriage, much less an intimate relationship. It is the **unconscious** expectations, which are nearly always **unrealistic**, that start working to destroy a marriage even before the ink on the contract is dry. In my previous book, I used four chapters to illustrate how little **rationality** is involved in mate-selection. We decide, by instinct, that **he will make me happy, (and vice-versa.)** Love at first sight involves not so much selecting someone we want to **be with,** as it is selecting someone we want **to be.** That someone we want to be, unfortunately, could have all or most of the qualities that we repudiated or got rid of in our own infancy and childhood. In that early environment, we adapted or adjusted what we thought, felt, or did in order to get along, prosper, perhaps even to "survive." If the person we now automatically and unconsciousness select has so many attributes we long ago categorized as **faults,** that is, dangerous, undesirable, or unacceptable, should we be surprised when we sooner or later experience **disappointment** with the person chosen. Such disillusionment is the universal emotion presenting in marriage therapy.[3]

Despite the obvious truths in the theories of mate selection, it is perfectly understandable for married people to look back at the **romantic** interval of their marriage and remain mystified as to how it all happened. But if **unconscious motivation** excuses an apparent mistake in our choice of a partner, there is little excuse for a bride and groom's failure to see and note the **two dark clouds** that hang over virtually every wedding. If they would but look up and notice them, the lovers might proceed with the ceremony anyway, but at least they could get out their umbrellas and prepare for the rain.

The *Dark Clouds* on the Horizon

One ominous cloud on the marital horizon is the **groom's** perception that marriage will be nothing more than a distraction (perhaps a permanent one, but only a distraction, nevertheless) on the path to his life goals. Attending to his bride's wants/needs definitely satisfies his need to feel competent. Her respect for him, and of his efforts in her behalf, beats almost anything else he knows, or has had in his life, up to that time. All this wonderful affirmation provides him with the sense "that nothing gets any better than this!" Most often, the new husband's assessment is right. Things do get worse. First, he begins to see that many of his efforts, even those requiring a lot of energy, elicit less and less appreciation. "Thank you's" from his wife eventually become a distant memory. His performance of the bread-winning duties seems to be entirely taken for granted. "Other" services at home keep being added, often in such a way as to suggest that if he doesn't provide them, he is a selfish and unfeeling lout.

Another commonplace annoyance: his wife's suggestions for "talking and relaxing" now somehow means bringing to his attention unpaid bills, troubles in school, household repairs, or her aching back. If a mutually acceptable time for bringing up such matters could be agreed upon, the husband might look forward with greater zest to the relaxation breaks. In many marriages, one other very disturbing element is introduced, typically by the wife, into the couple's private conversations: issues and concerns that have already been resolved are rehashed or second-guessed, or re-experienced. The wife's resurrection of old problems generally threatens her husband with the same unpleasant and negative emotions from which he ran away the first time the difficulties occurred.

Recalling past tragedies, reverses, mistakes, depressions, or transgressions is certainly, on the face of it at least, a very sadistic way to approach any friend, especially if you want to achieve an intimate relationship with him or her. What is a wife (or a husband) to reasonably expect by resurrecting issues that have been resolved? Granted, an essential precondition for intimacy is that there can be no preconditions. Therefore, there can be no conditions on what either partner is "allowed' to say, as long as they are telling the truth. But "painful memories?" What's the purpose? When anyone looks back, he or she becomes locked in the past, where possibilities no longer exist, only guilt, shame, or the second guess.

In defense of the wife, her recall of past unpleasant events may be motivated by her desperation to see her husband show *some* emotion. Thus, she will even settle for his **harsh emotions**, that is, reactions like discomfort, irritation, and even anger. "Trying to live with an uncommunicative man is like trying to live with a Pet Rock," sums up well the feelings of wives whose husbands never speak to them about anything.[4] Remember, men typically use **silence as a technique for managing (sic) their anger.**

A second dark cloud over the marriage ceremony, that is given little or no attention in premarital counseling, is the notion that **self-sacrifice** is women's true nature! I am not referring to the desire of most women to yield to their lovers sexually, the truth to which Victor Hugo was probably referring when he wrote, "One of the magnanimities of woman is to yield." Rather, I am referring to the expectation that a good and capable woman is one who will be the guarantor and the preserver of marital harmony. As Somerset Maugham scornfully noted, "A woman will always sacrifice herself if you give her the opportunity. It's her favorite form of self-indulgence." Sadly, a wife would prefer to be indulged by reverence and some devoted service. Though the law now guarantees her equal rights, which law guarantees a wife such reverence, affection, caring, and sensitivity, or even a husband who will do a reasonable amount of the housework and child-raising duties?[5]

Ironically, a man's flight from helping his wife with any of her day to day responsibilities is not typically due to laziness, at all. Giving a husband things to do that are not important, and which a wife could easily do herself (or, worse yet, the kids could do), can, if done often enough, constitute one gigantic **turn-off!** Unfortunately, women see a totally different reality: "Almost all household chores are simple. **Are men above simple chores?**" Apparently, there is

only one kind of man who can appreciate that it's the **sheer volume** of simple chores, not their complexity, that causes wives to compare their lot as a housewife to a **concentration camp** (Betty Friedan) or a **tomb** (O'Faolain): a man who has had to take care of a house and kids alone, either because he has lost his wife or because a wife has had an extended illness.

The prevailing consensus is that simple chores simply to not "appeal" to the typical American husband. He needs a **quest.** When there is nothing worthy of being designated a quest, or no specific mountain to climb, a boy/man often looks for just about any tangible, visible, presumably-attainable goal that requires some skill, courage, and fortitude, in order to maintain his sense of adequacy, or even to become one-up. Winning any competition generally makes a man's day. Also acceptable is any activity that will keep him from thinking about his biggest concerns: his past losses, **who** is getting ahead of him while he does nothing, or **what** is ahead of him. When a man is not "doing something," or convinced that he is "keeping up," he soon begins to feel anxious about such things, or even to feel inadequate.

Why Must Everyone Deal with Feelings of Inadequacy?

Why do boys (and girls, at least when they don't have a friend) from nine to ninety feel inadequate much of the time, even those who have been consistently honorable? Freud offered one explanation that is still very widely accepted. He theorized that anyone can feel anxiety, guilt, shame, and the other feelings that can come with them, in the present moment, as a direct result of feelings, desires, and impulses that were present long ago in his/her unconscious or subconscious mind, and which never reached **awareness.** Since these desires never reached the conscious part of the mind, they have never been faced or handled. Because of the Boy Code boys/ men cannot readily admit to **any negative emotions.** So, they must **deny** their inadequacy, shame, sadness, or guilt. **Men typically remain boys at heart,** that is, they retain well into middle age the **great expectations** that are the stuff of dreams. Their dreams of success always include bravery and heroic sacrifice. In lieu of a heroic task or a worthy project, a boy or a man will dream of winning, earning esteem, capturing prizes, being respected, or "becoming someone." Boys/men always take a **starring role** in their dreams. I never heard any boy confess to dreaming about failing, being a coward, losing or even coming in second. Eventually, the dreams of success involve a "fair maiden," to whom they can dedicate their service.

❖   Then, one day, often just "out of the blue," the man, usually young in age (but not always) finds that he has become the hero of someone else's dream. With little or virtually no effort on his part, he achieves a "quick fix" for his anxieties about measuring up to his peers in the very important matter of being wanted and respected and admired by a lovely and desirable woman.

This wonderful woman values him, affirms him, and "loves" him **just the way he is**. For a time at least, he can actually "see" all his good points through the eyes of his beloved. When he extends the same affirmation to his beloved, both are happier than they had ever thought possible.

Most of us have lived this dream. A blessed few are still living it.

A man's bride may have her own story to tell. If marriage, family, and children are to be her first priority, her background would probably fit the following description:

❖   Mary sometimes felt anxious, insecure, or even inadequate, too. But, unlike her brother in the same circumstances, Mary generally felt inadequate only when she lacked a friend. She dreamt mostly of becoming beautiful and admired, and of having many friends. There were, of course, fewer footballs, baseballs, and such, in Mary's reveries and fantasies, than in her brother's; but, there were more castles, kings, queens, and masked balls. And princes, too. But, instead of dreaming primarily, or at all, of prizes, winning, esteem, bravery, or being the conquering hero, Mary's fantasies emphasized friendship, sharing, and love. Lots and lots and lots of love.

Chesterton concluded that the great lesson of *Beauty and the Beast* is that a thing must be loved **before** it is lovable. Granted, a person can feel loved because he or she is a special person, for example, a prince or princess. But, I believe it is much more accurate and noble to say everyone is special simply because they **can be** loved and **can** love. Girls are born with this insight. (Those who believe in a Personal God know that they **are** loved.)

A girl/woman definitely prefers a world where everyone, even the baby animals can exchange love, and where each lady meets the "Prince Charming" who will love and protect her forever. Lo and behold, one day the lovely maiden does meet her Prince, who will have her and hold her, and "they will live happily ever after."[6]

Presently, we will discover what happens to that dream when the wicked witch and the dragons (and the unrealistic expectations) make their appearance . . . or when the bride discovers that her prince is really a frog.

10

Fall From Grace? . . . "My Fair Lady" to "The Little Mrs." to "My Old Lady"

> *"The tragedy of the modern woman is not that she is not allowed to follow man, but that she follows him far too slavishly."*
> —G.K. Chesterton

Leaving Out the *Rights* in a *Rite of Passage*

Zsa Zsa Gabor's response to the request that she share some of the knowledge of sexual matters that her first eight marriages had provided her—"How would I know anything about sex? I've always been married."—reflects the common notion, promulgated for several centuries, that most of the sexual knowledge, the sexual need, and the sexual satisfaction, was reserved for the man. A woman claimed otherwise at her peril. Yet, a girl's introduction to intimidation by a male culture certainly does not begin when she becomes sexually-developed or when she gets married. Most experts still insist that the "pressure to be feminine" begins at birth, even while admitting that marriage certainly "ups the ante."

From the moment a woman makes the decision to become a "wife," she assumes, in her own mind, responsibility for the "obligations" of this role and proclaims to the world that she is fully qualified. To search for norms by which a bride, or the bride's family, are to be judged, start with the wedding or, more precisely, with the wedding preparations. The seriousness of the marriage contract as a guarantor of a woman's future hopes is offered as the justification for the bride and her family assuming most of the work and expense for the wedding. The prospective groom who fails to appreciate the depth of emotions that accompany these preparations may find himself looking for a new bride.

While adolescence and motherhood, representing the other **rites of passage** in a woman's life, are obviously very important and challenging, the **main** drama of a woman's life begins when she marries. Marriage, at least for most women, still marks the turning point in their lives, changing forever their goals, priorities, feelings and emotions, reaction patterns, and behavior.

Why Only *One* Caretaker for a Marriage?

After a "Miss" becomes a "Mrs." the success of the marriage seems to become "her responsibility," reflecting her qualifications, breeding, and character. Her sense of accountability for this new entity, the **us**, that is, the married couple, becomes stronger and clearer each day. In addition, when his new wife's actions and attitudes change, as an inevitable consequence of her perception that every action is now being scrutinized, it is not long before the typical husband becomes baffled by his mate's unprecedented concerns, anxieties, and preoccupations. [1]

As a wife struggles to change her former "single" ways to conform to her new role, she suddenly needs more support. One crucial need is to see evidence, on a very regular basis, that her mate is sensitive and interested enough in her thoughts and feelings to notice and appreciate her new concerns, and ante-up the added support which she needs. The typical husband is mystified, confused, and "ignorant" of these concerns, as his wife suddenly starts to respond and act differently. He eventually reacts to her ever-increasing demands for affirmation and approval by a variety of tactics well known to any serious observer of American marriage. Husbands are "famous" for their passive-aggression in forgetting important things, and for their apparent inability to stay "focused" enough to "see" or "hear" their wives for more than a few minutes per day.

Regrettably, it is the psychological **child** (explained in Chapter Twelve) who generally signs the marriage contract, so the marital partners now cry, sulk, fidget, withdraw, or seek more immediate sensual gratification in drugs, food or alcohol—and begin to openly express their **anger.** In fact, any adult who refuses to make the commitment to grow up takes his/her repertoire of "child" survival tricks to the grave.

If there is one characteristic that best reveals our level of maturity, it is, surely, our ability to express our own anger in ways that do not produce harmful consequences. Unfortunately, ninety-five percent of those married never achieve enough skill at handling their anger to be able to achieve a great marriage. Few men or women achieve the **insight to see anger as a gift,** alerting them to a hidden and unfulfilled need. If anger could be seen that way, the solution to the anger might be found much more readily. The challenge is to find the need, the grievance, or the wound, and express or **share it, as one's own problem,** before all the angry words are spoken. However, for a considerable number of married people, anger is simply taboo. You will meet several such couples in some later chapters. Buried anger causes just as many problems as anger that is freely vented. Anger can be disguised in any number of ingenious ways. For examples, anger can be taken out on fellow employees or subordinates, on relatives, neighbors, or minorities. It can be buried under an addiction to food or to other women. In many marriages, there are no fights because only one spouse ever gets angry. (Unfortunately, the *never-angry* spouse is usually an expert **provoker.**) Many wives have never been allowed from earliest childhood to express their anger, and simply get "sick" instead.

Except for "a precious few" husbands and wives who manage to get beyond the **conflicted stage,** the anger is there in the marriage, but is being **handled** in a way that prevents a great marriage or an intimate one. Sooner or later, and following the second law of thermodynamics that states every closed system runs out of energy unless some more energy (for example help or insight) is added, many of these conflicted marriages come to a stage of **gridlock,** that is, no one or anything changes for the better. Even when no changes are noticed, the relationship is generally getting worse.

During the "romantic" part of the marriage, when the focus was on only the positive aspects of each other's character and personality—making mutual affirmation easy—energies were devoted to spontaneity, creativeness, romance, or the spirit of adventure. When the marriage partners' former feelings of inadequacy return, the shame and blame that generate anger come, too. Like Adam and Eve in the Garden, who suddenly realize they are naked, the differences each now sees in the other become part of the problem, as **acceptance is replaced by criticism.** The child-like affirmation of the other is replaced by an awareness of the **"baggage"**—the past pain, shame, guilt, mistakes, insecurity, fears, anxieties, grievances—which the spouse has brought into the marriage. Inevitably, a more wary, more guarded, and more business-like atmosphere is adopted—of negotiation and reciprocity, leading to more and more "arrangements" to keep the marriage the best, or most practical option, for both of them.

A woman's argument that her husband married her only for her looks gains a lot of credence when her mate's level of avoidance goes up with the size of her waistline. **Chapters Twenty-one, Twenty-two, and Twenty-three** will provide some sound principles to show why romance and mutual attraction should have little to do with fading beauty or flabby biceps. Obviously, if a man's only interest in his wife is to **use** her sexually, the marriage is essentially over. In **Part Four,** the tragic loss that a man incurs by such an attitude of uncaring and selfishness is vividly contrasted with the possibilities inherent in a committed relationship in which love is exchanged. Whether a man ever comes to realize it or not, his wife can easily become his greatest blessing, and loving her the source of his greatest joy. Any man who has a loving woman at his side is a **success** in the ways that matter most.

11

The Woman Beside Every Successful Man

"When I am faced with a family in which there is a depressed woman, my first move is to empower the woman. When I am faced with a family in which there is a depressed man, before beginning work with the man, my first move is to empower the woman. . . . [O]ne needs to invite him to . . . increased relational responsibility, a move he may not be inclined to make if his partner allows him to avoid it."
—Terence Real, *I Don't Want To Talk About It*

No *Married Man* Wants to Be an Island

In the section *Before Proceeding* . . . , depression or addiction in men was revealed as a major problem in at least one of every five marriages at any given time, and in nearly one-half of American marriages at one time or another. But whether the addicted or depressed person is the husband or the wife, the **wife's active cooperation** will generally be essential for successful treatment of either. The reason is that "**real men just don't get addicted or depressed!**" Men simply deny the problem, because to admit it would stigmatize them as weak and incompetent failures. Thus, they do nothing constructive or remedial. So, when they **do** get addicted or depressed, how can they do anything on their own about it?

While professional help is almost always needed, a wife's under-standing of the male psyche is never more useful than when her husband is addicted or depressed. While a wife's understanding of male pride, and the one-up/one-down world in which he lives and struggles, can be a wonderful plus in **every** marriage, this under-standing is generally crucial when her husband is depressed and/or addicted.[1]

Lying at the root of traditional masculinity (in this country, perhaps more than any other, because American women have full equality by law), is the concept of **control**. Having a wife who, by mandate at least, is "equal," can be very threatening to a man who has been raised to control or manage his family. A **boy** who finds himself one-down to anyone, or in any situation, will do just about anything to deny, to hide, or to correct the humiliating state of affairs. A **man** will simply do it faster. The male dynamic of "better than/less than" often obscures consideration of "equal to" in a man's interpersonal contacts. Male pride is an ever-present motivator lurk-ing in the wings, ready to be used as a "first defense" to ward off any criticism from an "equal," which criticism, by its very nature, would put the **critic** one up.

Strangers in the Dark

If a man is aggravated by criticism from his wife, and most men are, he will almost always be enraged by judgments that are not true, or that are inaccurate. Yet, the **stupid generalizations** about men, that provide so many knowing smirks when normal women get together, have become a permanent part of the language and cul-ture. Ignorance in print is easily demonstrated. Both the general and the sexual how-to-please-your-husband articles written by women for women in most of the leading women's monthly magazines provide ample reasons to declare that a lot of supposedly intelligent and educated women don't understand men, or what men want. Such writers consistently evidence a deep misunderstanding of what goes on in the mind of a man.

Never mentioned, for example, is the simple truth that a man welcomes the opportunity to do something that he knows will make a woman happy. In Chapter Six, I pointed out that a man or woman who is **mature** wants to be desired or **wanted**, but has no inordinate, or excessive need to be **needed**, that is, to have his or her spouse become a dependent. Providing a man with a clear and worthwhile project, for example, will often bring out manly qualities a wife may have considered long atrophied. Mutual **needs**, obviously, exist in every relationship. However, when needs are perceived or presented as **demands**, they can become a focus of conflict. Most husbands deplore being asked to perform tasks or "piddling little nuisance projects" that a wife (or one of the kids) could easily do, putting such projects in the same category as the repetitive "donkey" work that characterizes many American workplaces. They rarely realize that **their wife has a million little piddling projects and needs help.**

Most men prefer to attend to a wife's **desires**. Being able to lavish her with a fancy bracelet or necklace she doesn't need, but which she is delighted to receive, usually makes a man feel worthwhile and happy. A man's **sensitivity to his wife's desires** is a fact to which women would do well to pay more attention. Another example: a husband's motor for romance will usually run much faster if his wife makes it clear that she welcomes or desires his attention. A husband is inspired by his wife's affirming response to his sexual advances primarily because he values her **respect** for the talent, the competency, the correctness of his actions. Failure to understand and appreciate or accept that a man's highest priority is to be **well-regarded** (translated: competent, correct, right about virtually everything), has spawned countless angry and destructive responses from husbands when they have encountered or experienced disrespect from their wives. This need to be competent or right is also responsible for a man's refusal to consult road maps, or even ask for directions.

Deborah Tannen emphasizes that because it is **independence** that American men strive for above anything else, while **intimacy** remains the dominant focus and goal of women, the two sexes have a different view of every situation. It is as if, to use Tannen's words, "their life-blood ran in different directions." Eventually the habit of going in different directions a large part of the time can make it very difficult for two people to "see" each other clearly on even the important issues. This distance can have results that are, **at least**, "troubling," and a source of apprehension.

❖ At the height of my career, I decided that I should get more training on some of the newest surgical techniques. Since my business partner at the time refused to increase his own work load so that I might take a bunch of post-graduate courses, I was forced to make a major career decision. Should I leave the partnership and the practice entirely (and all the patients who knew and trusted me) and join a totally new group at a "teaching" hospital that was thirty miles away, or, should I stay where I was? I eventually decided to change.

For the two years prior to making my decision, I sought as much expert advice as I could get. The possible consequences of my decision were scary enough to motivate me to seek psychiatric counseling. My wife Marianne (who, as the world's best listener and best conversationalist, remains my chief claim to fame) agreed to the psychiatrist's conditions for seeing me, namely, that she must be available to talk to him if he decided her input was necessary to help him guide my decision.

To my utter amazement, the first question from the doctor, uttered before I even had a chance to sit down at my initial consultation, was: "Do you love your wife, Jim?" I surprised myself when I blurted out without thinking: "Yes, I do. But I don't think the ways I show that love is good enough for her, now, and probably never has been good enough!

"I fully admit, I have always done my thing. So, if your question means, can I expect my wife to ante-up more support for me, while I risk both our futures,' the answer could be 'no.'"

Since that day, I have thought often about my spontaneous response. For more than twenty-five years, I had done "my thing' and had never once asked my wife if she would want a different kind of life than that as the wife of an extremely busy obstetrician-gynecologist. Undoubtedly, a large part of the problem prior to my first heart attack, a decade ago, was "my mistress"—delivering babies, performing surgery, and responding to emergencies. My profession always took first priority. For thirty of the thirty-five years that I performed those duties, there was (for reasons I cannot get into) **no time off**, that is, no leisure time when I was not subject to emergency call.

Most of the men I know closely and admire, and who have entered marriage for the duration, rate themselves as "darn good husbands." Yet, several have expressed regret at the priorities they chose early on. Like me, success took first place in their lives and their wives knew it. We share the humbling impression that our choices left much to be desired.

Apparently, few men realize that being a husband and father doesn't end with being a great provider or a business success. In my reading of the feminist literature over the last thirty-five years, a vast number of luminaries from the "male story" (**his**tory) of civilization are rated as authentic failures in marriage by their wives' accounts. Rousseau, Tolstoy, and Tillich come quickly to mind. Despite their impact on history, they didn't get any "husband of the year" awards. It is clear that not much has changed. If there were such awards, and even if **men** did the nominating, present-day nominees would be difficult to find. Since men have been programmed for success, not happiness, it should not be surprising that men have "better things to do" than striving to be a **great** husband and father. In fairness, it should be noted that a woman, too, can place her spouse well down on the list of her priorities. She might do this for any number of reasons, but her most probable justification would be to get even for her husband's inattention.

The de-emphasis of marriage and motherhood as a career, and the anti-male rhetoric which has confused men have not brought couples closer. The dogged persistence of both the traditionally inferior status of women and the "entrapment" of men in a patriarchal society based on power[2] hasn't helped either. When you add the gender differences, the challenge of matrimony seems as demanding as Perceval's lifelong search for the Holy Grail. It is hard to believe any married couples ever achieve intimacy. Chapter Twelve will put two of these marriage challenges in perspective.

12

The Core of the Marriage Challenge: Staying Free and Equal

> *"Love and intimacy. . . . I am not aware of any other factor in medicine—not diet, not smoking, not exercise, not stress, not genetics, not drugs, not surgery—that has a greater impact on our quality of life, incidence of illness, and premature death from all causes."*
> —Dean Ornish

Does Anyone Still Believe in *the Noble Savage*? Unfortunately, "Yes"

To understand and appreciate the forces in the human psyche that move people toward or away from relationships would be, for most of us at least, an incredibly complicated assignment. Humans are characterized by their intense yearnings for relationship, while at the same time driven to attain and maintain their freedom. Husbands especially fear any loss of freedom or of being controlled. A woman or a man's tolerance for intimacy is quite limited, for reasons that will be explained in the next two chapters.

A brief look at recent history reveals the drama of man's struggle to maintain the social order or the common good without sacrificing his freedom. The key dogmas of the **Enlightenment** were that man, not God, is at the center of the universe, and that every infant is born free and noble. These assertions have been used to justify the subsequent "wars of liberation." For the most part, theorists have persisted since then in teaching that the infant who is **born free** is often enslaved by religious dogma, the state, society, or any of their surrogates. As a corollary of their theory, the most effective, useful, and **mature citizens should be produced by an educational system that enables the students to discover their underlying true selves** by helping them escape from all the "outside" biases and controls. Thus, the psychology of man that guides most of our public education is that every child can become a better and better person and eventually reach his potential through knowledge alone.[1] If a student can accept these ideas and endure in this struggle long enough or well enough to uncover the free and noble person that he is, he will be better prepared to achieve his (or her) potential.

The message of much of modern psychology stresses that an individual who is consistently affirmed and encouraged, is willing to learn, and avoids all bias or prejudice, especially religious ones, will have a happy and fulfilled life. By simply exploring for data and processing it for him/herself, the individual can become a better person. The success of this principle—that education can lead us to discover the beauty we all possess—has yet to be demonstrated (the kindest evaluation I can muster). Even though our educators have devoted one whole century to an unsuccessful effort to have our schools graduate better and better citizens and neighbors, they continue the systems that are based on a faulty view of **what motivates people** to act the way they do, as well as what **should** determine their priorities. In **Part Four**, the **values,** that is, the principles or priorities that would be more likely to be successful in producing good citizens (and good spouses) will be suggested.

Ironically, the science of Psychiatry essentially disagrees with Psychology's proposition of **man's initial innocence.** Freud and his successors insisted that every infant is born with **a dark side**, that is, a propensity for evil. The rationale for psychiatric treatment is that religion, parents and other early "traumas" can, and invariably do, **amplify the problem produced by the dark side's bad choices.** So, all the bad influences of infancy have to be removed, along with all the problems produced by an infant's or child's bad choices. All of the millions who have paid a combined fortune for psychiatrists **could justifiably send some of the bills to their pastor or to their parents.**

Transactional Analysis and the *Role of Inadequacy* in Our Relationships

Totally ignoring the question of God's existence, and operating generally outside the limitations of the scientific method, modern psychology has provided another concept that is totally in the humanist or enlightenment tradition. Referred to as *transactional analysis (TA)* this technique has been used as a tool in individual, and especially group therapy, for four decades.[2] TA is a perfect tool for explaining where ninety-five percent of our marriages end up, so I will use it for that purpose, though being firm in my belief that the system is of little value, in itself, as a solution for troubled marriages.

According to Transactional Analysis, **all human activity is motivated** not by a sexual drive as Freud defined it, but rather **by one's sense of inadequacy.** In transactional analysis there are only four possible **positions**, or ratings we can give ourselves **relative to another**: These positions are:

1. **I'm not O.K., but you are. Every** child is in this position initially.[3] By the end of the second year or during the third year the child settles into this position more or less permanently, unless, or until he can reach the fourth position; or, if the child is very unfortunate, he could assume either of the next two positions—again, more or less for the rest of his/her life. These positions are:

2. **I'm not O.K, but you are not O.K., either.** This is a position of withdrawal and denial that can eventually lead to **psychosis.**

3. **I'm O.K.,** but **you are not O.K.** This is the attitude and approach to others that characterizes the **criminal mind**, the violent, or the sociopath.

Since good strokes are needed to escape any of the first three positions, and only O.K. people are capable of giving those good "strokes," the second and third, both of which deny anyone else is O.K., have a poor prognosis and are usually permanent. They are definitely not satisfactory approaches to others, or for reaching the fourth, or adult position. All three of these positions represent one's conclusion about a **relationship** in which one or both parties is inadequate.

When the **infant** assumes the **first position**, that is, you're fine but he is not, and realizes you are needed to supply his needs, the infant's **first thought is how to get your continued support despite his inadequacy**. Thus, everyone starts his (or her) life as a **con-artist**, that is, acting like he deserves your help, when in fact he thinks he doesn't deserve it. From infancy the options are to stay a con artist to get his (or her) needs met, to assume the dangerous second or third positions, or to reach the adult position, in which he becomes "worthy," or adequate and supplies virtually all his/her own needs.

The **adult** position of Transactional Analysis is

4. **I' m O.K., and so are you**. In this position we value ourselves and others, essentially without conditions.

The fourth position is the successful or "grown up" position. According to the principles of TA, this level of human maturity can only be attained by a prolonged sequence of conscious decisions, most of which require a considerable amount of information and data processing of the past and present **transactions** in our lives. **Transactions represent the basic scientific unit of behavior, the result of a person's response to contact by another**. The stimulus and response together is a transaction.

TA insists that **most of us spend our lives in the first position of inadequacy**, that is, you're O.K. but I'm not. So we have to get good strokes or affirmation or support from others. To get approval and support despite our inadequacy we must resort to using "ulterior motives" in many or most of our transactions. Hiding our inadequacy requires that we employ some sort of deception. **Acting with an ulterior motive**, that is, acting in such a way as to conceal our inadequacy is referred to as playing **games**. All games might be said to proceed from an attempt to show that we are better than we see ourselves, so that someone else will accept us. The principle being: if we judged ourselves to be adequate or O.K., we wouldn't have to impress anybody, and thus we would not have to play games. **The games people play** only increase their misery, and represent their acknowledgment of inferiority.[4]

The adult position of deciding that you are worthy of regard by others—those people whose opinion you value—requires that you have a considerable amount of affirming data about yourself, and about those others, to whom you are comparing yourself. Much effort in "learning," referred to as data and reality processing, is involved in order to become an adult, again **emphasizing the value of education.** Insight into the transactions of our earlier years are crucial to our ever attaining the adult position, because it is in childhood when the **damage** is done, that is, when the caregivers, teachers, and mentors effectively sabotage or misdirect the child's attempts to move toward adequacy.

In accord with the humanist idea that infants are unspoiled, TA holds that the only intrinsic, or universal **badness,** that is, the **flaw in our nature,** is our inevitable **awareness in our infancy of being "not O.K."** All sin, including the original sin described in the Bible, is the response to this awareness of inadequacy.

Each individual exists and relates as three separate realities: a **child,** a **parent,** or an **adult.** The "child" is that part of us that **feels.** It is also the creative, adventuresome part of us that reacts with sadness, fear, anxiety, curiosity, or creativity. The child cries, sulks, laughs, fidgets, withdraws, and wants to eat, drink, and be merry. It is even the child who has the "religious experience," the mystical, ecstatic awareness of being enough, through a relationship with the eternal. But it is also the child who is capable of any **irresponsible** act, even **murder or marriage.** Indeed, it is usually the **child who signs the marriage contract** after he/she has received from the other that long-sought-for acceptance that signals that he/she is O.K.!

The "parent" is the **taught** part of us, the part which carries around all the **directives** given to us in our first five years. Because directives, rules, beliefs can be flawed or biased, the parent is seen as the real obstacle to our reaching the fourth position, where we correctly **value ourselves** and others. In TA, the acceptance of any rules or principles solely on the word of another, without personally processing the data, is never a good idea.[5] The traditions, or culture, that the parent transmits or plays to us, must be personally verified, and each directive thoughtfully accepted or rejected by the adult. An objective standard of morality exists, but the adult has to find his/her parts of that standard for him/herself. The "adult" is the **thinking** or thoughtful part of us. The **adult** is best occupied with **replacing the parent or parent tapes** with data about reality, that he/she has carefully processed and verified.

For the purposes of this book, the **fundamental insight of Transactional Analysis** is that unless we allow our adult to function as our guide, and to **be responsible for our thoughts, feelings, and activities**, we will never achieve a **great relationship** with our spouse. Of necessity, we must also reach the **adult position**, that is, the position of **self-acceptance** that allows us to accept others as equals.

Consistent affirmation is the magical ingredient in **TA**. Approval and encouragement keeps us motivated to seek, or to retain a sense of adequacy and therefore keeps us relating as an adult; and, it is those affirming others who keep us from being overwhelmed by too much data from our environment, especially before we are capable of processing it.

When we make **others responsible** for our development we are falling into the trap created by the **family of origin victimization of virtually everyone** that has been so much a part of twentieth century thought. To their credit, those who employ TA in therapy acknowledge that escape from the first three positions is made more difficult by endless reviews of past trauma; and, they also agree that accepting personal responsibility is the key to a sound relationship. Thus, TA fits in perfectly with the solutions offered in this book for saving a marriage and for creating intimacy. Accepting personal responsibility is indeed the essential requirement for relating without ulterior motives, "acting from an adult position," or achieving a great marriage. **The bottom line:** regardless of how often **your parent or child** calls the shots for you, the accountability for whatever you do, rests with **you.** The primary functions of a **focus group** are to foster awareness and acceptance so that the members of the group can move toward the adult position, while avoiding affirmation of anyone's **I'm not O.K. position**. The same approach must be used by marriage counselors who find that the child and/or parent in each spouse is playing "games" all day, because of their feelings of inadequacy.

Addiction: Forfeiting Our Freedom

Even though denying or hiding our faults makes us feel like phonies, most of us still do it. But, when we say or do things we do not mean often enough, we eventually become quite anxious. Obviously, some people's relationships can get quite anxiety-producing and complicated. As the saying goes, liars have to have incredible memories in order to keep all their different stories straight. Only those relationships that are built on honesty and what is authentic stay healthy and continue to deepen. On the other hand, if either partner in a marriage buries or denies or cannot accept his (or her) own truth, that person is soon disconnected, or isolated, because authentic communication becomes impossible. **Addictions make all the denials easier to sustain.** By helping a person stay disconnected from his true feelings, the addiction enables him to **keep his heart closed**, that is, allows him to avoid facing anyone openly or honestly. **The concept of addiction as a defense mechanism, that is, as a way to avoid facing our inadequacies and our shame is an important concept.** An understanding of this process of isolation from others as a consequence of the resort to addiction is key to an understanding of the vital importance of self-acceptance, the first step to building a relationship.

Introducing the *Ideal* of Maturity

Despite the difficulties in using TA in the treatment of any addiction or anyone with a psychiatric disorder, the concept of the four positions can provide a simple formula for looking at how he (or she) relates to people, especially those with whom he wants to create a relationship. Does he act as though he values himself and values anyone else as his equal? Or, are all his relationships loaded with ulterior motives, or people playing games? Does he constantly struggle for the "on top" position? Is his marriage still locked in the **power-struggle phase**, that is, still constantly conflicted, where differences are eliminated by battles in which he (or his partner) **wins** as a result of an resort to strength, shame or blame, and therefore one partner **loses.** Unfortunately, such **victories** are almost invariably

pyrrhic ones, representing a **no-win** situation for the relationship as the right to equality is infringed and **the bond of trust and fairness is weakened.** Without this bond, generosity and commitment decline and eventually vanish, along with passion, enthusiasm, and affection. On the other hand, if the potential protagonists are **"mature" enough to tolerate or accept differences,** there are **no battles** and therefore **no losers,** so that both partners win, and the friendship blossoms.

Everyone has his/her own ideas about the meanings of "mature," "grown up," "adult," or a "well-developed personality," so achieving a unanimously-accepted definition is not possible. For example, swindlers, or con men, can have great personalities, while some totally charitable people are impossible to abide up close. Even if no one agrees on a list of characteristics that precisely define a "mature person", most of us have a pretty clear idea of the qualities we admire and would like to possess. **We** certainly want to be regarded as mature or grown up. But, if we fully realized that maturity can lead not only to great marriages, great sex, intimacy and love, but also good health, we might give the quest for growing up a lot **more attention.** I suggest we first direct our attention to the topic: "**How to become mature,** or, to use the psychological term, how to become **differentiated**.

13

Self-Awareness—
The First Requirement for
Reaching Maturity

> " A man can be a fool, and not even know it . . .
> unless, of course, he is married."
> —H. L. Menchen

A man and woman can celebrate most of their lives sharing the same bed, and remain **total strangers** in matters of the heart. Why is this possible? It is possible because of their refusal to **be aware of,** to think about what they are doing to each other by **the way they relate.**

Four Little Tales of How Love Blooms in America

❖ Jenny, short for Genevieve (a name now used only by her husband to "pretend" respect), fumes all through breakfast, as her husband, Max, reads his morning paper in silence. Daily, Max alternately hums and grunts, feigning unawareness that his deliberate inattention to anything his wife does during the thirty-minute breakfast ritual is creating a problem. Within a few minutes after he leaves for work, she will need two aspirins to manage her headache. The anger will last, or be "stored," until she can find a way to get even. Max allows himself a few seconds for some departing banter, even venturing a less-than-robust peck on the cheek and a barely audible, "see ya," as his "larger-than-it-should-be behind" goes flying out the kitchen door. She repeats to herself, "If I never see it (or him) again, so what" (or unprintable words, expressing the same thoughts)?

One can predict, with some confidence, that five or ten years hence, this scene, or some variation of it—that retains all the sado-masochism and irreverence—will still be enacted, regularly, on the kitchen stage.

❖   Candy and Ed have driven 1200 miles to a winter vacation in Florida, every one of their twenty years of marriage. She just came back, reciting to the next door neighbors another of the major grievances that always seem to occur in the car during the drive down or on the return trip. This time the "big fight" involved the timing of a powder room stop. Candy asked, as they are driving, "Ed, would you like to stop?" "No," he answers tersely, but without hinting at any emotion or any thoughts of his own.

Not realizing, despite two decades of traveling together on the exact same route that hers was not a multiple choice question at all, but a request for a dialogue, specifically when she might reasonably expect to relieve herself, he continues his "hell-bent to Alaska" pace without so much as a sideward peek. Or maybe, just maybe, he **pretends** not to realize—in order to pay her back for some grievance. After what seems to be an eternity of waiting, maybe even twenty minutes, the fullness of Candy's bladder if matched only by the fullness of her anger, as she produces a horrific scream. Later, when his hearing returns and while she is still wondering if her bladder might finally have been "broken" by his stupidity, she rebukes his pitiful attempt at an apology with a scornful "shut up." The next two days, while each is imprisoned in a very small space with a hostile spouse, are passed quietly. To describe the situation more accurately, they are passed silently. Only when the driving is finished, and they are free to do their own thing at any time, do Cindy and Ed return to talking to each other, and to civility.

Our friends who live next door to this obviously-conflicted couple say that they have never observed either partner acknowledge his or her own weaknesses or sins. Every conversation on their relationship—Ed with the husband, or Cindy to my friend's wife—has been devoted to criticism of their spouse. Is insensitivity of this degree commonplace or rare? I do not believe anyone really knows. One thing is certain: such a scenario should never occur between two civilized adults!

❖ Fred, the only retired member in a bridge club which meets the second Tuesday of every month, regularly accuses his wife, Ruthie, of "rudely interrupting," when she tries to say anything, during one of his five- or ten-minute monologues, which he regularly fits in before and after the actual bridge competition. But, the few times that Ruthie initiates a conversation or ventures any sentence sequence longer than ninety seconds, she hears the "authority" (the neighborhood women's name for her husband) proffer one of his patented "clarifications," that obscures any point she may have intended to make.

Ruthie's girl friends tell her that she is a fool to let her husband interfere with her right to contribute to the group's conversations, and she agrees that she is being foolish. But she is afraid of Ed's temper. Ed senses that his treatment of his wife offends even the other male members of the bridge club, but his lifelong sense of never quite living up to his potential has always made everything he says, and the skill at which he says it, more important to him than to any of his listeners. When his wife interrupts, he feels she is exposing **his need**, and **his inadequacy**, to everyone listening. He would like her to be proud of him, but he knows that will never happen—especially now that he has retired, and there will be no more opportunities to achieve any higher status.

❖ At a recent men's weekend, thirty-one husbands confessed to the near impossibility of listening to their wife explaining a problem in its totality. They each would provide her with a solution as soon as they grasped what she was "going to explain."

As you might expect, the general confession of this male impatience with wifely conversation, elicited some prompt "defenses." One man put forth an explanation for this typical impatience which prompted a lot of affirmative head nodding within the group: **his wife,** he pointed out, would frequently use "the presentation of a problem" merely as a ruse to get him to pay some attention to her. A husband who detects his wife resorting to this ruse often adopts his own technique: he will hold off his full attention until he is sure she **is** saying "something." Then, if there actually is a problem, he will jump in with a response that will solve it. All husbands agreed that they would try to select a response that would be most likely to end the conversation, in order that they might get back to their own agenda as quickly as possible.

A spotlight of self-awareness on the thousand-and-one **insensitivities** that comprise so much of marital relating is badly needed.

The Bravery to Look Within

Marriage itself is unique in constantly challenging the partners to be better human beings. This is especially true because each stage of marriage brings a whole new set of challenges as partners disengage from their families, raise children, and reach old age together totally alone. Unless we plan to marry three times—for romance, then for a child supporter and manager, and finally for a companion and care-giver—our spouse must grow up with us. Thus, the necessary precondition for progress and success throughout the course of the marriage is for each partner to maintain an accurate assessment of him/herself and thus continue to grow.

Carl Jung said that "shock" is the inevitable reaction to seeing ourselves clearly for the first time. Facing each flaw is an experience fraught with embarrassment. Yet, self-awareness is the first principle for success in every psychological system's plan for human development. Denial, suppression, repression, depression, addiction, projection, and identification head a list of techniques we all use from time to time to avoid the trauma of facing our past and present feelings more clearly. Anyone who claims that courage is not required to search into one's buried feelings is thereby declaring that he/she has never done it.

A clear example of what buried feelings can provoke, and of the need for courage to look back on our lives and motivations, is provided by David Lisak's research on men abused as children. His research showed that there were two basic ways actively-abused male children handled their overwhelming feelings of shame and anger. Initially burying these feelings, of course, was akin to having a hurricane pass over warm water. The buried feelings became powerful enough to shape forever the individual's entire approach to others. Lisak referred to the boys' abuse as a "domination—[creating] a crisis in masculinity." Some of the abused boys, referred to as the "first group," became "rigidly male," or "hypermasculine." They forever after identified with the aggressor and forever found it difficult or impossible to admit weakness, fear, or pain, even to themselves. Many of these men became substance abusers, that is, they did violence to themselves. Unfortunately, too many were also violent toward others. Thus, those of the first group carried on—"absorbed"—the parent's feelings of contempt and shame and imitated their violent denials. The second group, Lisak found, responded to their victimhood—their pain of being "unmanned"—by "rewriting in their own psyche and in their actions the criteria for manhood. . . . [They did] away with any form of domination or violence."[1]

Each of us has a unique story to tell. But for many of us, the fear, shame, guilt, anxiety, or doubt constitute painful obstacles to our ever discovering our own life story. A person who destroys his/her health, or the lives of other family members, by drinking or abusive and violent behavior—by definition, a person with addictions—is acting out his refusal to look at his own life story. He (or she) is able to abuse himself primarily because he sees himself as already flawed. Yet, if pressed to name one "sin" that would deserve such punishment, he/she might not be able to find one. For some, slaying dragons might have demanded less courage than that demanded for the search into the unknown depths of their own hearts and souls, especially for those who discover that handling the sadness of remembered childhood abuse can be a lifelong cross. Tears from fear, shame and humiliation, guilt, sadness, or remembered pain can drown some searchers in sorrow, and immobilize them on their life journey, while for others the tears can wipe the slate clean and enable them to begin to finally live their own lives.[2]

The Largest Class of People in the World: Victims

What, do you ask, does a person do when a stage is reached in his search for self-awareness at which he discovers that he has been a

victim of his parent's sins, or of a harsh environment, or of religious and cultural repression? In the twentieth century it has been the psychiatrists and psychologists who have insisted that they had the answers to that question. The psychotherapy in Focus Groups is aimed at helping a larger number of victims cope with past trauma. The **problems** with all these disciplines arise when the designated victim uses **past traumas** for **present failures and failings.**

How many friends have told you that the reason they have essentially **given up** on life and/or their relationships is because one of their parents was an alcoholic, or too strict, or "abandoned" them when they were children?[3] My answer to that excuse is that nothing apart from our free will—certainly not our family-of-origin, a "sick" society, nor even religious repression—can make our adult choices for us.

Everyone has a dark side. Those of us raised in a religious tradition take comfort from the knowledge that guilt and sinfulness make us all brothers and sisters.[4] Denial of our imperfections, or burial of fears, sadness, weakness, guilt, shame, and pain can bring anyone to ruin, even though the person being destroyed hasn't a clue about his own motivations. Problems must be faced or acknowledged, then accepted, before we can deal with them. Help or guidance from an outside perspective can lead us to insight, but we first need the humility to initiate the process.[5]

Eliminating the Final Excuse for a Bad Marriage

It is especially important to avoid blaming scapegoats when our marriage is deadlocked and not getting better. The fact that childhood issues come up in marriage conflicts does not prove such issues are either the sole reason or the main reason for the disharmony. Each bride and groom is responsible for the success of his and her marriage, regardless of anything in their lives preceding their free choice of each other. To deny that truth is to believe that married people somehow give up their freedom of choice. Unfortunately, a lot of otherwise smart people do think that. They either blame the problems on each other or they blame the "institution" of marriage itself. As evidence, they point to the men and women who appeared to get along very well, until they married.

What do you say to anyone who doesn't see at least the obvious reasons why the **marriage commitment** can ruin a good thing. The formal commitment to stick it out until death, no matter what happens, terrifies most men as few decisions could, especially when they realize that their mate now has exclusive rights, forever, to their sexual apparati. For some men, perhaps **most** men, the ritual of courting (or seducing) a woman makes life much more thrilling than it becomes after his mission or quest is accomplished. **The bottom line:** a man may flee when his wife's youthful beauty has faded **despite** the solemn promises of marriage, certainly **not because** of those promises.

Since we all tend to be blamers from time to time, it should not surprise us too much when someone blames the binding marital commitment for his (or her) problems in getting along with a spouse.

Once we have gotten rid of all the scapegoats, we can get down to the essential business of working on the culprit, the enemy, the cause of our problems, namely, **ourselves.** Working on that project could lead us to unbelievable blessings.

14

Some "Growing-Up" Dividends

"When you are with someone whom you can trust and show your 'shadow' and still feel loved, it's like shining a light in the darkness— the shadow diminishes and we don't project it onto others."
—Gail Gross

Remembering a Few Basic and Vital Principles

Carl Jung referred to the repressed, disowned, defended parts of our selves as our "shadow." An essential part of his psychiatric approach was to help a person become aware of his hidden self and accept or "own" it, as a way to becoming "whole" again. There is still general agreement that repression or hiding of those parts of ourselves we do not like, or that we are ashamed of, requires a lot of our psychic energy, and causes sickness and unhappiness. As discussed in Chapter Nine, marriage greatly complicates this problem of repression, since our selection process usually leads us to marry someone who possesses the very qualities we no longer manifest. For example, as a child she may have been a carefree imp, but totally abandoned that approach to others because her family wouldn't tolerate it. Now, the only men to which she is attracted are disorganized risk-takers.

Clearly, marital conflicts can spring unbidden from unconscious forces over which we have little or no control, unless or until we can understand our motives and accept ourselves. Even though self-awareness and self-acceptance is an ongoing and life-long process, gaining insight into the source of our thoughts, feelings, and actions, and thereby gaining some mastery over them, enables us to **relate more successfully** to others. This is why "growing up" is so important.[1]

Hopefully, by the time you finish this book, you will accept as valid several basic propositions:

✓   If partners are to "grow-up" together, it remains essential that they maintain their separate identities. Two people cannot achieve happiness together unless they are happy as individuals. Each person must work on his/her own project to become "whole," so that he (or she) can accept himself and be free to relate to others. No one can give to a mate the missing parts or traits he has disowned.

✓   Intimacy is impossible between two persons unless each values him/herself and the would-be intimate. Thus

✓   Only "grown-ups," or those who see themselves **and their mate** as valuable, that is, as 0.K., can hope to attain intimacy. And

✓   Only insofar as we accept our total separateness from all others, and that we are solely and totally responsible for our lives, can we be free to love.

The **ultimate** meaning of being "grown-up," and the importance we give to getting to that level, depends, of course, on your view of human life. This book's answer to **life's purpose** is provided in **Part Four.**

The purpose of our marriage, that is, our goal as a married man or woman is to be a **lover** and to **be loved.** The stronger the bonds of love, the fuller and more satisfying our lives become. The fate of the children in any marriage is determined in large measure by the quality of that married life, and the maturity of the two individuals that comprise it.[2]

The Best Marriage Partner: the *Differentiated* Person

In this book, "being mature," "growing up," and "acting like an adult" all refer to the ideal of human development that psychotherapist Murray Bowen called **differentiation.** As a corollary to his concept of differentiation, Bowen also theorized that a man or woman will unconsciously select someone who is at the **same level** of differentiation as he or she is, a point discussed in Chapter Nine.

Some practitioners and/or theorists claim that the independent or autonomous aspect of a supposedly-differentiated person is an illusion, while others insist that most of what has been written about differentiation discounts "affiliation" and thus describes men, not women. These disputes can safely be ignored, because we include the recognition of the need for relationship, and the yearning for relationship, in our definition of differentiation. The formation and preservation of committed personal relationships based on "values" of duty, patience, and self-sacrifice are essential to our concept of maturity.

The **selfism** or **isolated individualism,** already discussed, for example at the beginning of Chapter One, and in the Notes for this chapter, is not **acceptable.**[3] As Chesterton observed: "Vanity is not only **not** the same thing as self-consciousness, it is very often the opposite of it. When a man becomes self-conscious, he very often becomes painfully and abominably humble. But so long as a man is healthily unconscious, he is almost certain to be . . . vain" (emphasis mine.)[4]

Differentiation is a life-long process of developing one's human potential (including the social talents), and of developing a sense or awareness of self that seeks always to be correct and true, that is, that seeks to avoid distortions or delusions. This latter quality is referred to as **integrity.** In addition, the **self-soothing ability** of a differentiated person enables him/her to handle the shame or sadness he feels each time he/she honestly faces a personal fault, including the sad and painful memories for which he, rightly or wrongly, feels responsible. This differentiated self, which he can know, or be aware of, as distinct or separate from everybody else, has the consistent ability, or the integrity, to maintain his/her values, and to present who and what he/she is, regardless of the challenges. This person can allow him/herself, by his own choice, to be close to, to be connected to, or to be affiliated with another/others.[5]

Thus, the differentiated person is capable of **interdependence.** Cooperation is easier, in fact, because he/she does not have a destructive fear or anxiety of losing control of his/her life or goals. His/her thoughts, emotions, and behavior remain under control. The differentiated person can certainly choose to sacrifice *some* personal goals for the good of another/others. Insofar as he or she is mature or differentiated, he or she will understand and experience the incompleteness of isolation, and will want or desire to experience connection in some way to others. Such persons will readily sacrifice, if necessary, to maintain the possibility for relationship. Appreciation of one's aloneness sharpens the perception and sensitivity to others. It is precisely this clear awareness of yourself relating to another that is lost when people get too "close," or "emotionally-fused, and thus react to each other's emotions automatically, that is, **mindlessly**.[6]

Differentiation Embraces Affiliation and (Voluntary) Interdependence

Autonomy, independence, individualism, or assertiveness are **not** synonymous with differentiation, or maturity. Such terms omit one-half of the meaning of differentiation, which always connotes the self-in-relation. Someone who is differentiated does not "use" people. Such a husband, for example, would not relate to his wife as if she were an "object," or his property. He would not demand or insist that she do anything that she didn't wish to do, and he would maintain reverence and respect for her as a person.

Differentiation does not lead to **closeness**, the **foolish** ideal of couples who seek to lose their own identities by investing all their energies "in the marriage." The maintenance of closeness in marriage is a formidable task. Each partner must monitor, and strive to preserve, the trust, acceptance, mutuality and reciprocity in the relationship because virtually every transaction, even most of the mutual disclosures, is motivated, and measured, by a quid pro quo, that is, a "what's in for me?" or a "give to get" standard. This **problem** with closeness does not mean some measure of closeness is not desirable or beneficial. Our common sense tells us that it is. But each partner must maintain the right to negotiate, **and to re-negotiate**, the level of closeness, or the degree of mutual dependence that he or she is willing to accept.

Equally important, couples who get their validation and acceptance as wonderful human beings solely from each other—without facing and correcting their personal failings, as a first priority—might avoid divorce, especially if at least one has the patience and the self-sacrificing ability of a saint, but they will never achieve intimacy, which requires two equal persons working on differentiation, or on growing up.

However, differentiation is not **the opposite** of being closely connected to others. A differentiated man and woman, that is, a couple who are not attached to one another by bonds of dependency can still choose to maintain consistent awareness of each other. Spouses who are differentiated and committed to building intimacy are rarely too far apart, too isolated, or too "distant" to see each other well. Rather, to say people are differentiated means they can stand on their own two feet, believe in themselves, and can stay focused on and hold to their principles. Such persons are potentially wonderful friends, as they are free to **choose** interdependence. "Connections" between differentiated couples proceed from their strength, since the connections are freely chosen, and are not motivated by any need, or ulterior motive. Thus, there is no need to control.[7]

Differentiation Is What Makes Intimacy Possible

It is precisely the sharing (again, as a freely-given gift without any strings attached) of one's thoughts, feelings, and actions with another person, that is the essence of love, and demonstrates the skill of intimacy in action. Thus intimacy can be the fruit of a man or a woman's decision to grow up.[8] The American ideal of rugged individualism includes varying degrees of **indifference**, which a differentiated person would not manifest or hold acceptable. Murphy Brown or Dirty Harry, as portrayed, may have been brave and assertive, but neither was differentiated. Cold and calculating is **not** what maturity is all about. Failure in our popular culture to stress the **social aspects of maturity,** that is, becoming a (grown-up) man (or woman) **for others**, is simply a reflection of the "what's in it for me" mentality of virtually all of modern psychology. Maslow and Rogers, among many others, "fatally forgot" that it is not enough for a man or woman to be **fully alive and fully human.** He or she **must be able express that aliveness and humanness to another,** that is, to be a **lover** and to **be loved.**

Theoreticians who claim that differentiation is a **masculine concept** fail to see that a man who is sensitive, gentle, emotionally open, and who listens patiently without giving advice, is more differentiated than a man who lacks such qualities. The ability to cry is not a requirement for becoming a man, anymore than saying a man who cries is not a "real" man. Both statements miss the point by a mile.

A mature man is not required to share all his feelings, or even many of them. He has probably spent his entire life repudiating in himself any "taint" of femininity. A man is **not** required to develop his **feminine side** (generally translated as an ability to nurture, or to share his negative emotions and feelings), in order to be able to meet his wife as an equal, whether in the bedroom or outside the bedroom. Admittedly, those qualities would probably help his intimacy skills, but he doesn't have to become more like a woman to treat his wife as a woman. Thus, a man need not possess the ability to cry to be a great and intimate lover. **Intimacy** is a skill practiced by separate, free, and equal individuals. As such, it **does not require anything** from the person with whom we would be intimate. Thus, it is not necessary for a woman to be **assertive** to practice the skill of intimacy, either. Apparently, the sage who said: "It can be dangerous to mess with Mother Nature," had the right idea.[9]

In the next chapter, the consequences of confusing closeness with intimacy will be placed on a very practical level.

15

Simple Recipes for Marital Disaster

*"But humans communicate with exquisite precision.
We read signals too subtle to be captured in language. . . .
In large part, we are transparent to one another."*
—Peter Kramer

Dependence, Independence, Interdependence: Much More Than Words

Recall that, in the **Preface** I promised that our discussion of marriage would be divided into three parts—**he, she,** and **us**—in order to emphasize a conviction that in marriage each partner remains a free and responsible human being, maintaining his and her private and distinct world of thoughts, feelings, and actions, while at the same time entering a relationship that is unique and separate from any other.

Married persons can foolishly give up their autonomy to the "us", and thereby forfeit any chance for intimacy. As long as decisions and sacrifices made for the benefit of the "us" are thought out, deliberate, and freely made, there should be no problems. **Interdependence** is the backbone of efficient and well-functioning marriages. But every time you "give in" on some issue against your will or your best judgment, you may be, in effect, giving up permanently your free choice in that matter. Sacrificing choice, or your own way of thinking, feeling, and acting in any particular area of married life can legitimize a sequence of actions within the relationship that you didn't foresee or intend, and which then starts breeding anger and resentment.

Understanding very clearly the long-term effects of **giving in** on any issue is vital to anyone even thinking about a permanent relationship.[1] Each decision to surrender your subsequent free choice in a particular matter, for the sake of the relationship, should be carefully thought out. Chances are high that you will eventually regret, or resent, many of those negotiated settlements, or standing agreements, which were made with great generosity and good will in the glorious and romantic early days of your marriage. The groom who gives up his bowling night with the men with whom he has competed, and with whom he has shared as much of himself as men are capable of sharing with each other, or, the wife who gives up her regular meetings with the sorority sisters with whom she has often exchanged many secrets and women's "stuff," have both made decisions that they may later regret.

Devoting too much mind, will, talents, and time to each other means both could wake up one day to the realization that they have very few free choices or free time left. Then, they will no longer "own" their lives and choices; another entity does, over which they have only partial control. Such devoted lovers often soon discover they have come to rely on each other's cooperation and good will to the extent that they need each other more than they want to, or now choose to. When the focus of one's thoughts, feelings, and actions has been narrowed to one person, then finding or pursuing one's own goals becomes difficult, or downright impossible. At that point, too, there is little opportunity for **free and unconditional** sharing, by which love is demonstrated. You are now doing things for your spouse because you **have to**, not because you **want to**.

In Chapter Eighteen, I will describe my first experience, in 1951, of the way married men of that day spoke of the wives to whom they had "sacrificed their freedom." Most of them expressed deep regret. Many resented what they had done. All seemed to hold their wives responsible for the "ball and chain" they had to carry! **Wedlock,**

padlock, as the old English aphorism had it. While the craving for human attachment is a biological and spiritual drive in both sexes, it does not wear well with men to give up all opportunity for adventure and independent daring. For the factory workers that I met then, a sense of being "locked-in" was an apt description of their relationship with their wives. Most felt that their wives were very parsimonious with the **key,** that is, with their free choices.

Intimates Retain Independence, Couples Who are Close, Often Do Not

The natural and inevitable **push-pull** of marriage as created by the human yearnings for autonomy, freedom, and independence and the corresponding desires for dependence, attachment, closeness, or intimacy should keep every marriage vibrant, challenging, and interesting. The fact that these dynamics can be aborted by a **cop-out,** that is, an abandonment of either the push or the pull by one or both partners helps to explain why so many marriages lose their life and vitality. Let's look first at a couple who forsook any pull toward autonomy.

❖ Fran's childhood insecurity and desire for "closeness" intensified with the death of her parents when she was still in her teens. Now, her style of relating was finally driving her husband, Johnny, to try to find some "breathing room" in the company of his friends from high school.

Despite Fran's intense anxiety whenever she and Johnny disagreed on anything or if they were separated during their free time, she reluctantly acceded to his request for some evenings out, convincing herself that "perhaps every man should have a little time with his friends." Still, each time he went out, she became more anxious, and more irritated. She also thought it quite reasonable to have an accounting of where, what, and with whom.

Their whole approach to each other seemed to take an entirely different direction, as he sought some time away from her to be with his friends. Fran could not understand why her husband didn't prefer spending his time with her. Their marriage had seemed to her to have been built solidly, on mutual trust, and the sharing of everything. This sharing had included virtually all of their leisure time.

Now, unfortunately, Johnny had decided to be "selfish." At least, that's the way Fran saw it. At first, her annoyance led merely to introspection. "Maybe, he doesn't love me as much as I love him. Maybe all men look at the marriage relationship differently than women do."

During the next several months, with little sign of change (and not many pleasant exchanges), Fran moved through feelings of inadequacy, disappointment, resentment and anger, to a state of bitterness. Fran finally demanded that they see a counselor, and Johnny agreed, but very, very reluctantly.

Their problems increased when the counselor to whom they turned for advice convinced them that their problem was primarily a lack of "good" communication, and an "unwillingness to compromise." "Poor communication" was the family therapist's incorrect, and unfortunate diagnosis. He based this diagnosis, he said, on Johnny and Fran's "failure to reach a consensus on what each needed to change, or to give up."

Regrettably, the therapist missed the reality that they had already given up "too much" of themselves over the years, in their mistaken belief that mutual dependency, or emotional and psychological closeness, or sameness, or agreement were what marriage and intimacy was all about. Instead of acknowledging that there was no way a man and a woman could agree on everything, he allowed them to continue to expect that **all their needs** could be met within the relationship.

Fran and Johnny had always believed that their love for each other was indisputable. They still believed that it was. They had always tried to get their thoughts, feelings, emotions, and activities in sync, and to watch that their "marriage energies" were going in the same direction. Both recommitted themselves, in desperation, to attempts to come together, to agree, to forge even more compromises, to "save the marriage"—in effect, acting on the marriage counselor's advice.

But the **obligations** of their marriage were all that Johnny could see. He was not only bored, but also exhausted and "smothered" by the pressures to conform in everything. The thought that Fran couldn't be happy unless he was with her was becoming a burden he could no longer carry. Between his family

and his job, it seemed that life was just one continuous responsibility.

That the "he" and "she" should be sacrificed for the "us" of the
marriage was something they had sought as a kind of ideal. Both
had clearly recognized, but had been denying for years, that they
seemed to have less and less to talk about, and also that they now
rarely did anything that was new or challenging. The relationship seemed totally devoid of vitality In truth, they were **both
bored** most of the time.

Each, from time to time, had dismissed the doubts that would
arise suggesting that their style of **total commitment** might not
be the best route to happiness. They were so good at giving up
their choices and cooperating according to plan, as evidenced by
their spending all their free time with each other, that they even
made love in a style and manner that was totally predictable.
Since the first months of the marriage, when that "arrangement"
was negotiated, there had never been one change in the script.
While they never "worried" about getting along in bed, they
never got very excited about it anymore, either.

Fran and Johnny could have been cited as authorities on
compromise, mutuality, sharing, trust, sensitivity, closeness,
reciprocity, sacrifice, duty, and commitment. These wonderful
ideals were the brick and mortar of the rugged marriage they
had built. These ideals had certainly preserved the peace. Fran
and Johnny had never once raised their voices to each other in
anger.

The counselor's advice that they must "compromise, come to
some agreement, stop acting foolishly, or acting in their separate
interests," simply added fuel to the flames of anger and resentment. That fire of anger had been building up for twenty-seven
years, during which time, out of love for each other, no sacrifice
was too great, and no price was too high, to make their marriage
a success. The negotiations and compromises added by the
counselor were to be the last log on their marriage fire. Since
Johnny's "he" and Fran's "she" were now so totally fused into an
"us," it seemed that only by destroying the us—the marriage—
could they stop arguing, fighting, hating each other. They separated.

The first few weeks were "nightmarish" for both. A gamut of
emotions prevented normal eating, sleeping, and a host of other

customary activities. Some friends took sides, but most simply vanished, at least temporarily, from their lives.

Finally, Johnny was advised by his boss that "a few weeks off might do him, and the company, a lot of good." He fled to a mountain retreat—an old cabin near a fresh stream, that a friend from church was in the process of selling, but which was still available.

Johnny initiated a search within to find what he was feeling. And he was relentless. He eventually got in touch with virtually all his feelings—of fear, sadness, guilt, shame, anger, frustration, and pain. He tried to experience each of them, and look for origins or reasons. One by one, he was able to experience acceptance and healing. After twenty-seven days of doing more thinking, walking, crying, and praying (and fishing) than he had in his lifetime up to that point, Johnny finally realized what he had done wrong. In his desire to please he had become **selfless.** In devoting nearly all his time to fulfilling "obligations, he had "numbed" his feelings in order not to experience (thus, not to express or reveal) his frustration and resentment.

Encouraged by the discovery that he could face his **present** feelings, he was finally able to examine the "wounds," "scars," or "defects" that he had repudiated (as a way to be accepted), as he was growing up. He faced each of these "issues," with an eye to closure. Eventually, he had thought about most of his good and his bad qualities, past and present. Though it was exhausting work, Johnny found it exhilarating. Johnny especially noted that, from his earliest childhood, he had **lacked the courage to express his thoughts and feelings, whenever he judged that they might be criticized or rejected**. Johnny's mother and father were both extraordinarily-fine people, but they were unswerving in their insistence that **everything be done right!** They did not at all believe in compromise. Johnny's response to that type of parenting was to consistently **give in** on matters that were very important to him, rather than risk rejection, opposition, disapproval, or criticism. That one failing alone had led him to a kind of slavery, especially emotionally. The only emotions he would express were those which were virtually pre-approved. Johnny's high intelligence qualified him for leadership, and he knew it. But, he was afraid to risk it as a result of his habitual style of relating.

Now, for the first time in his life, Johnny dared to look deep enough into his heart to realize that, although his sins were few, they nevertheless could not be dismissed, ignored or hidden anymore. He had to "see his sins," to regret them, and also to cry over them, as a way of letting go of them. Finally facing what he had done throughout most of his life, Johnny considered the major decisions he had made in the light of his present priorities, options, responsibilities, and goals.

Fortunately, unlike Narcissus, who remained **selfless**, and died from lack of food and sleep because of his obsessive "love" for the person he saw reflected in the water, Johnny was now fully aware of even his deepest feelings and was also able to see himself and his life beyond the tears. One fact stood out in his mind. He saw that leaving a wife and family, besides filling him with pain and sadness, was not very admirable.

Johnny also realized that he had been wrong in believing love was essentially a sacrifice. It was part of a love ideal to which he had wholeheartedly subscribed. But after making a lot of painful sacrifices, he found that he was mostly resentful, not content. Too much of his day had come to be committed to what he considered mindless routine. Spending most of his days in "loving service" had added confusion, boredom, and depression to his resentment.

Remembering the Christmas-spirit-like joy and expectation he had experienced when he and Fran first met, he searched for, and found, the one key difference between the then and the now: then he could **freely** give out of love; now he **had** to give or else. More importantly, John saw that the primary motivation, in fact, the only motivation for love, was to make the one you love happy. But, he had given love (he saw it clearly now) in order to get love and approval back. He also saw that Fran had done the same thing. Thus, both young lovers had brought their own **conditions** to the marriage. For example, each had to reciprocate and evidence their appreciation of the love that was given to them. Like any conditional love, the seeds of resentment were being sown even as loving actions were exchanged.

Dropping all consideration of the part that Fran may have played in the change from then to now, he resolved to take total responsibility and control of what he did or did not do, regardless of any past promises. But, never for an instant did Johnny consider being unfaithful to the woman who was still his wife; and, he made sure he discharged his obligations to financially support the family. He also recognized, once he stopped being resentful and angry, that he had been a lousy father. Since his children needed him most **now**, not when he had finished his growing up process, he began immediately to participate in their lives.

His daughters' shame at having mom and dad living in separate homes was short-lived, because Dad was showing up all the time, keeping his promises to them, demonstrating his love and regard for them in ways both big and little.

Fran and Johnny started meeting each other for lunch, for walks, and finally for private dinners together. Neither made any demands, but a lot of happy memories were recalled. Each avoided talking about what they were thinking about their relationship, since that always seemed to take them back to the past. Instead, they shared their feelings at "this point in time." Fran had never heard her husband share his **negative feelings** before, only his happy ones. She was flattered to think that despite what he had done, he still trusted her enough to open his deepest heart to her.

Seeing Johnny's determination and effort in becoming a person who cared about himself, whose efforts in his own behalf were paying obvious dividends in terms of his confidence, his joyous outlook, and his appreciation and sensitivity to what was happening in his life, Fran made her own discovery. Since Johnny was **becoming the man Fran thought she married**, and without **any help** from her, maybe she could become "the wonderful woman" he thought he married, without any help from him. In opening their hearts once again to each another, they were being healed themselves.

Many married people share Fran's and Johnny's lack of appreciation for the need to maintain control over most of what one does every day. Separation allows each to **see** the other more clearly. Maintaining **personal responsibility or accountability** for only one's own thoughts, feelings, and actions, helps to keep out the criticism, the "shame" and "blame" approach that ruins the marriage. Admittedly, perhaps not many husbands and wives retain as much **good**

will as Fran and Johnny had retained. Because both were highly motivated to succeed, a simple change in perceptions regarding their approach to each other and their own deep-seated needs, was enough to turn the marriage around.

Not enough real-life stories have happy endings, or so it seems. But Johnny and Fran's story did. Few couples I have known in my life are as obviously pleased in their relationship, as they are now. Their marriage was transformed as Fran gained insight into her excessive need for closeness, Johnny recognized that honesty with oneself and with others was essential if any relationship was to grow, and as **both understood and accepted the very real differences** that existed between them. By working on just one or two glaring deficiencies in order to make themselves neater persons they were improving **the gift,** that is, themselves, which marriage allows them to share. Finally, because they now **share by choice, not out of some childish need,** Fran and Johnny are creating a new marriage bond built upon the highest human ideals.

A Fool's Approach: "Giving to Get" Respect, Love, Attention and Appreciation

A man (or woman) who enters marriage having the spouse's affirmation, respect, and regard as his only source of **self-regard** is headed for disappointment and frustration for at least two very good reasons: Whenever you need something from somebody, that other person is going to make you pay for what you need, eventually, if not sooner. The second reason is both more basic and more important, because the lack of self-regard is emotionally crippling: **you cannot love anybody, including your husband or wife, if you do not love, respect, reverence, and honor yourself.**

Self-Love Versus Selfishness

The **self-love** proposed throughout this book is **not selfish** at all. The "me first, everyone else second" of twentieth-century psychology was never based on enduring values, so it's worthlessness could have been predicted. The **message** of my book for women made **self-**

love the key to a woman's health and well-being. [2] Here are two brief examples that show the results of the lack of self-love.

❖ Mary C. never took any time for herself "because that would be selfish." Now her five grown children are distinguished by their selfishness. For example, her two sons and three daughters always manage to go to the in-laws for all the holiday dinners.

Originally, Mary's children went to the in-laws for all the important dinners because they knew Mary "would never get angry with them and the other parents might." Now they do not go to Mary's because they can't abide her resentment of their past neglect. However, Jack, Mary's husband of twenty-seven years, wins the prize for self-centeredness. His vacations (yes, all of them for the last ten years) have been spent with his deep-sea fishing buddies.

Mary would qualify in the national census figures as a "non-person." That is, she would qualify, if they had such a category. Knowing Mary, as she relates now, I can understand why she is being avoided. She has never developed any of her interests or talents, even though, for example, she had evidenced musical and acting talent in high school. She has never talked about anything but her family, and now that conversation is solely critical and resentful.

❖ Wanda always **needed** love. When she married, getting love was her major priority. She would do whatever she thought would earn her this love. Compounding her difficulties, the thought had never occurred to Wanda that married women now have legal equality under the terms of the marriage contract and do not have to sacrifice everything to the will of husbands and/or children. Both errors prevented Wanda from being loved. Always present in her service to the family was the urgent need for getting something back—love, regard, appreciation, or affirmation. Because everyone in the family knew or sensed this, relationships were strained, or always "on the verge." If only Wanda could have **appreciated herself**, and thereby have learned the **first lesson** in the creation of a relationship. [3]

Self-Regard: The First Talent for Creating a Relationship

If you lack self-regard, then the need to have another, or others, tell you that you are somebody, that you are worthwhile, or that you are worthy of love, becomes an insatiable craving that no one person can satisfy. People will sense your need, and avoid you, if they can. If it is true that the essential first step in the path to maturity is accepting personal responsibility for what you do, and not blaming your parents, your spouse or anyone else, then it is equally true that the essential first step in building a relationship is to build a strong sense of personal worth.

Seeing yourself as already "flawed" can justify all kinds of self-destructive practices. Not just the self-immolation that many wives and mothers choose, but also the substitutes to which men flee, such as substance abuse or over-achievement priorities, neglect or violence toward others, and substitution of **acquisitions** (translation: things) for **personal** relationships.

Doing something that is self-loving does not mean doing something that is fun or is easy. It often means doing something that is difficult, painful, or labor- intensive. Self-discipline, as well as sacrifice, may be required. Self-love of the proper kind always proceeds from, or is always based on, an examination of one's assets and liabilities. However, the introspection is motivated by a desire to be a better person for others. The criteria for evaluating decisions made as a result of one's search within is whether or not those decisions are **reasonable,** and not based on feelings or emotions.

The Bottom Line: Happiness or Misery

One simple explanation for the pathetic rate of marital success is that few brides or grooms expect marriage to be so incredibly confrontational, and so challenging to each partner's **preferred opinion** of him/herself. If his (or her) sense of self-worth is not firmly established or has been dependent on the opinion of someone else, the level of self-worth can diminish as the amount of affirmation received is reduced. When no affirmation is forthcoming, the individual who cannot supply his own self-regard starts disconnecting. Inevitably, married people start lowering the level or amount of affirmation they accord each other so that eventually those who cannot justify their own self-regard become isolated from one another. Although you can fool some of the people all of the time, and all of the people some of the time, you certainly can't fool your spouse for long. In fact, in many marriages, he/she starts looking through your "baggage" even before the honeymoon clothes have been put into the drawers, and soon finds a slew of reasons for withholding any further accolades.

It is a rare **newlywed** who will take the time and effort on a regular basis to see and appreciate, and do something about, his/her offensive and socially unacceptable, or at least disturbing, qualities. Because self-awareness seems unnecessary when the other person "loves" everything they "see" in you, you are not inclined to change anything. By the time you might conclude that improvements are needed, your husband or wife has beaten you to the punch with criticism. Unfortunately, for **most** couples, the mutual admiration and total acceptance society, that began with one bride and groom, unravels, as the frailties we all share begin to be recognized. These frailties are the egg and sperm, the seeds from which **criticism** is born.

When the spouse who affirmed us becomes our severest critic, possible responses are: **self-sacrifice** (grin and bear it), or **self-affirmation** (explained below and in **Part Three)**, or the **adoption of a negative or a dependent approach**, which could take the form of angry retaliation or resentment, feelings of frustration, sadness, or depression, an emotional withdrawal through boredom, or, an actual withdrawal by divorce. Men and women can be equally sensitive to criticism, but their response is most often quite different. While a women will fight back, sometimes viciously (if only to maintain a **connection** with her husband) a man will most often **run away,** that is, use an assortment of **avoidance techniques** like silence, the passive-aggressive strategies of forgetting everything she thinks important, or shifting his priorities so that his wife is placed a few notches lower on his list.

John Gray emphasizes that virtually every woman makes changing her husband a passionate project that begins as soon as the vows have been exchanged, if not sooner. Ah! If only a woman were wise enough to know (or to accept on faith) that a *man is empowered by the woman who does not criticize him or try to change him*, especially his priorities, his attitudes, his habits, or most specifically how he relates (or doesn't relate). As the resident expert on relationships, it is very easy for a wife to quickly detect every one of her husband's nineteen **relational flaws**. In the beginning at least, men are not at all inclined to be deliberately or purposely critical. Few men have an agenda of traits they want their wives to change, although they may have a list of expectations of things they want their wives to do for them. Even those men who might have an agenda, for example, those who want their wives to be more "organized," more interested in outdoor sports or activities, or their hobbies, typically expect their wives to respond to their suggestions as a man would, weighing the pros and cons, and providing clear reasons for acceptance or rejection. Because the **gender differences** are not factored in, men either fail to make a good case for what they want, or their wives have so many other priorities they want to deal with first, that a man soon decides the **wife change** is a project "out of control." His wife, in these cases, presents as a very complex puzzle that lacks an accompanying instruction manual, handles, or keys.

In the beginning virtually all the criticism from our spouse is **for our own good.** It is only later that criticism is utilized as a weapon to inflict harm or as a defense against the partner's attacks. Whatever differences there may be, and using the same logic that James Thurber referred to when he said that the problem with sex is "the other person," **both** spouses eventually resort to exchanging critical thoughts whose primary intention is not for the other person's good. Rather, the primary intention of the criticism is **to inflict pain.** It is this pain which invariably evokes a "fight" or "flight" response in the spouse's midbrain, or hypothalamus. The neurotransmitters that are produced in this part of the brain, independently of the mind and free will, affect nearly all the body's physiological responses, and therefore impact not only the marriage relationship, but also the mental and physical health of the "combatants." For example, once **hostility, cynicism, or distrust enters the relationship** the rate of depression soars as much as twenty-five times and the number of heart attacks triple.[4] Once the table is set for trouble, and trouble comes, trouble stays as a permanent guest. That is, trouble stays until one of the partners decides to **grow up**, that is, the process that begins with self-awareness, and which should lead to self-acceptance. **The first step in the establishment of a relationship** is **not** **acceptance** of your partner, but **acceptance of yourself!** If it is true that you cannot love anyone else more than you love yourself (It **is** true!), so it is equally true that you will not be able to fully accept anyone until you fully accept yourself.

Accepting Yourself as *the Designated Lover*

Self-affirmation or self-regard are the terms often applied to the acceptance of yourself. By simply seeing yourself as **somebody unique and acceptable,** someone worth working on, you can avoid the path to misery and loneliness that Wanda, in the example above, experienced. Unlike Wanda, your self-sufficiency leads you to consistently do what needs to be done to make yourself a better and better person. Because you see that you are worth the effort, even the hard work that is required, you look for reasonable projects for self-improvement, to keep yourself exciting or interesting, lest you become less and less interesting or appealing. Unless you work at it, the "boring sameness" you witness in the lives of so many of your friends will come to you. To create and maintain interest or vitality in any relationship, "work" on yourself is at least as necessary and important as any other work you could do. Any worthwhile and enduring relationship ultimately depends, then, upon a conscious awareness that you are somebody special, and intend to remain so.

Admittedly, polishing your own talents and making yourself into a fine and caring person with both feet solidly on the ground—in effect, making yourself a valuable "gift" for someone—does not guarantee that you will ever achieve an intimate relationship. Having a valuable gift to share only makes your gift-giving **possible.** Always, you have to find or keep someone with whom to share your gift. The Love of your life may be just around the corner, but if you do not go around the corner, you may not meet him or her.

To have an intimate relationship with anyone, your love has to be given unconditionally or **freely,** and not as a way to get loved back. Gifts, like love itself, that are attached to an expectation or to a demand for reciprocation are **never** expressions of unconditional love. Rather, such "supposed-gifts" are little more than **purchases,** or barter, and not real gifts because we are "giving to get" something.

Moreover, while **good will** is basic to a successful marriage, it should never take precedence over **good sense**. When this idea of "giving to get" starts contaminating other key areas of a committed relationship, and too much priority is given to establishing routines, to "getting along," and to bartering to get what each partner wants, both partners can suddenly find that enough **conditions** have been introduced into the relationship that the "he" and "she" of the relationship have become totally subordinate to the "us." The consequent loss of autonomy by both husband and wife reflects their failure to realize that conditional giving and sharing in a relationship, however well-intentioned and whether recognized as conditional or not at the time it is done, does not lead to intimacy at all, but dependence.

Giving and sharing "works" to create intimacy only when the gifts proceed from **a desire to make another happy, and are not subject to any conditions**, especially not by a need or expectation for a gift in return. That truth explains why choices, decisions, and sacrifices should not violate good sense and should be made thoughtfully, carefully, freely, and without conditions.

Every love story you have ever read is only believable and inspiring to the extent that each lover maintains his or her distinct identity and freedom, and as long as the love between the partners remains mutually unconditional. Tragedy becomes possible only when one lover wavers, decides to be selfish, or "gives in" against his or her better judgment.

The wonderful truth to be seen from this approach is that it is based on sound psychology, and conforms to the highest moral principles. Love offered without conditions brings with it a built-in safety feature: only one spouse has to maintain a **commitment to seek maturity** in order to keep in view the goals and promise in the relationship in times of crisis. Since the interdependence of the free and equal lovers does not include strings that have to be re-negotiated or severed, each maintains control of his/her own destiny.

A man (or woman), in the system being proposed, knows clearly that he can only demand perfection from his mate when he has achieved his own perfection. That means he or she can **never** demand it, even though he is, in fact, working to be perfect. A husband who loves himself enough to work on his own improvement can confidently expect two immediate benefits: the first benefit would be plenty of justifiable self-regard, joy, and satisfaction; in addition, his efforts to improve his own self-regard, would very likely inspire his lover to increase the value of her gift, too. That is simply the way "love" works! Imagine the reaction of your wife if you start giving her attention and <u>respect</u>, and little tokens or gifts of caring and affection. You know, as well as I, that her first reaction will be that "you are having, or have had, an affair, and your wonderful new attitude has been prompted by guilt." So, tell her up front, as evidence of your new honestly and openness, that your new attitude is not prompted by guilt, but by love!

Simple, but Not Easy[5]

The formula for success in marriage is simple, but surely not one that is easy to execute. It is not simply a prescription which reads: "do good, and avoid evil." In marriage, as in parenting, sometimes it is the things we **fail to do** that cause most of our problems. The sins of omission, or neglect, are surely just as common, and as lethal, as the sins of commission. And, countless evils visit every life and every marriage. The only thing worse than sickness, bills, taxes, mistakes, depressions, job loss, and accidents is having several or all of them occur at once. Still, we should always maintain the hope that achieving a **great marriage**, even a **great sexual relationship**—both goals now achieved by only a select few—are attainable in our own lives.

Recall another huge obstacle to intimacy in marriage: the narrow ideal of manliness to which boys/men/husbands subscribe. Any man who makes **independence his highest priority** is forced to bury all human emotions except anger, which typically gives him the social skills of a pet rock. A man's emotional isolation tends to be directly proportional to the talent and effort he expends to achieve success. His consequent loneliness and isolation, can, and often does lead him toward violence to himself and/or to his family. Precisely because **women typically give priority to persons** rather than things, most of them do possess the skills, the desire, and in the present state of society, even the cultural permission to re-connect men with themselves and with their own buried feelings. Hopefully, women will persevere as they have done throughout human history, and will not use their hard won equality in many areas to turn away from committed relationships with men, including guiding them back to re-connection. **Women can help**. More importantly, **women must help**.[6]

But women as well as men can have **misguided goals** and **unrealistic expectations**, many of them unrecognized or even unconscious. Cited several chapters earlier, these unwise goals and unconscious expectations represent the most common cause of marital conflict and divorce. But, they are not, obviously, the only causes. Women can have the same human frailties as men, including selfishness, pride, and laziness. They can also possess personal repugnance or intolerance for a man's natural or learned differences, differences that may be impossible for him to change. Ironically, it may be the woman's (occasionally, a man's) need for closeness, which produces the **most damage**. A couple's strong need to be close can provide such strong **motivation** to succeed that autonomy or freedom is sacrificed. Good reason to examine this problem of closeness or attachment, one more time, but this time from the viewpoint of what the couple expects marriage to give them when they make closeness, sharing, cooperation, getting along, and eliminating differences and conflict their top priorities.

16

Re-Searching What You Want from Marriage

"When there are no boundaries, intimacy can be dangerous."
—Dean Ornish

Getting Too Close for Comfort

In the last several chapters, I tried to provide some **compelling reasons** why married men and women might seek to profit from an examination or search for any **unnecessary dependencies** in their relationship. I pointed out that the chief source of these **intimacy-destroying** arrangements is the presumably-good intention of achieving a **close** relationship.

The vast literature on intimacy is really about "closeness." Two people can be close without being **mature, independent, or equal**, which are the three conditions necessary for the skill of intimacy. Partners might be described as close when a large part of their free time is spent together, and their number one priority is maintaining harmony and agreement. In such relationships, the emotions that are expressed never generate conflict or any form of unpleasantness. Couples seeking closeness quickly learn to avoid showing any emotion that causes "trouble." In that sense alone, they become closer, but their closeness also depends on maintaining comfort and safety. Without this commitment to safety, being together all the time could easily generate too much anxiety. Without a well proven track record of acceptable reaction patterns, the closer a couple comes to each other in terms of the thoughts and emotions they share, the more damage they can inflict should they ever get "fed up" or angry. Thus, in a close relationship, **doing your own thing** (as Johnny decided to do in the example in a previous chapter) is apt to generate all kinds of anxiety-producing reactions. The conditions required to maintain closeness prevent intimacy, which requires total separation and independence, and no conditions. Obviously, when a husband's emotional life is largely a reflection of what his wife is feeling, or vice-versa, the variety, the vitality, the spontaneity, or the freedom that is required in intimate human relationships is missing.

Why would anyone seek a close relationship, instead of an intimate one? Chapters Thirteen, on **self-awareness**, and Fourteen, on the **growing up dividends**, should have provided you with some good answers to that question. Surely, we all desire an atmosphere in our home where we feel safe, where no one shouts or bickers, and where everyone seems to be pulling together. Another benefit: if I make my emotional life totally in sync with my wife's, I do not have to face, deal with, or "own" my emotions. I thereby avoid taking personal responsibility for any guilt, sadness, or pain that I have brought into the relationship. Unquestionably, married couples can "use" each other, and often do as a way to avoid **personal responsibility** for their own sadness, anger, anxiety, or uncertainty. One very common American example: a husband who fears he will lose emotional control if he releases his anger or who steadfastly avoids expression of his pain, fear, or anxiety will somehow gradually transfer his personal feelings to his wife. Thus, observers of that marriage will see a wife with **all kinds of emotional problems** and a husband without any. Unfortunately, this dumping of emotions is almost the same as hiding behind an addiction, since like addiction, it allows the person to avoid **facing his (or her) own feelings**. Men are generally much better than women in dumping anger.

The **transfer of feelings** in a long time relationship almost invariably becomes **unequal**. It is usually the wife in our culture who gets too many of the feelings, and breaks down, or explodes. The couple in a close and loving relationship who are sharing one boat are reluctant to believe that closeness can be dangerous even when the point is reached at which one spouse has become very emotional and the other shows no emotions. But, it is virtually **impossible to convince either** that their journey **could become a perilous** one if the spouses **remain in emotional sync,** that is, each reacts to the other's emotions in an appropriate way. Two examples: the sadness of one depresses his (or her) mate or the pain of one evokes empathy in the other.

Although those married couples who pursue an ideal of closeness generally start in emotional harmony, their emotions can become "conflicted" at any time. For example, eventually her sadness can make him angry, or his anger make her depressed. Her frustrations might bring out his impatience, while his resentment can make her cry. Either partner in such a marriage might well decide to **rock the boat,** that is, decide to react in a new, unacceptable, or unloving way. When separateness in the matters of self-awareness and personal accountability has not been maintained, one or the other spouse may suddenly realize as the boat starts rocking that he (or she) can't swim!

❖   Beth and Ned were very close. Within months, the newlyweds had negotiated agreements on just about everything. He drove, she took care of their social life. He shopped for food, and she cooked it. Ned took care of the lawn and garden, Beth took care of the furnishings. They had decided how many friends they could handle and had proceeded to fill in all the available slots the first year. Their social life, they chuckled together, from time to time, was in "perfect balance," just like their marriage. The picture of their marriage looked wonderful.

The couple in our story were blessed , with no major illnesses, financial worries, or natural disasters to shake things up. Both the children—a son who was fifteen and a daughter who was eleven when the event occurred that changed their lives forever—reflected their parent's organized and efficient lifestyles.

Neither partner had ever thought seriously about questioning any of the **personal qualities** that not only made their relationship **so much better** than that of their friends, but also **so much different**. Of course, both Beth and her husband had occasional "misgivings" about this or that arrangement in their marriage—

aspects that they would have liked to change or improve. But, Beth considered conflict or "differences" as the antithesis of love, while Tom desperately needed the reassurance that he was a "great husband," and, as a result, was not going "to make any waves." Thus, both would invariably choose to be silent, rather than disturb the perfect relationship that made them the envy of their friends.

Unlike their friends, this couple **never** fought. To release the anger that was generated by the inevitable frustrations and resentments in their lives—that arose either from within the marriage relationship itself, or from those connections with co-workers, friends, neighbors and the like— Beth and Ned "attacked," in their private conversations, many subjects, people, and things. But, even in those instances, they were always on the same side, always in agreement.

Her "bad' guys and his always matched. At least one villain got skewered at virtually every evening meal. The "terrible increase in murders," "fires," "prices," or "natural disasters" were some of the topics that could get the kid's juices pumped up, too. Discussions "on the morality of the kids today," would usually be the topic of the meals at which their children could not be present. As their twentieth anniversary approached, they could look back on twenty summer vacations in Ocean City, one thousand Sunday brunches after the church services, and the same number of Friday night movies.

Yes! Beth and Ned Conington, Senior, were a smooth functioning team with a regimen for living that "worked." And, they firmly believed they could satisfy **all** of each other's needs without help from anybody else.

The Sunday morning when Beth and the two children came to the church and the brunch without Ned, thirty-three people asked one or the other of the family where he was. They explained that "he was at the doctor's office." Beth told her questioners that Ned had complained of a painful headache, and had told Beth that their best friend, who just happened to be an internist, had advised him "to get right over to the office, and be checked out."

Ned insisted to Beth that it was "nothing," reminding her that he had such "migraines" since he was a teenager, and "they always went away in an hour or two." Beth and the children reluctantly followed his request and went on to church.

Ned never saw the family doctor. He never saw anyone else, as far as anyone knows, in the entire town of sixteen thousand people. (And, apparently, no one saw him.)

Five years later, the mystery of Ned's disappearance is still unsolved.

Only Beth—no one else—ever saw, or will see, the "pink slip" that Ned placed under his pillow:

Dear Beth,

   I have been writing and rewriting this letter for ten years. Since I have always been a coward when it came to refusing you anything or doing something that might ruffle your feathers, I am only being in character by taking this coward's way out of our marriage.

   You just "expect" people to do whatever it takes to keep things in the prescribed pattern, even though you never really give orders. Isn't it ironic that after 20 years of doing everything to please you, I am giving you the ultimate hurt any husband can give, by walking out.

   Please use this letter as my permission to divorce me. There is no doubt in my mind that you will find someone else as quickly as you want. You are still beautiful and you have a great personality.

                                                                    Ned

Within three months, the church council voted to give Beth a very good job that was suddenly available with the retirement of the parish Secretary/ Treasurer/ Manager of Social Services.

Beth asked the police and the FBI to drop their investigation of the matter almost before they started, because "she could not bear to know with certainty that he was dead, or worse, that he had been the victim of foul play." When she was reminded that she could not remarry for seven years if his status was uncertain, she answered that she could never marry anyone else. She could endure only if "I have the hope that he is alive somewhere." **That** much was true. The FBI did investigate for a few months, but since there were absolutely no leads and Beth always seemed too distraught to supply them with any help at all, they eventually turned the files over to the "missing persons" section, where the case was simply ignored.

I am aware of at least fifty couples whose marriages ended in a fashion similar to the tragic couple just described—although in two-thirds of them it was the wife leaving without a trace. While the motivation for the men appeared to be avoidance of intimacy or confrontation, in the cases where the wife was eventually located, there was always another man. In a life in which care and affection are the only food or pay received, a woman who receives little food or pay will search elsewhere until she finds some.

Co-Dependency Precludes Intimacy

Though I have been challenged from time to time when I have offered my assessment that most marriages **miss the possibilities** by a mile, that is, they are not highly fulfilling relationships by any stretch of the imagination, I am invariably supported by the experts. The consensus is that only about five percent (or less) of married couples actually achieve the stage of unconditional love and the skill of intimacy. But, what about the other forty-five percent of marriages that at least endure?[1]

Most of the marriages that survive, I firmly believe, continue to be what they have been throughout the history of the human race— **arrangements** that are sufficiently **mutually beneficial** to the parties involved to keep husband and wife together under the same roof, if not necessarily in the same bedroom. Once the marriage contract is signed, the sexual discoveries have been made, and the patterns of sexual exchange implicitly agreed upon (I realize that nowadays this sexual agenda is often taken care of before the walk down the aisle), the first priority is typically to decide who does this job and who does that, and what are each other's most pressing needs. Obviously, two should be able to live almost as cheaply as one, and mergers can work many other wonders, too, as most CEO's will attest. Thus, before the ink is dry, most newly-joined couples are knee-deep in mutual dependency, generally referred to as co-dependency.

Co-dependency is the term used to describe those aspects of a relationship where **need**, not choice, determines what is thought, felt and done. Obviously, we all have needs that require outside help. Thus we are all co-dependent in some ways. Unfortunately, except for those instances where another's help is essential, a more apt term for codependency should be **emotional immaturity**. When we look to others to satisfy the needs we should be taking care of, ourselves, we are being dependent, and selfish.

Emotional immaturity also describes a person whose self-regard, emotional life, and course of action, depends on someone else. Thus a focus group of codependents should more properly be referred to as an "immaturity group." Such a group readily give its members a place to hang their hat, and to feel normal. But, **unless sponsors are provided** who understand the basic immaturity, and keep the focus on self-correction, such a group, in and of itself, may do little or nothing to get anyone to "grow up"—at least to the level at which a successful relationship becomes possible for them.[2]

The most effective group therapy must insist that "growing up" is each person's personal responsibility, just as it is in marriage. To "heal' your co-dependency in a marriage, you do not have to distance yourself, ignore, or reject your partner, anymore than a teenager must do any of those things to escape the "control" of his parents. Rather, the project is to gain knowledge of what you think, feel, and do (and why). You definitely have to identify what you are feeling. Self-control, patience, and courage are needed in order to perform such examinations. Whatever happens in the process of searching within, you have to **accept full responsibility** for what you find.

If you are overwhelmed with confusion when you try to analyze your feelings, or when you try to understand why you are so isolated and unfeeling, a good solution may be to start **writing down** what you think or feel. A simple **journal** can become a powerful technique for sorting things out and bringing you back into contact with your feelings and thoughts.

One of the first talents to be sought is **self-control**, which means, among other things, staying calm when everyone else is upset. This ability is of fundamental importance in marriage. Since we all keep in our repertoire a list of at least a few of our spouse's **buttons**, that is, the words or actions that make our partner "lose it," it is a gloriously effective advance in one's ability to be intimate when he (or she) can remain calm after his spouse "pushes a button" in an attempt to control or manipulate his emotions. The ability to stay calm does not mean that he "tunes out" his partner or feigns indifference (a typical male ploy in American marriages), but rather that he (or she) **stays totally present**, and shows himself as aware of what his wife has done. When he (or she) achieves this level of control, he can stop his wife (or husband) from ever pushing the same button to hurt him again. In marriage, men and women frequently use the press of a button to release, or transfer their own anger.

In an ongoing relationship like marriage, virtually every conflict of interest can generate anger. Each difference in goals or priorities can raise concerns involving freedom, being controlled, or being used. Especially is this true for men, who view any hint of manipulation as an attempt to take total control. As emphasized in **Part One**, men will get angry and try to eliminate any circumstance that could put them one-down to anyone.

Obviously, couples must constantly cooperate and negotiate, if only for practical reasons. My point is that from the beginning of the marriage, each decision to **depend on** the spouse for something should be made consciously, carefully, and **freely,** that is without any use of intimidation. For example, if a wife keeps giving in to her husband's demands on her time and energies because she is afraid of his explosive temper, the days for the success of her marriage are numbered. Besides being based on justifiable and reasonable grounds, each decision to do something for a spouse should include at least the implicit stipulation that it is not written in stone. Any "arrangement" that has you doing something for a spouse that he (or she) could do for him/herself should have an escape clause. In that way, the path to **irreversible** dependencies is avoided.

Skill at cooperating with another can be praiseworthy, and a sign of personal growth, if the agreements are made consciously and without intimidation, and if the cooperation doesn't involve rights that should never have been negotiated away. On the most practical level, the time you spend honoring past agreements is time you don't "own" or control any more. When someone else, or a bunch of standing agreements control or decide how you spend large parts of your time and energies, you are probably going to get bored or bogged down. If you decide that you have sacrificed your freedom of choice too often or unnecessarily, you are almost always going to come to resent both the person who shares your life and those agreements you made with her (or him).

Ned, in the clinical case just presented, felt totally "enslaved" by all the independence he had given away. He arrived at the judgment that **too much** of his day was spent doing things that he not only felt that he didn't want to do, but that he now believed he shouldn't have to do. But, by continuing on the path of least resistance, which he had always chosen, he avoided a confrontation with Beth that would have required him to face or to overcome his cowardice.

Growing-Up, Not Better Communication, Is the Answer

Marriage counselors are mistaken if they believe that better communication is the answer to most marriage problems. Communication does not automatically give either partner the increased self-mastery, courage, perseverance, self-respect, and wisdom that is required to consistently avoid marital deadlocks, especially if the partners think **every difference** between them has to be eliminated. Resorting to negotiation and compromise to definitively resolve every difference that arises inevitably increases the couple's dependence on each other to intolerable levels. When the point is reached when one or the other says, "no more concessions," the couple's approach to differences or conflict has to change or the marriage is finished. This is especially true in those marriages where the spouse who now refuses to concede anything has been **giving in** most of the time.

The **self-regard** needed by at least one partner to break the cycle of mutual dependence, is generally **decreased** when anyone— whether spouse or counselor—exerts more pressure to communicate, negotiate, or "reach a consensus." When we see the married couple in the restaurant **not talking** to each other, we must realize that they are **communicating** volumes. He/she is already **hearing** all that the partner has said or "**can** say," and knows that the spouse has heard every possible response. Talk under these circumstances is often taunting, or cynical, or a sick form of pretending. It is certainly much better if conflicted couples spend more time on examinations of conscience which could lead one or the other to make the decision to become a better person to live with![3]

Summarizing . . .

Certainly knowledge provides the raw material for achieving wisdom. Both "how-to" and "what if" books on marriage should provide insights leading not only to wives and husbands who are smarter, but also to those who are wiser. But a man (or woman) also has a will. It is the will, or heart that decides what he or she is going to do. Thus, **knowledge alone** of what it takes for a great marriage does not produce a great marriage. Correcting a man or woman's lack of knowledge is not nearly as difficult as dealing with a person's **lack of will to wholeheartedly seek** a great marriage.

Marriage is, and should always have been, the best way to become fully human and fully alive, and the best forum for expressing that aliveness in relationship. While success requires the acceptance of personal responsibility, the virtues of perseverance, good judgment, kindness, courage, humility, honesty, and generosity are obviously important. A good sense of humor can make up for a multitude of sins. Marital success also depends on the preservation of the **he** and the **she**, that is, the preservation of the independence, autonomy, separateness, or freedom of the persons who signed the marriage contract. Each must be allowed "to paddle his/her own canoe," that is, be allowed to think, feel, and act as a free and distinct entity. Otherwise, intimacy is impossible. Those who give up their own identity in marriage, or more precisely stated, their own integrity, are paying too high a price. Beth and Ned in the example just cited, and millions of couples like them, demonstrate that truth every day. The realization that one has sacrificed "too much" automatically evokes resentment. Unless the partner is a saint, such resentment will be met with a response equally negative, divisive, or unpleasant. **Giving in** to get a spouse's affirmation or validation is paying too high a price. But, **self-validation**, that is, self-regard earned by hard work on yourself, can take away much of the anxiety, fear, and insecurity that prevents the **loving choices** that lead to intimacy. It has been very wisely written that, "Without the ability to persevere when validation from the partner is not forthcoming, couples bog down."[4]

An issue of control almost always demands negotiation and compromise, and, some surrender of one's free choice. Over the course of a marriage, maintaining a sense of togetherness, while holding on to control of one's own life or choices, can be the most difficult challenge of all. This task of **staying together (**and cooperating), **but remaining separate (**and in control of your own life) can seem too formidable unless the meaning of differentiation and intimacy can be learned and appreciated.[5]

Heretical as it may sound to those who wish and dream it should be otherwise, the two candles at the marriage ceremony, which are used to light the third candle representing the marriage, should never be extinguished. The fact that they are extinguished is a graphic reflection of the fallacious idea that in marriage we somehow lose our separate identity.[6] The **three marriage candles** must burn on brightly. The first two reflect the reality that husband and wife must continue the lifelong process of perfecting their own unique gifts. The third candle reminds us to be attentive, caring, involved, and knowledgeable about the "needs" and "wants" of the one we love, and to persevere in our commitment to work together on our mutual goals.

17

Keeping Your Own Candle Burning

"Walking hand in hand in a relationship means walking a fine line between giving too much and giving too little."
—Steven Carter and Julia Sokol

Handling Issues of Control <u>Inter</u>dependently, Not <u>Co</u>-dependently

In most marriages, it is not sexual issues that keep couples in an adversarial approach to each other. Most couples greatly fear making sex an issue, and quickly compromise and "settle-in" on how their sexual exchanges will proceed. Indeed, if they don't, the marriage usually doesn't last long. Rather, it is the **non-sexual issues of control** that relentlessly grind the forward progress of a marriage to a halt.

Not all differences between a man and a woman need to be resolved. As the partners move toward maturity, each develops more and more tolerance for differences. As long as trust and fairness are maintained, differences should pose no threat to a relationship of independent equals whose highest priority is each other's happiness.

Unfortunately, all but a "precious few" couples see differences as a burr under their saddles, and persist in fighting to eliminate them. Thus, sooner or later, these daily struggles for control destroy half of

126

our marriages and seriously obscure the path to intimacy in forty-five of the fifty remaining ones.[1]

There are **only three approaches** to **resolving differences**, whether the power struggles are over finances, leisure time, outside interests, personal hygiene, how many children, or "what's for dinner?"

The first method is **giving in.** Whether out of weakness or as an act of love or as an heroic **sacrifice,** giving in represents a giant leap away from intimacy. The second approach is trying to achieve a **perfect compromise** in which each partner gives up precisely the same amount of freedom or control. Both of these methods of handling conflict represent, in effect, a step in the direction of co-dependency.

The third, and last, approach to settling power disputes is the conscious and deliberate decision on the part of both partners to **test interdependence** on that issue by a **tentative negotiated settlement,** that is, an explicitly experimental and temporary agreement, one that is always subject to re-negotiation at the request of either party. The difference between the second and third solutions above is subtle but crucial. Very few, if any, compromises are perfect. Those which aren't "perfect," always contain the seeds of later resentment. But, being explicitly assured that any settlement can be changed at the will of either party, makes "control," and a resentful response, a non-issue.

This is not academic nonsense we are discussing here. Depending on how long the couple stays together, there are thousands to millions of differences of opinion, needs, wants, and priorities. Unless these issues of control are handled by mature adults, the marriage gets more and more conflicted rather than less. The third solution demands the acceptance of **total equality** between the parties. This equality is never negotiable, and should **never be sacrificed**.

Love, Not Sacrifice

The model to keep clearly in front of you: "lovers" demonstrate their "love" by the sharing of **valuable gifts,** rather than by the offering of personal **sacrifices.** Even the God of the Torah, and of the

Christian Old and New Testament, said "I want love, not sacrifices."[2] Watching the one I treasure "sacrifice" for me is definitely affirming, but it is painful, too. I would much rather see her do something she delighted in doing, even though I received no other benefit.

Understanding how **reciprocity,** that is, giving to another and receiving from another alternately and mutually **leads to co-dependence** is equally fundamental to our understanding of the kind of love to which I am referring. Gifts given because of an expectation of reward are not expressions of unconditional love. Nor is giving to another out of a sense of gratitude and appreciation. Love for another can inspire or motivate you to be full of gratitude or appreciation for their past and future gifts and thus such gratitude or appreciation are possible **fruits of love,** but they **can never be preconditions. There can be no preconditions.** Unconditional love cannot be purchased. Expectations that your partner will sacrifice for you, as a repayment or prepayment for your sacrifices, threatens intimacy and love by placing preconditions—appreciation, demands, needs, or contingencies—on your gift-giving.

A very important note of caution—**the exercise of "unconditional love" does not mean one is totally loving.** There are always things you dislike, or perhaps even hate in the people you cherish most. The only love worthy of the name is trying to provide a benefit to someone else without attaching any strings. The fact that you do not like them at that moment does not prevent an intimate exchange. Even expressing your hate can be a demonstration of your intimacy skills. If you think that hatred negates the possibility of loving exchange you substitute a condition, namely, an intolerance for hatred, for honest dialogue. How many couples do you know in which it is obvious that one spouse's defiance or anger would end the marriage (or, at least, cause the offender to be "shot down," figuratively, if not literally). As long as "hatred" is not tolerated in a marriage, intimacy remains impossible. Integrity, or honesty, is necessary for that skill, and hiding our authentic feelings qualifies as an act of dishonesty.

The *Only* Absolutely Essential Element in Unconditional Love

Mother Teresa was perhaps the **greatest lover** of the Twentieth Century. Clearly, there is more to "Love" than that experienced, or written about, in the magical world of **lovers,** in which both partners exchange love, that is, both give and both receive. While Mother Teresa was unique in the power and steadfastness of her commitment, the world is full of examples of unconditional love in which there is only one **lover** and one **loved.** Whether referring to "Doctors Without Borders" or "The Missionaries of Charity," these examples qualify as expressions of unconditional love because the only absolutely essential element in **all loving acts** is that **a benefit is intended to the one being loved to which there are no strings attached.** This **other kind** of unconditional love is in many ways nobler, or more praiseworthy than that exchanged in **committed relationships**. The command to love our neighbor is found in all religions. "We are commanded to love our neighbor, but we do not have to like them," is the lecture we hear in our churches. This truth recognizes that serving and helping others in some way—even if we do not see them, or are repulsed by their contagious disease, by their filth, by their anger, by their physical deformities, or by their attitude—is still an act of unconditional love because a benefit is intended and nothing is asked for in return.

Mother Teresa was criticized for her apparent lack of a structured social ethic, that is, not providing a political or social agenda, or for not using her prestige to effect reforms in her country. But, this saint was a lover and not a political activist. She demonstrated by her life's works that the bottom line in matters of love is not words, but service. When Mother Teresa was asked "What do you say to these people who are the "poorest of the poor," "the lowest of the low," her reply was: "I sweep their floor!" Clearly, this was her way of saying, in as few words as possible, that God wanted her to embrace them, wash them, feed them, and attend to their obvious and tangible needs. Through her inspiration, many thousands throughout the world are proving their love for the abandoned in the same way.

When I write about **unconditional love** in this chapter and in the last, I am talking about love **between persons seeking to be intimate**.

Each lover benefits, or receives something, from the expressions, exchanges, and actions of love. Otherwise, what sense is there in loving anyone with a view toward intimacy with them, other than experiencing the self-regard and personal joy that comes to everyone who loves. Who would believe any love story that didn't make it clear that both lovers benefited from, or delighted in the gift of love from the other? Applying this essential element of love to marriage—serving and being served—provides us with **the best prescription for marriage success**. Seek, as your highest priority, that level of personal development that will make you a wonderful "gift" for your spouse, then *freely* share that gift (your service and talents) as often as you can, and do this sharing without any conditions! If you need to do something with strings attached, go fly a kite.

Courage, Honesty, and a Generous Heart, Make Love Possible

Perhaps no area of marriage proves the shallowness of the **barter, or exchange method of loving** (which isn't love at all, because it is conditional) than the fruits of its use in the bedroom. The boredom, disenchantment, or divorce that eventuates when "lovers" **use** sex for their own purposes should be obvious to anyone who takes the time to think the matter through (if he or she has not already learned the lesson the hard way through his/her own experience). **Using sex** for an ulterior motive is, by definition, a neurotic game. **Anything** that comes between the lovers diminishes the union. For most couples there is so much going on that has nothing to do with giving, or with making the partner happy, that it is no wonder that sex often becomes a form of mutual exploitation.

Ideally, if the husband and wife could each get his/her own **baggage** (translation: pride, anger, fear of failure, and all the **selfish priorities**) out of the marriage bed, they might be able to "touch" again. More on the connections between sex and love in **Chapters Twenty through Twenty-Three**. But since several chapters of the book have been devoted to the problems and violence resulting from a **man's need to be free**, and several to those caused most often by a **woman's desire to be close**, let's return to those obstacles to marital success for which **both genders** can take full credit.

18

Why So Many Things Go Wrong for So Many Wonderful People

Do you take this woman, from this day forward, for better or for worse, for richer or poorer, in sickness and in health, until death . . .? I do!

The Natural History of a Marriage: From Expectation to Disenchantment

While the comic may claim the marital vows are multiple-choice questions, and thus opts for the better, richer, and healthier marriage, most of us see a lot of the alternatives. "For better or worse" definitely does not mean that we can keep all our bad habits and do nothing to change our failings or weaknesses.

We all begin marriage with a strong desire to be "fulfilled," even if we do not characterize our motives with such an all-inclusive word. Because our mate accepts and affirms us and delights in our company, we experience joy and serenity, and have great expectations that this blissful experience will last forever. In those moments, we are fulfilled. But living happily ever after is the promise of fairy tales. Sooner or later, most of us find that our **preferred view** of ourselves, that is, what we would like to be, does not match how our spouse sees or experiences us. In fact, our preferred view would not even match what we would actually find if we took the time to look at who we are now. Perhaps looking at what we have become would make us feel uncomfortable or guilty. It is usually much easier to focus instead on our partner's deficiencies.

Our permanent relationships **begin** in an atmosphere of mutual admiration. Someone else accepts us as we are. They like us, love us, appreciate us, or enjoy our company. When we share the same feelings, we move logically to a commitment. But, sooner or later, the man and woman in a committed relationship will start looking for **reasons** for his or her commitment to **this** person instead of someone else. Inevitably, he or she starts finding things that makes his/her choice more and more dubious. Once the compliments start becoming rare, and criticisms come on the scene, the velvet gloves come off, to be replaced by boxing gloves.

It is fairly easy to show that any relationship built upon the partners' exchange of **unmerited** affirmation and acceptance will start to dissolve the day either partner finds a reason to complain about the other. Cinderella's or Snow White's expectation that "someday the prince will come" reflects a very common fantasy. We all dream of living happily ever after. As Chesterton wrote many years ago, fairy tales are simply the happy side of commonsense. Sagaciously, he added that commonsense is a common sense among women, but that men typically lack it. At any rate, the young lady expects that her prince will ensure her happiness, he will take her away from all her problems. If she is young and beautiful and virtuous, and he is young, handsome, courteous, gallant, rich, and a son of a king, chances are the marriage will work. But how many of us have all this going for us?

A man also expects that the woman he marries will always love, affirm and accept him, according to her promise. If the goal of a rapturous and ecstatic "connection" with his (or her) spouse is seen as an "impossible dream," and is therefore forgotten or abandoned, the marriage can "go south" quickly. When all the factors described up to now come into play that make conflict inevitable, that is, when the lovers open their eyes, or come to their senses, and the honeymoon is over, then the child-like faith, hope, and love that made life so wonderful is replaced by the sobering realization by both partners

that neither is now being affirmed. Each partner sees that the unconditional love and acceptance he/she thought had been found was
only an illusion. Conditions, demands, second-guessing, heated
discussions, fights, anger, negotiations, and compromise become the
issues of the day, and consume most of the energy. The husband
withdraws to his work or addiction as a way to conserve his energy
in order to survive. His wife finds her own form of denial, often
repressing the feelings of disappointment, isolation, fear, or anger,
which can start her walk on a path to depression.

Ironically, both the husband and wife always steadfastly maintain total agreement on one very important point: the marriage
would be wonderful again "if only my spouse would change!"
"Saving the marriage" means improving the spouse or solving his/
her "problems." Many couples, working from the premise that they
are both in the **same boat,** fight over who is to be the Captain. Those
who are sensible enough to realize that there are two boats running
parallel to each other, still can't avoid toppling their own boat in
their attempts to reach over to steer their spouse's boat. Apparently,
the simple idea that the relational ships would move more smoothly
and efficiently if everyone handled their own oars and used them
properly, never catches on.

Criticism: Intimacy's Mortal Enemy

By far the most common way for a man (or woman) to react to
feelings of inadequacy is to **criticize** others. If he is married, the
handiest target is obviously his wife. A **man** who perceives himself as
being criticized too often or too vehemently, will generally simply
dismiss his wife from his life—figuratively, at least, if not literally, as
his way of defending himself. A wife, too, can manifest an allergy to
criticism, but typically she will do it by **exploding** with invectives,
eschewing the husband's favorite technique of withdrawal and
silence. Many marriages never get off the ground because of the
defenses used by both spouses to counter even the **perception of
being criticized.** Effective defenses include emotional numbness,
sadness, boredom, depression, and condescending or controlling
attitudes.

Who of us has not witnessed rebukes delivered by one spouse to another? I am not referring to the callous remark, the disgusted sneer, or the mocking gesture, as common and as reprehensible as they are. Anyone of us can do horrible things in the heat of the moment because of anger or resentment, things that we later deeply regret. It is the deliberate, calculated, and abusive "speech, the literal, verbal "chopping down" of a spouse which virtually assures that the relationship will not bloom again that year, if ever. Even pleading temporary insanity can't undue the pain that such speeches inflict.

The fact that a man (or a woman) can easily rattle off ten or twenty grievances, faults, criticisms of his mate is simply a reflection of **his** level of maturity, tolerance, acceptance, or love. His **list** could also be evidence of his effort to control his spouse, or to control her priorities or values.

❖   There are **two exceptions** to the rule that criticism is of no value in inducing change in a spouse. The first exception occurs when a complaint from a wife, for example, sends her husband into a rage. In this situation, one can be almost certain that the fault that has been described is one that the husband himself would very much like to change, a fault the he finds very unpleasant or unacceptable. How can a wife accept her husband's fault if he can't even stand it? If he refuses to admit to what is true, and to accept those faults he is not going to change, why should anyone else, especially those who have to live with him? The very fact that his **greatest resentment** occurs when someone points to the trait which he most dislikes in himself, and which **he** would most like to change, can be used to light a clear path to self-improvement. Another exception to the "no criticism" rule is, of course, when the spouse is resorting to addictive or destructive practices. Silence can constitute "tacit approval " and be a collusion in his (or her) abuse of self or of others. **The bottom line**: if we can accept an *undistorted* view of ourselves, we would no longer need to react, defend, be anxious, or resentful when another person calls attention to our faults.

Criticism, while a reality in virtually all long-standing relationships, can be **motivated by good intentions**. Everyone thinks his (or her) way is the best way. One obviously good intention: some people's simple faults (I'm not talking addictions, here, as they were cited in the previous paragraph) are dangerous to themselves or to others. The criticism that is so reprehensible, the kind that eventually destroys a relationship is **that criticism** which is deliberately **intended to be hurtful**. Searching for the reasons a person might choose to hurt his or her spouse by being critical can be a very complex undertaking. At the same time, a search for reasons can be very rewarding to anyone serious about changing the relationship for the better. Insights have been provided in several earlier chapters suggesting why a man (or woman) might use hurtful criticism. He (or she) might desire revenge. He could use criticism as a defense against being controlled or belittled or to keep a partner from getting too close or too affectionate. Repeated disappointments resulting from a partner's lack of any response to our "suggestions" for a change in his (or her) attitude or priorities is probably the more common motive for "lashing out" with destructive criticism. The most tragic scenario in this matter of criticism is probably that in which one spouse attributes **selfish** motives to the partner's actions, when he (or she) is acting entirely out of love. This probably occurs most often when a wife (or husband) is **hypersensitive,** that is, has "problems" with, or an allergy **to control**. For example, the husband may handle the checking accounts to give his wife more time for other chores, and his wife fumes inside at his "control" of their money. Or, a wife may make some suggestions about the time and place or the husband's approach to sex, with the intention of being a better sex partner, but the husband sees these suggestions as "an attempt to control him," and responds with hurtful criticism.

With the two exceptions noted, unless and until there is the recognition that you accomplish nothing when you try to change your partner through criticism, you will probably never **get with the program** suggested in this book, that is, **cleaning up your own mess.** Even should you decide now or eventually to "get with a program that your spouse suggests", in order that you might more quickly placate him (or her), or get him off your back, you should be forewarned! It should be clear by now, that trying to please others by being untrue to yourself, is just another "quick fix," and will lead you back to the same gridlock you were in before you got with his (or her) program.

If your answer to the question posed in the last paragraph is "No, I will not follow my mates suggestions at all," and then you suggest that the better way is to "get with it" in the way **you know you should,** you get the cigar. Make that a **Cuban** cigar (or a bottle of the most expensive perfume) if you are able to admit that **you are the problem,** and that **you** need to start growing up. Obviously, any husband or wife would reject without hesitation the **marriage therapist's** criticism or accusation that his or her marriage is not doing well because he/she remains an emotional child. In fact, making such a claim could get the doctor shot, even if what he/she advises is true. Like any advice, suggestions only work when they are "seen" as totally accurate, then fully accepted and acted upon.

How do couples move beyond the confrontational, or power-struggle, phase of their relationship? Where lies the path to a great marriage, to enduring love, and to fulfillment?

Fortunately, those husbands and wives who have shared many happy times, typically resist giving up totally and permanently on their investment in each other when the conflict-stage arrives in earnest. All the **bonding experiences,** that is, all the successfully-shared **crises** are remembered. We feel a deep kinship with the spouse who saw us through, or shared the pain. Even memories of the horrendous fights evoke "grudging respect" for the partner who took our best shots, and survived. Because all these "credits" create good will, almost any genuine effort made by one's mate to be civil, polite, or approachable, in dealing with an impasse, tends to evoke a like response in his/her spouse, and puts the faltering marriage back on course. Sometimes, putting a faltering relationship back on course doesn't take a whole lot of fancy techniques. Maybe, just a little more mutual appreciation, and the simple recognition that the essential first step in resolving any human dilemma, whether it is alcoholism or a conflicted marriage, is to **accept personal responsibility** for everything one does, and everything one should do, but fails to do.

Parts One and **Two** provided practical illustrations of how a marital dilemma could be resolved if just one of the partners accepted his or her contribution to the problem, and then attended to the work of fixing it. Many reasons were suggested that might explain why a man, who **was** a wonderful person, by everyone's account (perhaps even by the judgments of **all the women** in his family of origin), might become, as a husband, the angry tyrant, the TV recluse, or the sullen family skeptic reported regularly by surveys of wives. Go to any bar and you should be able to find at least one unhappy husband, or ex-husband, anxious to tell you **his** sad story. "The bitch never appreciates my pain and suffering on the job." "It's not enough she criticizes every thing I do, she criticizes who and what I am. Man, that sucks." In my bachelor days, I think I heard a hundred such monologues on "my side of the story."

What Is Marriage For?

It is fashionable to suggest that in earlier generations husbands and wives got along better because "he did his job and she did hers." I know that claim is not true. Having worked closely with several thousand different men in a large factory during the course of seven summers—the years from 1950 to 1956, now considered part of "the golden age of the family"—I can state with confidence that men have been 'bad-mouthing" marriage and their wives to other men for a very long time.

Admittedly, there is now more **open** infidelity, and more homes with only one parent (twenty-eight million of them) than fifty years ago. But, in the seven summers I worked in a factory with middle-class, blue-collared, religiously-affiliated "family" men, the only references to wives I ever heard inside the factory were neutral, rancorous, or demeaning!

❖ After the first month of work, I started listening intently for someone to say "I can't wait to get home to my wife." Or "I'm going to surprise my wife with flowers (or candy)." Or hearing anyone say to a co-worker, "You should meet my wife—she's terrific." It never happened.

Since, I've thought often of the possible explanation:

The men in that factory were virtually slaves. Most of them worked a different shift each week, which, for most, included weekends. The jobs were unskilled, repetitive, frenetically-paced, boring, dirty, or dangerous (or all of the above), with only two ten-minute "cigarette breaks" and one twenty-minute lunch period per eight hours.

I remember thinking, before I entered the factory the first time, how green the grass and how beautiful the landscaping. Regrettably, to this day, I cannot forget the smells, the heat, and the profanity, that overwhelmed my senses, **inside** the factory.

How many wives of these "disposable" men really knew what her husband had to endure? Not many, probably. "Being a man," he probably never told his wife how bad the conditions were. Men are typically stoic about providing details of their own abuse. Yet, it is equally likely that he came to resent the fact that she didn't appreciate what he had to undergo for the sake of his paycheck.

You could object, "You were just a kid and not paying much attention to men's comments about their wives," or, "This didn't really happen the way you describe it." **But it did!** With nine sisters, eight of them older, I remember being concerned about what could happen to them when they got married, especially that they be respected and well-regarded. My interest in marriage matters was publicly demonstrated over five decades ago by my **1948** composition for the high school oratorical contest, entitled: "The Sad State of the American Family." I still remember the good sister who asked me, in that sophomore year, if I really wrote the article myself, or if I had copied if from something already published. I told her the truth, that the talk was not taken from one book, but rather from a hundred books and from my personal observations.[1]

However, what husbands think of their wives, in my system of evaluating relationships, reflects only on the husbands, not on their wives. As the three single professional men who wrote the best seller *What Men Want* put it, when you say a woman doesn't suit your tastes, you are actually making it clear that you don't suit her tastes, either. With rare exceptions, the feelings in a relationship tend to be mutual, eventually, if not sooner.

In **Part Two**, I discussed some of the reasons the gentle, affirming, devoted brides whose later pregnancies I managed, might change into the bitter, sad, disheartened wives whose only references to their spouses eventually become negative ones. Many real justifications for a wife's thumbs-down attitude toward her mate have already been provided. The myriad of missed possibilities for demonstrating love can become instead the fertile source for anger and bitterness. Both the possibilities, and the consequences of missing them, are limited only by one's imagination. One point is clear: **we have never gotten marriage right!**[2]

Tragically, the **consequences** of messed-up marriages keep getting **more and more devastating** to the men and women involved, to their children, and to society. Who or what's to blame for our failure to use all our wealth and natural blessings and access to the latest knowledge to improve the quality of our marriages. In the next chapter, I will dare to at least suggest that some of the usual scapegoats are **not goats** at all, but **red herrings**.

19

Who Can We Blame?

*". . . [I]t's usually through some sort of shock that the psyche begins
to realize how superficial [its] life has been and begins
to seek out something more meaningful."*
—W. Brugh Joy

For many, married life settles into a routine, without apparent conflict or anger, but without vitality or passion either. Neither partner in such marriages seems to care too much that there is little sex, little sense of adventure, and few new ideas or suggestions. The word **boring** seems to be an apt description for such relationships. The marriage seems to be on "auto-pilot" and out of the couple's control. If there is never a separation or divorce, the union will probably be filed under the "successful marriage" column. But, is it? I don't think so.

How can so many marriages reach a state of affairs just described which no one, certainly, ever intends or seeks? What forces or circumstances or persons could be blamed for bringing or keeping two educated, motivated, healthy, initially-compatible, presumably sane adults of the opposite sex from readily achieving some kind of relationship that would be a hundred times more interesting and satisfying?

How Do the Problems in a Committed Relationship Get So Far Out of Control

Wisely or unwisely, the men and women of the twentieth century have listened better and more often than any previous generations to those "experts" who profess to understand the human psyche, and how the personality of the individual is formed. With little or no dissent from anyone, the principle is proclaimed that our parents, family traditions, and cultural priorities, are largely responsible for who we are as adults, and how we relate to others. As a result, we consult psychiatrists, psychoanalysts, psychologists, and family counselors to help us undo the harm and trauma of our upbringing. As a corollary, these professionals in the matter of relationships have provided all of us with an excuse for our failure to connect warmly and wonderfully with our mates. In the process, the experts cite evidence that even the choice of our life-long partner has been, in the psychological sense, "thoughtless."[1]

Undoubtedly, there is consolation in blaming either past traumas, the marital and sexual therapists, or even the **binding** marriage contract, itself, for the failure of our marriage. An entire "tradition of sexual ignorance and repression" is another favorite scapegoat, even though anyone with a modicum of good sense can see that the basic problem is not so much a lack of knowledge as it is a lack of good will.

Doesn't Anyone Realize That *the Pearl of Great Price* Is not a Pearl?

Unless the couple described in the first paragraph above is suddenly visited by some trauma, for example, cancer or other serious illness, or death in the family, which shakes them out of their complacency and forces them to re-evaluate their lives and what each means to the other, they will probably reach a point at which change is virtually impossible. Because each has lost sight of the "value" of himself or herself, the value of the spouse, and the value in the relationship, neither sees sufficient reason for changing anything. If questioned, each would blame the absence of "worth" in the relationship on their spouse. "My (fault-filled) spouse is ruining everything and destroying my hopes for a better life and future."

Obviously, a successful marriage is impossible unless, and until, at least one spouse comes to his (or her) senses and realizes he is wasting the most important opportunities of his life. If life is a precious gift, then he is precious and so is his spouse. Once he sees that he deserves love as a unique and incredibly marvelous complex of possibilities, he should quickly be able to see his companion in the same beautiful vision. Despite his/her past history, anyone who reaches the point where he sees **the pearls,** can then say "yes, I will begin," and commit to the process of **growing up,** as it was defined in Chapters Thirteen and Fourteen. An example of the wonderful changes that can occur if one spouse decides to grow up was provided in Chapter Fifteen. The disastrous relationship that can be created when neither partner chooses to work on self-improvement is described in Chapter Sixteen.

If one of the participants, and eventually both do not commit to personal work on themselves, no one, therapists included, can effectively bring any marriage to the level where the participants can see that the wonderful possibilities overshadow everything else.

Fortunately, even adults with deep-seated "family of origin" issues arising from sexual or physical abuse, or from childhood neglect, can almost always take that important first step toward healing, themselves, by accepting that despite their abuse, they are worthy of love. They can then proceed to take responsibility for what happens in the relationship. Most of us have known, or read, of individuals whose home life was so sad and dysfunctional that it seemed impossible to believe that they would ever talk about it or admit it. Some of those abused people even came to despise the feelings of sadness or shame that they felt every time their family dynamics came into consciousness. Yet, we became aware of their past because they were able to rise above the abuse, the violence, or the neglect, and share their experience with us.[2]

The Past Can Be Faced, and Closure Achieved

Facing and dealing with the past requires dauntless courage, worthy of a knight. A successful marriage lies within the reach of any husband and wife, regardless of past experiences, when each has the courage to begin the hard, and often frightening work of facing their feelings and their motivations in an attempt to find out why they react as they do, for examples, why they get angry, sad, anxious, or afraid so easily or so often. From courage comes the development of **integrity**—the openness and honesty to admit one's insecurities and fears, and to still remain committed to the search.[3] No matter how troubled the marriage, either partner retains the power to change the relationship for the better. Again, **no one** outside the relationship can help, until the partners have committed to changing themselves. A key principle is that when one partner works on himself/herself, the "relationship" is changed. The other partner must either change, too, or get out. Integrity is vital in every area of our life. The next four chapters will show the absolute necessity of integrity (honesty about oneself) to successful communication, for achieving a great marriage, and even for achieving the ability to experience great sex.

20

The Communication Games Married People Play

"Who we are, in truth, is a simple fact of who every person is, a loving being. . . . When we are not expressing ourselves in situations which allow us to feel loved . . . we are disconnected from who we are."
—John Gray

Communication—a Double-Edged Sword

Clearly, few men ever completely adjust to a woman's use of words. But, this ignorance of the gender differences in communication is not nearly as lethal or destructive of relationships as the "skillful" use of communication to wound or injure. Despite all that has been said about a man and woman's vastly different approach to the marital commitment, and all the obvious problems of language, the cause of marital problems has **never been** primarily a defect in communication In fact, in conflicted marriages, there is **usually too much of it, especially of the hateful or sadistic kind.** Mark A. Karpel, in his text written for **couple therapists,** insists that ". . . relatively few couples who present for treatment are suffering primarily from communicational deficits."[1]

For most couples, in fact, the communication problem is not speaking, but **listening.** When each partner thinks only of expressing his or her grievance and does not listen to his spouse's complaint, the "dialogue of the deaf" begins. Besides the need to listen, what is **not said** (not saying sometime hurtful or destructive) is obviously as important as what **is said.** Thus, even if it might be true that as much as half of the world's problems are caused by **poor** communications, then it is also a certainty that at least half are caused by **good** communication of anger and resentment. Remember, too, that body language, intonation and our actions (or inaction) constitute a language of their own.[2]

The **goal of communication** is easily summarized: to allow the feelings of connection, cooperation, and fairness to be expressed and heard. But this goal can become impossible to reach when the transactions between married people are loaded with **ulterior motives,** that is, with selfish, dishonest, hidden motives. Such **duplicity** (dishonesty, misrepresentation, or, in psychological terms playing **games)** eventually weakens or severs the bond of trust. Mutual **trustworthiness** may not be the most important asset in a marriage (**reverence** is), but the marriage will not survive without it.

Playing *Games* In Bed Can Be Dangerous to Your Sexual Health

David Schnarch, who insists on an **integrated** treatment for marital and sexual problems, that is, treating them together as one and the same problem (see **Acknowledgments**), also reminds us that "only in marriage can you 'screw' someone twice with the same act. The second time is the pretense that you didn't enjoy it, when, in fact, you did." One of his major hypotheses is that the sexual part of the marriage generally reflects the condition of the marriage itself. Since men often give up all non-sexual ways of communicating regularly with their wives, women are often forced to resort to sabotaging the sexual exchanges in order to communicate their own anger and frustration.[3]

In fact, **feigning unawareness** of any actions that hurt, sadden, disappoint, annoy, anger, belittle, confuse, or frighten our partners, can provide a sadistic outlet for either partner, and quickly becomes the most-used and most energy-efficient way to exact revenge in marriage. Hiding our **gratitude or pleasure**, especially in the sexual area, is equally "sick." But then, why should any of the above be unexpected? Retribution for acts of commission or omission, both real and imagined, is a motivating factor in everyone's life. Marriage only makes it easier because there are fewer places to hide.

One popular marriage **game** is **controlling the partner by "submitting"** to his/her desires—but, precisely in your own way. The partner with the lower desire for an activity can always control the level and time of that activity, taking advantage of the other's need. The one with the lower desire is delighted to take advantage of the knowledge that concessions will be made. Even harsh conditions will likely be accepted by the mate if his (or her) desire is strong enough. When one is first presented with this concept of unequal desire, he (or she) tends to think only of its sexual applications, but it comes into play for the man who wants his poker nights with the boys, and the wife who wants her husband to learn ballroom dancing. Think about it. **Both** partners often use **unequal desire in many different areas of marriage** to blackmail each other.

The Japanese used this unequal desire in the attacker-defender relationship as a technique of self-defense, since the aggressor invariably allows himself to become vulnerable by his passionate attack. They called the skill of overcoming your opponent by an act of apparent surrender, *jujitsu*.

The same principle of turning the tables in issues of control has been raised to a unique **bedroom art form** by American women. Instead of allowing their husbands to sadistically "use" them like sexual pawns—the "wham, bam, thank you ma'am" stereotypical victim of selfish husbands—the wife becomes a sadist herself as she plays with his mind, feelings, emotions, and sexual "needs." The game is called, "Yes, dear."

The "Yes, dear" game is a natural for a wife, again because the only obvious strong **domestic need** a typical husband exhibits is a desire for sex (or, sometimes, for dinner). Sexual **favors** are often precisely that—the wife's only negotiable asset for use as barter for getting what she wants most. She will submit to his sexual attentions "as a favor," even though she's "not really in the mood," or she will "allow" sex, "distasteful" as it is, as her "loving sacrifice." For example: the wife must take care not to respond too passionately or enthusiastically, otherwise her husband might conclude that he is doing **her** a favor. He might then feel no obligation to be grateful, or to pay attention to any of **her** needs. If the wife evidenced delight, such a response could also give her husband what he might want most from sex—affirmation of his sexual prowess and expertise—which again will relieve her husband of **other obligations** of "service." Surely, she is not being **authentic**, that is, honest. Nor is she being loving by pretending. In fact, she is resorting to yet another sick game. But, why shouldn't the wife use the weapons that she has available— to help level the playing field, and achieve her own sense of adequacy? It is ironic that it is only in this matter of sex that the typical husband is most obviously not one-up—that is, not at all in control. Again, the reason is that the time, frequency, style, or intensity of any activity in marriage is controlled by the partner who desires or needs that activity the **least.** Human nature being what it is, husbands rarely complain if their wife is a lousy cook if she is good in bed. On the other hand, there are men who don't mind the lack of adventure in the bedroom because their wives are creative in the kitchen.

Part of the husband's stronger desire for intercourse results from his inability to communicate, or connect with, or **to keep in touch** with his wife in other ways. Our skin, and its sense of touch, is our largest sense organ. Touching is the universal standard for showing regard and affection. In every book on infants, the point is made that touching and holding the babies is more important than food. We never outgrow our need to keep **in touch**, even if we have convinced ourselves otherwise.[4]

Humankind's Noblest Method of Communication (*Potentially*)

Intimate sex, that is, when the heart, minds, and bodies are joined in a mutual, consciously deliberate act of total giving or sharing, is the consummate human communication. That this achievement may be as rare as someone reaching Mt. Everest is testimony to the skill, perseverance, and courage needed for both. When men and women give more time and attention to interests other than each other, it can be expected that their sexual achievements would fall quite far short of the possibilities.

Since men are not comfortable in two-way conversations, especially with women, they use sex as their way of keeping in touch. Lest he lose all form of communicating with his wife, a man's ability to function sexually is his most treasured talent. Impotence is so devastating and deplorable, that men who are impotent feel greatly diminished and inadequate . . . and *speechless.*

Unfortunately, the husband's use of sex as his main means of communicating to his wife what he is thinking and feeling, introduces a lot of conflicting emotions into the sexual exchange. His "goal-oriented," "bottom-line," "let's get to the point" approach to conversation—the one-way talking that boys/men prefer—can definitely affect his style of relating sexually to his wife. Sex is surely often used as a way to get the spouse's affirmation. Unfortunately, using sex to get your husband or wife to approve of you or to like you can introduce a lot of fear, uncertainty and anxiety into the relationship. Clearly, it is not very sexy. Eventually the sex becomes boring or is even omitted.

Summarizing Some *First Principles of Sexuality*

Wanting to be desired, or desirable, is praiseworthy and marriage-enhancing, as long as your desire does not become a **need**, that is, **something you must have**. When you must have something, somebody is eventually going to make you pay for it. More importantly, when someone has or develops a hunger, or addiction, for sex, he is surely not talking about intimacy as that term is defined in this book. Since intimacy requires that the lovers be free, independent, and equal, sex could only be intimate for the sexually addicted if the lustful ardor is mutual.

It may be well to remember the principle that **procreative** sex may be a biologic drive we share with reptiles and mammals, but **re-creative** sex can take many years of work, by both partners in the relationship, to do well. Proof that having babies is a natural or biologic drive is provided by the 3,000 new teenage mothers, which America has produced every day, for nearly three decades. Proof that a **good** sexual relationship isn't a very significant part of that biologic drive and not easy to attain is provided by the billion-dollar how-to industry on the subject. Obviously, if any book or magazine article had an answer for achieving consistently good sex, no further books or articles would be needed! Perhaps even more convincing is the consistent discovery in sociological surveys that the likelihood of sexual dysfunction in married adults increases as the age he or she became sexually active, decreases.[5] If sexual **adequacy** is more likely if boys/girls wait until they achieve some maturity, it is obviously reasonable to expect that the **most mature** lovers would have the best sex.

The reality is that **intimate sex** is an acquired **skill** and a **developed taste**. With few exceptions, before you can be sexually intimate repetitively or consistently, you must develop the maturity and independence that intimacy requires. Erotic pleasure or passionate lovemaking is a human accomplishment requiring creative minds much more than firm thighs, abdomens, or genitalia, and is one of **the growing-up dividends** described in Chapter Fourteen. Any discussion of human sexuality must acknowledge that virtually **every act of relating between a man and a woman has sexual potential or overtones**. Men's consistent failure to recognize that fact has wrecked millions of sexual encounters, and prevented even more from being considered. That point is the theme of the next chapter.

21

The Problem: Foreplay Includes Everything But . . .

*"I have loved, and I have been loved,
and all the rest is just background music."*
—Estelle Ramey

*"If the psyche is unwilling, no amount of technique can persuade it;
and if the psyche is willing, no lack of technique can dissuade it."*
—Ann Aldrich

Always Gamesmanship, Too Much Resentment, Rarely Malice

Friedrich Nietzsche wrote that nothing on earth consumes a man (and presumably a woman) more completely than the passion of resentment. Not only does resentment play a large part in the day-to-day motivation of those who are married, it also plays a large part in what is written about marriage. Feminist writers have even expressed resentment that the question "What do women want?" is asked.[1]

In *It's Your Life: a Gynecologist Challenges You To Take Control*, I wrote that the husband who acts as though he "doesn't get it," is not trying to get it. He is rarely "thick" or "stupid." However, he very often has totally different priorities. Unfortunately for him, his **care-**

lessness typically prevents him from connecting his wife's cold shoulder in the bedroom to his coldness to her in his free time. The responses to my "questionnaire on husbands" (see Appendix for the questions) make it very clear that women are more dissatisfied with their husbands' performance **outside** the bedroom than inside it.

Is this rampant dissatisfaction justified? My answer: undoubtedly, **some** of it is eminently justified (and I have the written evidence to show it). But, many of the gripes are **unjustified** because they are criticisms of the ways a boy/man has been "programmed," whether by nature or nurture. Hell will probably freeze over before our society has changed sufficiently for all the women who oppose the **present male-programming** to be satisfied.

Why Can't We Accept that Gender Differences Are Real?

Much of what wives **deplore** in their mates is due to the fundamental **gender differences** that I have already discussed. Whether they are natural differences or the result of socializing influences is not the issue here, but rather their affect on hundreds of husband-wife interactions all day every day. For example, John Gray makes the point that marriages would be vastly improved for wives if men continued to share their thoughts and feelings as much as they do on the third date (statistically the time of their greatest sharing), thus fulfilling one of a woman's strongest needs.

In Chapter Three I explained that, while sharing **feelings** is almost always safe (though few men think so), sharing **thoughts** about the relationship will probably always be dangerous, partly because women don't like men's pompous, authoritarian way of conversing. Men simply hear and speak language as a means to maintain status and independence. I will say more about the distinction between feelings and thoughts later in this chapter. Gray provides another good reason for a man's silence: a man apparently **stops talking** because he is no longer interviewing for the job of husband, and typically has decided that both he and his wife can now get on to being, and doing things, together.

Because men don't realize what women enjoy most, they **stop listening, too**, at least in the way they listened before marriage. Because their relationship is sealed by a marriage contract, a man can decide that he will now begin to relate to his wife in the same way he relates to his best male friends, that is, using a side-by-side, or non-confrontational approach. This generally results in minimal eye contact, more nonchalance, and lots of apparent inattention. The anthropologists theorize that, from earliest times, men never "faced" anyone except their enemies in combat. They fought, played, and worked side-by-side with their friends. Women, on the other hand, have always related face-to-face.

Most husbands fail to see why their wives should be the least bit perturbed by their apparent after-marriage inattention, since a man considers such casualness and indifference as evidence of his accep-tance of his wife into a very narrow circle of friends. In many instances, he is simply excusing her from the obligation to engage in the inane or forced conversations she might find necessary with her other friends. He expects that she will understand that, and appreci-ate the compliment! Another gender difference to keep in mind: boys/men not only have a decided preference for "one-way" talking, but they also are **one-sided listeners,** that is, most men comprehend better if they hear the information through their better ear.[2]

Another and much more subtle explanation for a man's apparent inattention or lack of a reaction to some things his wife says: he may be so overwhelmed by what his wife has said, that is afraid to say anything, or to show any reaction. He might respond to the same statements from a man with a variety of approaches—from a punch in the nose or mocking laughter, to a verbal fight to the death using wrath-filled epithets. But with his wife, no reaction is often the best, and safest course.

When one looks at the way men "spar" with each other, espe-cially at play, both psychologically or verbally if not physically, and observe how men seem to enjoy the thrill of the competition, it is not hard to understand how men might consider ordinary, or non-competitive, verbal exchanges very boring. For example, women have often likened the competitiveness of men at large social gather-ings to the behavior of male deer, who bang their antlers together each spring, in order to discover which animals are the more domi-nant ones.

Sadly, any man who no longer gives priority to looking in his wife's eyes and talking to her, or, to listening to her with his full attention as a way of discovering more of his wife's mysteries, forfeits his possibility for a deeper and more satisfying relationship with her. Instead of longer, deeper, more intense conversations, for example, the mutual discussions become fewer, shorter, and more superficial. It's not at all surprising when their sex life follows the same pattern.[3]

On the other hand, whenever a woman blames her husband for "acting just like a man," she is confessing that she doesn't understand the reasons behind his actions. At the very least, she is proving that she doesn't **appreciate** the very different ways in which men "relate" to women, and to each other. Much has already been said about society's different approach to raising boys and raising girls. Boys/men who assume the role of "breadwinner" have been training from day one to be ever vigilant when dealing with others, ever ready to compete, fight, or protect their interests. "Acting like a man" unfortunately is what most men have to do for a living, or for survival—usually not for just their own sake, but the sake of their family.

Dealing With the Typical *Unfeeling* Husband

The separation of a man from his feelings is a very important part of a boy's **blueprint for survival,** which I sketched in **Part One.** As a response to an unfeeling husband, a wife has only a few choices. The optimal alternative would be to continue to be open and honest about her own feelings, including how his lack of emotional expression makes her feel. Short of that "adult" response, a wife could choose a very difficult and dangerous alternative: emotional silence. When she avoids expressing her feelings, the only possible ways for the couple to communicate are by the exchange of **thoughts,** or, by an exchange we can only describe as unemotional sex (see below). While **feelings** keep us in the present moment, where infinite possibilities exist, especially if those feelings are experienced as invitations to move closer to another, **thoughts tend to be heard as criticisms,** or as judgments, and keep us stuck in the past.[4]

Communicating(?) with an uncommunicative husband by unemotional sex might be compared to eating without an appetite, simply in order to stay alive. Or, it could be likened to satisfying an urge in the same way one might scratch an itch. There is certainly nothing distinctly human about it. Sex without human feeling is what eventuates when a man has separated himself from his feelings, and, as a result, is unable to share them. An emotionally-unequal relationship can never become intimate. The wife cannot supply her husband with feelings, any more than she could eat his food for him. Nor can the husband be forced to overcome his separateness. As Eric Fromm described such a man, "he remains in the prison of his aloneness." Thus, trying to sexually satisfy a man who is separated from what he feels will not only soon prove very frustrating to even the most well-intentioned wife, but such a course of action is, in fact, a collusion in the man's flight from himself.

The final choice for coping with an unfeeling husband: the wife **carries** her husband's repressed feelings, thus adding them to her own. Inevitably, the double load overwhelms her, and she becomes an overly-emotional, "hysteric," "overly-dependent," "neurotic," "bitchy" wife.[5]

Obviously, the best course of action is for the wife to allow the husband to take full responsibility for his own problems, and maintain her own integrity by staying in touch with her feelings and sharing them openly and honestly—keeping her own canoe moving forward, as it were. Surprisingly, when the wife keeps her own **canoe** moving forward, the husband will often come to his senses and start paddling his own canoe to keep up. Why? There are two clearly evident reasons. While it takes the non-action or unfeeling of two people to maintain the marital boredom, or to keep it conflicted, it only takes one person to shake up the status-quo. The second reason is that a husband wants much more from his marriage than the extremes of a totally unemotional wife providing him with unemotional sex and a hyper-emotional wife who is hysterical, dependent, or neurotic. This remains true even when most of what he says and does would indicate that he has lost heart and no longer cares. Lonely, isolated, unfeeling boys/men must never be taken at face value. A wife who perseveres, while maintaining her honesty and emotional integrity, often accomplishes miracles. **Unconditional love, after all, is the strongest force in the universe.**

22

Work, Sports, Sex—
Do Husbands Ever Think of
Anything Else?

> *"Civilized people cannot fully satisfy*
> *their sexual instinct without love."*
> —Bertrand Russell

Why People-Persons Tend To Be Better Lovers
Than the Sex-Experts

Women have consistently believed that men place **physical chemistry** (translate: looks, appearance, sex appeal) at the top of their requirements for a mate. There is no question that men's eternal weakness is beauty. They are beguiled by it. As the posters graphically advertising *Maidenform* bras all over Manhattan point out, "Inner beauty only goes so far."

In fact, both sexes consistently put "mutual attraction" at the top of their list of requirements for choosing a mate. But the skill of intimacy is a long journey from initial attraction. Thus, even though men want attractive wives, this fact does not mean that beauty guarantees intimacy, or that lack of physical attractiveness prevents intimacy.

There are many reasons why beautiful women tend not to marry well, but certainly one reason is that they do not attract the most mature men. As a man's self-regard increases, his need for a "trophy" wife decreases. Unfortunately, many women also tend to believe that their husbands pay much more attention to their bodies than to the emotional, mental, and spiritual aspects of their relationships. Perhaps this explains why half the featured articles in **Cosmopolitan, Elle, or Redbook** have as their goal teaching women **what men want sexually**.

The popularity of the "how-to-sexual-technique" books results from a conviction that the sexual problems between men and women are the result of sexual ignorance. The publishing industry has exploited the idea that learning sexual technique will result in great sex, and that great sex is the best and surest way to marital bliss and to intimacy. The version of intimacy to which they refer is the presently popular **feminine version of intimacy**—that is, involving intense emotionality and verbal disclosure of those emotions.

Surely, it should be clear, after forty years with the sexual revolution, that providing detailed instructions on how to "turn on" our mates sexually is **not** the solution to anything important. If lack of sexual information were the problem preventing great sex and great marriages, we would be hearing and reading, by now, about the wonderful improvements in everyone's sex lives and marriages. Unfortunately, sexual dysfunctions are rampant, and increasing, by all serious accounts, not to mention that "great sex" seems rarely to be associated with permanent relationships. The bottom line of all this is the truth that **sex is not the key to abiding love and fulfillment in marriage.**[1]

Although Cited, the Excuse for an Unfulfilling Marriage Is Rarely Sexual

I will return to the connections between sex and love in committed relationships in the next chapter, but it is important to stress now that in many marriages the connection can be a tenuous one. But even if the connection is weak, it is almost always a bad relationship that is ruining the sex. Those who work to save marriages in conflict, especially those counselors who are "not into the personal responsibility approach," can provide a myriad of other equally-**unconvinc-ing** explanations for the high rate of "unsuccessful" marriages—financial difficulties, a dysfunctional family, cultural or religious differences, too many children, childlessness, even the wrong environment. Blaming any of these **stresses** for a marriage's failure fits in with present day systems in which **neither party is guilty**. In **my system** of evaluating marriages that have fallen short of the inherent possibilities, **no one is innocent**, even though everyone has plenty of excuses.[2]

The length of anybody's list of excuses for marital discord invariably depends on how much time you have to listen. **First on my list** (writing as an author, not a husband): the typical marriage joins together a little boy, now "molded" into a real man (translate **macho**), and a determined, wary girl/woman who wants to be **modern**, but who has been assailed with so many conflicting signals about what that means that she typically sees marriage as her first chance to begin to define **herself**. The traditional **stereotypes**, that is, the dominating man and the submissive, sacrificing woman, have, of course, been officially repudiated. But, the **games** described in Chapters Eighteen and Twenty, which have replaced them are obviously just as "sick:" The husband must still be **tough**, that is, never show vulnerability, or weakness, and must separate himself from his fear and pain; and, his wife should not (at least in public), display too much intelligence, nor any competitiveness or aggression. A man's primary duty (no matter what anyone claims) is still to be the breadwinner, even in families where both spouses work. If a man's wife makes more than he does, the sense of being one-down is nearly inescapable. Husbands who support the family now have one-half the free time that their fathers had. And, there remain many physically-demanding, dirty and dangerous jobs that require **manly** virtues. So it should not be too surprising to find that the majority of husbands still expect the wife to do most of the housework, manage the social obligations, and nurture the children. Admittedly, some recent movement toward cooperation has been made, largely as a result of increasing flak from the wives.

Even if **post-modern** couples approaching marriage decide all the foregoing "roles" are no longer applicable to them and view them as old-fashioned nonsense, they remain confused as to an effective approach to a great marriage.[3] Since the assertion was made a few paragraphs back, that **a bad relationship usually messes up the sex,** what does it take to bring back the thrills, or at least some joy, pleasure, or satisfaction? Clearly, the most logical approach would be to improve the relationship!

23

Some Couples Don't Just Get Older, They Also Get Better

> *"I had realized long before that great sex is no substitute for an open heart. What I began learning is that an open heart can lead to the most joyful and ecstatic sex."*
> —Dean Ornish

Making Sex Better by Changing Priorities

A lot of comments have already been made about sexual interactions and conflicts in a marriage, primarily because so many people see "sexual incompatibility" as the basic reason why many married people stop loving each other. The point should have been made by now that sexual problems are almost always the **result** of, **not the cause** of marriage conflicts.

Everyone keeps forgetting that **great sex** requires creative ability, that is, intelligence. However, nowhere is it written that **knowing** we can use our intelligence (and our imaginations, of course) to create better sexual encounters with our mate will, in fact, insure that we will **choose** to do so. Instead of being wise and going for **better** sexual encounters, we often prefer to play the psychological **games**, referred to in earlier chapters to create new ways to win, control, get one-up, prove a point, get even, manipulate, belittle, tease, torture, punish, or pay back a spouse.

Both for fun, and with the intention of making some serious points as well, let's take some of the more common sexually-related complaints, and observe how different couples handle the same problem. Except for the last case—involving Brian and Sandra— fifteen different scenarios could have been reported for each complaint. Some sexual experiences that patients have reported to me will **not** be included, not only because someone in my practice area might figure out who the victim was, but also because the physical or sexual abuses were so atrocious and reprehensible, that sensibilities—both yours and mine—might not be able to abide it.

❖   Marcy is still enjoying the sex, despite her husband's ineptitude during these first two years. After a discussion with her close friend, Wilma, she decides not to let him know that the sex is "ok" the way they do it, reasoning that if she did that, he will never change anything, and she doesn't want that. She wants the sex to improve a lot. Since she expects to be sexually active for many years ("until she dies, if possible"), the thought that her husband will never get any better, is quite depressing to her when she thinks about it, which means every day.

❖   In the beginning, Anne, like Marcy, enjoyed the sex despite "Paul's stupidity." She also tried not to show any pleasure, reasoning, as did Marcy, that "otherwise he will never get any better." When he didn't get any better, despite her thirty-one years of patient waiting, Anne realized that her reasoning was not sound. Perhaps because of her silence (and some other issues), the only change was that he got worse, and she stopped enjoying it.

❖   Martha thinks her husband John is an "egomaniac." She has said as much to a lot of her friends at those times when comparing husbands is the topic. He gets his title primarily for taking the credit in those rare instances when sexual intercourse and the preliminaries are enjoyable to her, while blaming her—telling her she should see a doctor or a shrink and find out what her problem is—for the hundreds of times in forty years that she hasn't responded.

❖   Martha's closest friend, Gert, volunteers the information that her husband pays no attention to any of her obvious signals during sex, and has never read any of the how-to sex books she has left lying around the bedroom over the years. "If he doesn't learn the techniques somewhere, how will he ever get better?"

❖   Evelyn, a bride of eight years, has the same complaint as Gert, criticizing her "thick-headed husband, who doesn't pay any attention to any of her sexual signals." But Evelyn's husband simply doesn't know what to make of her "furtive and contradictory signals." He complains that "what works on Tuesday, makes her mad on Saturday."

❖   Gert's sister, married only ten years, declares her mystification at her husband's ignorance in sexual matters. As "the self-declared resident expert on everything," she believes that he should know what a woman needs. Alexis agrees that "if a man can't know what to do in this day and age, with all the information available, he must be a fool."

Obviously, the references throughout this book to the fact that women are capable of enjoying sex at least as much as men enjoy sex, are not intended to suggest that a woman has to enjoy sex the way her husband approaches it. The reason for presenting these cases is simply to point out that the remedy in each of these scenarios is not to be found in the husband's sexual technique, but rather in his **entire approach** to his wife **as a person!** (And, of course, her approach to him!) Alexi's (and Gert's sister, too) lack of response is almost surely not due to hormonal imbalance, or any problem with her pelvic organs, or even her husband's lack of knowledge of the proper sexual technique, but is rather due to the fact that her husband rubs her, **personally,** the wrong way. If he didn't, they could quickly work it out. The problem to be addressed is to be found in the persons **relating,** and not in an examination of her orgasms or his erections.

Differentiation (Growing-Up) as the Cure for Sexual Dysfunction

Although both sexes naturally experience anxiety before or during sexual exchanges of any kind, and this anxiety **does** heighten the "pleasure," too much anxiety can produce sexual **dysfunctions,** such as premature ejaculation, failure to achieve or sustain an erection, or, in the case of women, an inability to achieve orgasm. A man can't fake his performance, but a woman can, and will, when it suits her purposes. For example, a woman can choose to simulate an orgasm to persuade a disappointing partner that his job is finished, and that he can now go to sleep.

Few problems, sexual or otherwise, in a relationship can be successfully resolved until at least one partner is able to change priorities and accept full responsibility for his or her part of the problem. The most effective change of priority, **especially** in sexual matters, is to place the partner's best interests ahead of one's own. The treatment success for a common marital problem—**performance anxiety**—should provide clear evidence that changing an attitude, an approach, a perception, without at all suggesting a change in technique, can do wonders.

❖   Brian had anxiety to the point that he dreaded attempting sex with his wife, even though he "loved" her and found her to be very "desirable."

The first therapist to whom the couple went, advised several techniques first introduced and popularized by Masters and Johnson, nearly four decades ago, and used successfully since in curing the sexual dysfunctions just mentioned, as well as other dysfunctions, such as "lack of desire for sex," and "vaginismus," that is, vaginal spasm preventing intercourse or resulting in painful intercourse.

I will not describe in detail the techniques prescribed by the first therapist, since the three that were tried were all unsuccessful in Brian's case. The therapies prescribed can be found in virtually all the "sex therapy" manuals, and are based on the methods "to restore sexual adequacy" that were presented in Master's and Johnson's original works.[1]

As part of the therapy, Brian and his wife, Sandy, were first advised to perform the "sensate focus" exercises in which Brian was to "keep everything else out of his mind, and concentrate solely on his genitals."

David Schnarch describes this approach, at least as far as it was generally interpreted or applied, as the "keep the mind-desire-eroticism out-of-it, horizontal-eyes-closed, cadaver-like, pretend-your-partner-isn't-there approach to sex." Even when it allows the disabled partner to achieve an erection or have an orgasm, this "mindless" approach takes most of the fun out of sex.[2]

The "sensate-focus" treatment didn't work at all for Sandy and Brian, so after half-heartedly suffering through two more suggestions (giving each other a total body message, but scrupulously avoiding the erogenous zones; and, foregoing intercourse, but necking or petting every chance they could) they rejected any further proposals from the first therapist and sought out another "expert."

In the first two interviews the second therapist made it clear to both Sandy and Brian that the performance-anxiety had very little to do with sex or sexual function *per se*, but everything to do with **personal integrity**, specifically what Brian honestly thought about himself. Does that approach sound familiar?

Indeed, the second counselor suggested an approach nearly identical to the one presented in this book as the solution to **all** marital problems: **grow up.**

Since Brian was the one who couldn't "perform," you would think that the therapist would say that he was **the one** to initiate the process first, right? Well, the doctor said there was no marriage problem that he could think of, that didn't involve **two** people!

He made both Sandra and Brian acknowledge that, ultimately, each was responsible for his and her own "performance." "But," he added, "in the real world, any changes that Brian made as result of his examination—and his acceptance—of his own feelings, motives, emotions, desires, needs, or sense of adequacy, was going to effect Sandra. So, she better be ready for the changes, and be mature enough to manage or control **her** responses."

The therapist continued that "anxiety, or fear of failure, produces emotions arising in the part of the brain **between** the neocortex—where reflective consciousness resides—and the genital areas of sensation. These **negative emotions**, therefore, are in a position where they can block both initial desire, and also the **continuing desire** we experience as passion.

"Thus, the fear that you will fail to perform adequately, creates a self-fulfilling prophecy. Awareness of fear occurs in that part of the brain between the highest and distinctly human faculties and the part of the brain that logs in the sensations from the genitals. Fear thus blocks the **passionate response** that is uniquely human, and at the same time blocks sexual functioning, too."

When Brian initiated his soul-searching—what he felt, what he needed, what he wanted, what he lacked, what he feared—the first truth to hit him between the eyes was that he **needed** Sandra **too much**. So much that he was **using** her simply for his own pleasure, satisfaction, and ego. He was not being **personal** or giving or caring or responsive or **present to her** in the lovemaking.

If his selfishness in acting "entirely on his own" and in emotional isolation, set him up for failure (and it obviously did), then **having her** interests clearly **present to him** should help him to do his part in **creating love**.

The "wall-socket" sex that David Schnarch speaks about, and writes about in his books is not a reference to intercourse, but to being honest, open, or **real, and being present to each other** through awareness, sensitivity, caring, and sharing.

Fantasizing about someone who is **not there**—whether Paul Newman, Leonardo de Caprio, Sharon Stone, or a supermodel from *Victoria's Secret*—may work for a time, especially if all you are seeking is adequate sexual functioning. But, don't expect the level of passion and ecstasy that comes when two lovers who are **real** people (not one who is real and the other who is "reel") create love.

Fantasizing for your own sexual pleasure through the use of pornography, which portrays the subjugation of another person **against his or her will,** or the use of **erotic** fiction, which portrays an equal who **acquiesces voluntarily,** should be condemned or discouraged. As **surrogates** for a spouse (to whom love and reverence and service is owed), such fantasizing constitutes a pandering to one's most **selfish** instincts. They also provide an escape from the work of creative love.

Going through a process much like the one proposed in this book, Brian chose—after acknowledging personal responsibility for all the "bad stuff" in his personal "portfolio," and accepting it—to try to become more honest, more open about the feelings that he was discovering, to be more authentic and "multi-dimensional"—to be, in a word, more **real**.

A good reason for a man to expect success by being honest, especially about his vulnerability, is that a typical wife will find his male vulnerability a decided "turn on." The truth is that a woman **knows** her husband's ego is often fragile, especially about his **exposure** in sexual exchanges. She would **welcome** a chance to help him deal with his insecurity. The thing that "pisses her off" is her husband's refusal to admit his feelings of fear and insecurity. A woman will have great difficulty allowing herself to be open to a mate who is deceitful, who is a phony.[3]

Sex as a scheme to bolster your ego, Brian decided, was just as selfish and phony as putting prestige and money before personal integrity and self-control. Brian also figured along the way that he had "nothing to lose" by correcting some of his more questionable social habits and thereby making himself a neater person to have around. His goal, however, was not to have Sandra panting with desire, which is the "ego thing" again, but to place her desires and pleasure, as much as he could, above his own needs.

Brian found that by shifting the **primary focus** from worrying about failure, to bringing joy to his wife, his own **desire** returned. This desire was not only present before he initiated sex, as it was before, but the desire continued throughout the sexual encounter. By focusing on Sandy, he was literally able to avoid rubbing her the wrong way. He was, finally, "paying attention to her." Remember what the second therapist said about a spousal reaction to change? Sandy soon realized that Brian was "with her," both inside and outside the bedroom, and, that he was no longer hiding whatever inadequacies or fears he felt—including, in this sexual problem, his fear of his performance, or his need for her "affirming" response. When Sandy knew that her husband was no longer worrying about his failure to evoke her response, she stopped worrying about it, too. The level of her fears and anxieties kept going down. The old complaints of "her taking too long, or "why is he so impatient," became part of a forgotten history.

Since Brian's desires for genital sex now included equal consideration of where his wife was coming from, sex started becoming an expression of their love. For the first time, they were getting a sense of what **total union** could mean.

If You Want to *Create Love*, Forget the Books and Listen With Your Heart

As the Velveteen Rabbit was loved into "life," or, as great music comes alive when a lover of the music—like an Idzak Perlman, a Yehudi Menuhin or Fritz Kreisler—plays it, so do lovers have the potential ability to bring the minds and hearts of the one they love to life and to **create love**.

Creating love has little to do with knowledge or technique. The how-to-articles on better sex invariably miss the points that *human* sexual activity, by definition, involves the neocortex, that part of the brain that sets *Homo Sapiens* apart from all other animals. Though we share the same kind of genitalia as most animals from the **reptiles** on up, and the same emotional pathways as the other **mammals,** these natural stimulus-response mechanisms that are automatic (unless the mind gets in the way) can never be **erotic** or **passionate** in any animal but man (or woman) because eroticism is perceived in the human mind and passion is an action of the human will.

Human sexual activity takes place in a context of what went before, what comes after. It is the expression of a relationship that is most human when it involve equals (that is, persons who reverence each other), who are acting freely, and in the best interests of the partner. Intercourse itself, as the most "intimate form of **touching, can be** also the **most intense form of communication,** but only if the lovers communicate without holding back any part of themselves. This means the **mind must be clear**, not clouded by drugs or alcohol, and the **heart** (translation: will) must be acting without any element of "not wanting," that is, it must be **acting wholeheartedly.** Coming into the sexual mix are courage, motivation, caring, reverence, commitment, vulnerability, self-giving and sharing, trust, humility, openness, perseverance, adaptability and process-learning, negotiation, forgiveness, and even a little plain old-fashioned hard work.

The fact that **procreative drives** come naturally at adolescence does **not** establish that good sex comes naturally. A sixteen- to eighteen-year-old boy may be able to pole-vault into bed with his erection, but few women of any age would thereby grant him status as a lover. The creation of love involves **equals** exchanging, sharing, and exposing their **core selves**, that is, their authentic selves to each other. Our life experience—the sum total of all that we are, and all that we have done—is the currency, the gift that is shared in creating love. The more one has lived, and made the **good choices** that make one a neater or better person, the more desirable and valuable a gift he or she becomes. Using that criteria, a teenager "ain't much" as a sex partner or as a "life" partner.

Only men have the competitiveness we refer to as penis envy, and mistake **genital prime** with **sexual prime**. Any woman blessed with a sexually mature mate would know the difference, usually because his expertise in getting himself, and his life together, and becoming sensitive to **her** desires (but not necessarily learning any new sexual techniques) was a long time arriving.

When Is the Prime of Life?
That Depends on Your Priorities

When **firm flesh** becomes a requirement for a spouse's arousal, he (or she) is subscribing to the "piece of flesh" model of sexually relating, which uses an unreal person, a fantasy, to supply his or her pleasure. For example, when someone equates genital prime and sexual prime—that is, ignores the value of maturity and equality in the concept of love, or, even if he (or she) simply equates physiological responsiveness with sexual intensity—that person is, in effect, agreeing with those who claim that nudity can be the most effective form of birth control. Nudity could be a **turn-off**, perhaps, for the "lover" who needs firm breasts, abdomens, and buttocks to be ardent. Anyone who has these requirements for achieving sexual satisfaction and passion, rarely improves as a lover. On the contrary, as the firm flesh of his (or her) partner begins to sag, he gets worse.

The challenge of sex, like the challenge of marriage, is a challenge to the heart and mind. Great sex is definitely not a challenge to one's endocrinologist or physical training advisor. It is ignorance of **the possibilities** of sex that invariably leads a couple in a committed relationship to boring sex. How can they create love when they cease to be creative. Granted, it is possible for a lot of heat and emotions to be generated in **any** sexual encounter, as almost any sexually-active adult will agree. Wonderful sexual moments are certainly possible for those not in committed relationships, but only as long as the mind can supply some **creativity**, that is, some variety, or a sense of newness or mystery, and the will maintains the **vitality**, that is, the enthusiasm or whole-heartedness. As David Schnarch writes, "when the goal is to be seen as you want [to be seen], but not known as you are, marriage can never compete with part-time romance."[4] Both the problems, and the **ecstatic successes**, are born in, and depend on the mind. Eventually, what each participant in an affair **thinks** (What does this relationship **mean** to me?), will determines the ultimate fate of the relationship. Even the pleasure in the experience will cease being reproducible if the biological activity does not maintain some human relevance. As long as the lovers can pretend that their love is unconditional, sexual bliss remains possible. But, lovers cannot usually ignore for very long the responsibilities and consequences created by the relationship. Perhaps, when you are not living with someone, it is easy to pretend or to convince yourself that your love for each other is unconditional or will last forever or is unique. When you discover that it is not any of these things, then negotiation, settlements, grievances, bad experiences, doubts, resentments, suspicions, jealousy, possessiveness, frustrations, and a whole host of other mixed feelings and emotions come to complicate matters, and the relationship soon becomes like any other.

The Most Important Sexual Organ

The stories of all the couples in this book should convince anyone that the mind is where most of the sexual action is. The anatomical joining of bodies remains an obviously wonderful part of human mating, even though those bodies do fade too quickly. But surely the most ecstatic and memorable human love occurs when the union of two clear minds and two equally strong wills is added to the physical mating. Certainly, we know from the experts, and/or from our own experience, that sex for human beings, unlike other mammals, is not so much in the genitals as in the head. Many would claim ninety-nine percent of the pleasure of human sex is generated in the head. But, **do *you* believe it?**

Just as any estimate of how many babies I have delivered would be nothing more than a wild guess (on quite a few occasions there were as many as twenty-four babies in an equal number of hours), so also would it be only a wild guess to estimate the number of women who have said to me, "I have no desire for sex, would you please check my hormones." Even those who believe libido resides in the head still prefer to look for a remedy anywhere but there! People resist letting anyone see the private chambers of their minds even more than they resist letting anyone see their bodies.[5]

The term "eroticism" does not refer primarily to **genital** sex. Rather, **erotic** and **passionate** describe experiences that involve all three components of sexuality—the **physical sensations** that we share with all animals from reptiles on up, the **emotional accompaniments** that involve that part of the brain we share with mammals, and the **reflective awareness** that is uniquely human and spiritual. The **neocortex**, or newest part of the human brain, enables us, among other neat things, to be **aware of ourselves being aware**. That ability makes free will, or choice—and therefore love—possible. This **concomitant awareness**—to use the language of the philosophers— allows the separation and simultaneous weighing of several ideas, and enables a man or woman to freely choose a mate. He or she can be aware of why **that mate,** and not another is chosen, to appreciate that person's sexual difference, and, to experience the other's separateness, feelings, thoughts, and actions in relation to his/her own. The level of "eroticism" proceeds from the clarity and intensity of this knowledge and awareness. Any obstacle to either lover's free actions, including either attempts to coerce, control, or to "withhold," can diminish or eliminate the erotic experience (especially if fear or pain or anger is introduced).

One recent murder in my area was typical of the countless others we have all heard about. A successful professional man was impotent with his wife (whom he eventually drowned in the bathtub), but not with his paramour, on whom he lavished all his wife's money. Some people might callously conclude that this act of cruelty provided yet another proof that lust wins out over love every time, at least in the short term. The more profound truth may be that **buying** another woman's sexual responsiveness, as the murderer did, is not a **manly** deed, in anyone's culture. Perhaps the case also again proved that, in order to function sexually with a real, strong, or mature woman, you have to be a real, strong, or mature man.

Therapists who deal with the sexual dysfunction of **premature ejaculation** generally report that the man has no problem when he is alone, or even if his wife stimulates his genitals. It is only when he attempts intercourse that the sudden ejaculation occurs. A foolish therapist could proceed to tell the wife to change her "**castrating approach** to her husband," that is, to stop sending him the messages that his manliness, his person, his sexuality is no longer needed or important to her, just his financial support, his protection, or even his companionship. It is extremely unfortunate, but usually true, that neither husband nor wife in this scenario have an accurate idea of their contrasting needs. The man, as a result of her "care-less" attitude about sex, almost invariably feels he has been "dominated," "unmanned," placed one down, if he develops sexual dysfunction in this situation, ascribing to his wife motives that, in nearly every case, she would never even consider. For her part, in fact, she almost always is simply seeking some respect, some equality, some "say" or input into the sexual exchange, but **not control or domination!**

Again, the main principle involved in treating sexual dysfunction is that it is the person's perceptions of himself and of his relationship that produce the problem, and rarely either a problem of ignorance or a problem with the genital organs involved. The problem is in **his (or her) head.**

"The loving are the daring" said Bayard Taylor over a century ago. He was right, of course. While achieving the skill of intimacy demands a fistful of manly and womanly virtues, the best sex is still a form of mutual aggression, embodying in its own way the same elements that accompany a roller-coaster ride—courage, anxiety or thrills, and risk. So much more reason to embark on the journey with a trusted friend.

The Sexual Route Is the Toughest Road to Intimacy!

Several points should be re-emphasized:

Whether describing an affair or a marriage, the presence of adequate sexual functioning, including erection, ejaculation, and orgasm, does not prove a **good sexual relationship** exists, only an **adequate** one. Also false is the belief that couples whose sexual relationship is OK have a **good** marriage, much less an intimate one. Sex is certainly **not** the **best route** to intimacy, since sexual "exposure" generally calls forth every defense a person can muster to avoid failure or being found inadequate. **Integrity**, that is, presenting yourself exactly as you are, especially from a sexual perspective, can be quite threatening or frightening because it can have dangerous consequences. When risk is introduced, honesty or authenticity can become quite difficult and challenging (and as rare as hen's teeth).

The "wholesaling" of the nonsensical idea that **great sex** comes naturally, and leads to intimacy, has resulted in the failure of most of the men and women of two entire generations to achieve or maintain great sex. It has also led to their preoccupation with sexual functioning, and, inevitably, to their total frustration in the sexual arena because they can't find the supposedly-automatic connection between knowledge and performance or between responsive genitalia and passionate, fulfilling sex. Unfortunately, even though the goal of **intimacy** has almost achieved the status of a twentieth century religion, and many couples zealously seek to learn intimacy skills,[6] their goal of intimacy is rarely achieved. How can it be, unless the would-be-intimates learn how to grow up first?

If the absence of a sexual dysfunction insured even just a good marriage, why do so many couples who have no sexual dysfunction still confess to feelings of shame, disappointment, inadequacy, emotional deprivation or frustration, mental pain or anguish, boredom, sadness, or anger when describing their marriage? Satisfying intimacy or erotic experiences are not a natural or inevitable consequence of a man's and woman's commitment to love each other, unless they are both mature enough to work for those goals consistently and achieve some measure of unconditional love. Earlier chapters have stressed that shame and blame (**and laziness**) must be consistently avoided.

When the time comes in a marriage that the lack of intimacy seems to be a permanent probability, some couples in their frustration and disappointment, often seek counseling, only to eventually discover that their therapist is trained in communication skills and/ or sexual techniques which ignore the issues of personal responsibility, maturity, even passion and eroticism. Generally, and unfortunately for the couple seeking help, marital-sexual therapists typically have no more experience with intense intimacy and erotic bliss than the couple does, and are probably using the techniques developed in the 60s which were never intended to help achieve either great sex or a great marriage.

Few therapists would risk telling a patient, "Don't come back until you can face all your selfish habits and give up your self-deception," or "Start working on becoming someone with whom you would want to live;" The best advice for most couples in therapy would be to tell each of the partners to do whatever would be necessary to enable them to answer this question **accurately**: "What is it like for your partner to be married to you?" If the answer is not one of praise and satisfaction, then why isn't it?" Ah! **That is the question.**

Only a select few in committed relationships claim to be experiencing passion. Thus, when we tell teenagers that sex is "wonderful" and "beautiful" and thus should be saved for marriage, we may not only be increasing their curiosity and desire, but also describing something we ourselves have never experienced.

If you are not one of the blessed few who experience "wall-socket sex," passion, eroticism, or however you describe heart-stopping, glorious sex, then I suggest that you throw away all the how-to-do-it books, make an increased effort to clean up your vices and insecurities, attend to more of your responsibilities (if you are a man that probably includes listening without giving advice), and try any or all of the following over the next few months: hugging until relaxed, kissing your spouse without tension, engaging in any intimate activity with the lights on . . . then perhaps with your clothes off . . . then perhaps with your eyes open . . . then actually looking into/then beyond the eyes of your mate . . . then, doing any/all of this during orgasm/ejaculation.[7]

Patients coming in for **the pill** as part of their preparations for marriage have consistently dazzled me with their great expectations. Many of those same patients, after their divorce, have recounted depressing and bitter memories. (One of the primary uses to which I hope to put this book, is to present it as my gift to each prospective bride and groom. But, only if I have the groom's promise that he will read it.) The only change that I note in the last few years is that few of the ex-wives now seem to think that providing **any explanation** for their failed marriage is necessary or possible. Impossible to explain, perhaps, because the feminist revolution has made gender an issue in the specialty of gynecology. **Because I am a man, how could I possibly have the right attitude, or understand?**[8]

Still, I can't help thinking that their marriages could have been saved.

24

Yes, We Can Turn Our Marriages Around

"Others have seen what is and asked why.
I have seen what could be and asked why not."
—Robert F. Kennedy

Motivating Improvement in Our Marriage

Psychiatrists, psychologists, marital and family counselors, and even the experts on support, focus or encounter groups suggest that the most effective way to change the way you feel about anything, including marriage, is to **change your perceptions**—that is, your outlook—and then your unwanted feelings will disappear.

This **first option** was employed in drawing up **the original twelve-step program**. Alcoholics Anonymous has been the most successful approach to alcoholism primarily because the founders insisted that the **first step in treatment had to be a changed perception.** The person addicted has to acknowledge his problem and his inability to handle the problem without help. With the change of perception, the feelings of helplessness, fear, and loneliness were markedly diminished, and the rate of success jumped. The next eleven steps emphasize that a higher power is a necessary part of the solution. But it is the first step that is the key to change. Failure is inevitable in the battle with addiction if the first step is too shameful and the addict is not humble enough to admit that, yes, he does have a problem and yes, he needs help.

Pride, however, is not the only capital sin. The "dry drunk" who doesn't drink anymore but doesn't do something about changing his selfish approach to living, and thus doesn't develop personal relationships of caring, often relapses or finds another addiction. While it can be eminently courageous to stop drinking, the rage, fear, loneliness, or shame, that this addiction has been used to hide, sometimes demands as much, or more courage to face, accept, and to address as making the first step.

Intergenerational Violence: The *Gift* of Negative Feelings

More men would be motivated to do the painful work of searching their souls to find the cause of their negative feelings and emotions, which can include shame, fear, guilt, sadness, doubt, anxiety, or rage, if they could be convinced that they have transferred, and now are **carrying,** these negative feelings **for their parents** (usually the father), and that they are, or will, actively transmit the same destructive feelings to their own children. This legacy is a very common one and accounts in no small measure for our society's present level of violence.[1]

Those who deal with problem children repeatedly refer to a child's need to **heal** his (or her) parents, and to **deny** his parent's faults or problems. The child's fear of being left without a strong and capable protector can be overwhelming, so the child doesn't allow that to happen. When anyone tells you they "feel sorry" for a parent, you can almost be certain that they are carrying that parent's problems.[2]

All this baggage, unfortunately, can take a lot of energy to sort through. By the time it is all handled, the person may have missed a myriad of opportunities for fun and growth. Many people eventually give up. There are signs by which one can tell that a man or woman has given up on himself (or herself), and has stopped looking for explanations or improvements. For example, the mate who ceases to care about his/her personal appearance reflects a sense of hopelessness and worthlessness. Even those who now blame their inadequacy on a **scapegoat,** for example their family of origin or their poverty, are thereby denying their responsibility for personal growth or improvement. They cannot change until they can say, "It is **my** problem, now."

Because it is human to protect something we value, persons who see their worth and uniqueness will persevere in keeping themselves intact. Thus, self-appreciation, or self-regard can motivate us to improve ourselves on a regular basis. Self-destruction through any addiction, whether alcohol, drugs, anorexia, or bulimia, invariably reflects a self-judgment that one is already too flawed to care about. Why save our health, our bodies, or our relationships when we deserve to be punished, or to suffer for our faults. For an example of how our flawed self-assessments can destroy our lives, we have only to look at the millions of people with eating disorders. The latest wisdom about anorexics is that, from their earliest childhood, they feel responsible for everyone else's welfare, and keep punishing themselves for not doing a good job.[3]

The reverse is equally true. Regardless of the causes, if the spouse who pays no attention to his/her appearance could make one simple step forward, namely, appreciate or admire some of his/her own good points, then his/her personal habits would probably improve. When we are appreciating our own assets or our good points, we cannot simultaneously feel sad enough to self-destruct. In fact, self-appreciation, or self-regard, can provide the key to our motivation to improve ourselves. Again, if we remain aware of, and accept, our personal worth as valuable and unique persons—that is, if we see ourselves as potential gifts—and also acknowledge our responsibility for self-maintenance, it is unlikely that any of us would self-destruct.

When It Comes to Taking Advice, Everyone's a Teenager

Giving advice, under the best of circumstances, is fraught with frustration and with dangers. But giving advice to someone who doesn't accept personal responsibility for who he (or she) is and for what he does, is an exercise in futility. Pointing out to such a person the reasons why he (or she) feels or acts the way he does, accomplishes nothing in the way of improvement. Such criticism also usually strengthens his resolve to resist any changes, so the reward for our interference is often resentment.

There is another reason that giving advice fails, even when it involves specific suggestions to a "receptive" friend, family member, or patient. The person who is not functioning well—whether depressed or addicted—needs first to have some emotional independence and control. Your suggestions, if they are on target, will almost always increase the fears and anxieties that the person has been running away from. He or she, in other words, must do some "growing up" first. He must decide he is **worth the effort** needed to be a better person **and** admit that he, and he alone is **solely responsible** for where he is in his life now, and where his life will go from here.

In marriage, the problems with advice are compounded. Like addicted people, men and women in damaged relationships don't often respond very well to outside suggestion. Especially dangerous are directives that suggest partners work to achieve consensus, or that they be more "reasonable." Telling them to affirm someone they have come to resent, just adds fuel to the fire that is already raging.

David Schnarch compares the marital therapist's approach of giving his/her conflicted clients specific "assignments," that require them to spend more time together, to suggesting that someone might be able to jump-start an automobile engine that has no gas in it. The suggestions feel "phony," and they are because they encourage the couple to do more of the very thing—confront each other—that brought them to their present deadlock. Instead of working **together**, the clients need time to work on themselves. And each must recognize and accept full personal responsibility for his (or her) inability to control and manage his own thoughts, feelings, and actions. One fact is certain: the players in a hostile-dependent relationship will not profit from any prescription that will demand more **cooperation**. Such a suggestion only increases their dependency on each other, and invariably triggers more withholding, or other games.[4]

Since Feelings Are Involuntary, Why Worry About Changing Them?

The second option available for motivating anyone to make the first step to improve a stalemated or conflicted relationship: ignore any feelings entirely. The advice is to **keep feelings out of it**. Instead of researching your feelings, or using the first option of changing your thinking and your perceptions (and all that **that involves**, as we have just seen) in order to produce a change in your feelings, why not simply say "to hell with the feelings." The marriage encounter lectures stress that once we are no longer burdened, distracted, discouraged, or depressed by our negative feelings, we can begin to change the way we act. The theory is based on the truth that one's conscious or deliberate acts are more or less subject to personal control, but that **feelings just are**. Therefore, no one should be held accountable, or feel guilty about them.

The second option, that is, ignoring our feelings can lead to problems if one ignores feelings for any other purpose than **to promote change** in one's perceptions or actions. An exhortation to hold on to our feelings in most other situations is offered because **our feelings are valuable to us** in other ways. Feelings are the pathway to and from our hearts, making it possible for us to connect, to relate, and to communicate with one another, and to communicate in (virtually) complete safety.

Just Do It!

The **third option for effecting change is the one I prefer: start with a change in your actions.** Change what you do and that will change the way you think. Then, every other change, including a change in the feelings, will follow. How else can we explain why so many people seem to respond to the Nike slogan: "Just Do It!"? The same invitation to act applies to any man or woman lacking the desire to change, but who realizes that he or she must change if the marriage is to improve. Alcoholics Anonymous has a saying, "Fake it until you make it." If an alcoholic waited until he no longer wanted to drink, he would wait a very long time. Why can't one partner just commit to the few simple changes needed in the marriage, to bring back the good will with which it began? Or, let the good will of one inspire the other to try again? When couples confess "There's no good will left in our marriage," they usually mean there is "no love, only anger or bitterness." Someone should tell them that their **hate is a sign of life**. Thus, there is still connection. **If neither partner cares**, that is, if they are utterly indifference to each other, I wouldn't give the relationship a chance (as long as they are both being honest).

Earlier, I pointed out that the obstacle to fixing marriages resides primarily in the will, not the mind. As Sir James Dewar wrote years ago, "Minds are like umbrellas: they only function well when they are open." Unfortunately, when the mind is closed, it is invariably because of a **closed heart**, that is, an unwillingness to let anyone, including the person himself (or herself) see who he is. The struggle to create a **change** of heart, or **open** a person's closed heart means changing his (or her) attitude of unwillingness to face his thoughts, his feelings, or his behavior, as well as his unwillingness to acknowledge their effects on others. Opening a closed heart has always been the most difficult challenge of all.

Tragically, men and women consistently refuse to believe that failure to include their spouses feelings and desires in most of their daily decisions, or, to even consider the long term affects of those decisions on their mates, adversely impacts **both** their lives, and the lives of their children.

Ultimately, of course, our goal should be to have an intimate relationship with our spouse, to be **lover** and **loved**. To achieve this result we need to retain our separateness, but make the happiness of the other our highest priority. We need also to promise that our caring and love shall be shared with them forever. For many of us, such a lofty goal is light years away. But, **the first goal is just before our eyes**—and we need only to open our mind and our heart to see it.

25

Needed: an Open Mind and a Change of Heart

"Healthy self-esteem is essentially internal. . . . [It] presupposes that all men and women are created equal; that one's inherent worth can be neither greater or lesser than another's. . . . [Our] basic sense of self as valuable and important neither rises or falls based on external attributes."
—Terence Real

"When we act on our own choices, we define our own future. The good news is we have the sense of being in control of our lives. The bad news is that it's our fault and there's no one else to blame."
—Peter Block, *The Empowered Manager*

It's <u>Your</u> Life, Too, Man!

For most married people, taking individual responsibility for one's own happiness seems unnecessary and even risky. Isn't marriage the arrangement in which one shares personal responsibility with a partner?

The answer to the question just asked is: **"No."** Unless both partners retain total control and accountability of all that they think, feel, and do, the marriage will eventually flounder, even if it does not actually end in separation or divorce.

180

The main purpose of this book is **not** to save marriages any more than it is intended to provide you with techniques for correcting sexual dysfunction. There are ample how-to books on those subjects. Read them, if survival and adequacy are all that you seek from your marriage and from your sex life. In fact, **these 200+ pages are not about "how-to," but rather "what if. . . ."** Life offers us in marriage (and in our sexual exchanges) so much more than adequacy. Unhappily, for millions of couples, avoiding divorce or sexual dysfunction is all that is sought or expected. Even if that is all **you** desire, please read these chapters with a **mind that is open** to seeing much more.

Your Quest for Intimacy

The person whose mind is open to new insights should quickly understand and appreciate how essential personal awareness and accountability is to his or her relationships If the husbands and wives who are **shamers, blamers, or leaners,** rather than **owners,**[1] wish the skill of intimacy, they must **first** assume responsibility for their own destiny. It is quite easy for a man to lose touch with, to be insensitive to the consequences of his actions. Especially, if he never examines those actions and the thoughts and feelings that preceded them as his way of denying or overlooking personal weaknesses, frailties, and omissions. A judgmental, unpleasant or abusive person is invariably someone who has lost his or her sense of accountability.

Fortunately, as Charles Dickens dramatized so powerfully in *A Christmas Carol,* even a person as seemingly heartless as Ebenezer Scrooge, can be quickly changed if he (or she) can somehow face the consequences of his insensitivity, as the ghosts of Christmas Past and Christmas Future forced Scrooge to do. Scrooge's change of heart, brought about by his shame for the harm and havoc he was creating in the lives of those around him, quickly and gloriously transformed their lives, although not nearly as much as it changed his own inner level of peace and joy. The same transformation is possible to all men and women if they can face the consequences of what they have become and how they affect others.

The metamorphosis from tyrant to saint is remarkably easier to accomplish in someone who has once experienced **unconditional love.** Once received, the experience of this love can never be totally

forgotten. Ebenezer Scrooge had once experienced the unconditional love of a fine woman, but his love of money had blinded him
to the larger treasure she had offered. The truth that the fire of love,
once lit, is never entirely extinguished, makes it reasonable to expect
that even the most heartless individual **can change** the obnoxious
habits he/she might present to the world. The path to begin a quest
for joy, peace, serenity, self-respect, and intimacy is never very far
away from anyone who has once known love. Even the most appar-
ently-insensitive or unfeeling man, can regain not only much or all of
the childhood hopes, wonder, sensitivity, and thirst for adventure
that he had as a little boy, but also that yearning to exchange love. All
of that **little boy's** feelings and emotions and ideals remain, no
matter how deeply they may have been buried. Sometimes a man's
pride will lead him to look at his **preferred self,** that is, at his assets as
he once was, or as he wishes he could be now, not as he is. A proud
man cannot accept himself as he is now. Such a man will ignore not
only his bad habits and his selfish thoughts, but also, and most
importantly, he will hide his fear, pain, guilt, anger, or shame.

A man's (or woman's) path back to his best priorities can only
begin if he acknowledges, or faces, as Scrooge was forced to do, his
vulnerabilities or liabilities and their consequences. While drugs,
alcohol, sex, work, sports, or any other **thing** can be used as a
diversion to prevent a man from being a good husband, father,
neighbor, or friend, these addictions can be overcome, with help. But
first, the person addicted has to have a change of heart, which might
also be translated as a change of priorities. Of course, a man's
disappointment with himself can be so oppressive to him that he
eventually **gives up.** After that tragic decision, a man can wander in
isolation and emptiness for the rest of his life.

Admittedly, there are millions of husbands who are **not** addicted, who work hard, and affirm and discipline their children—
men who are never really unpleasant, and never abusive. If you are
like that, you can stop reading now, provided you also hug your wife
meaningfully every day, and regularly look into her eyes, and say
your equivalent of "You're my everything, my reason for living. I
would do it all over without hesitation. I love you." Remember, what
is being proposed in this book is the path to intimacy. This skill of

being able to consistently exchange love and reverence with an equal, and still maintain our separateness and our freedom to act, is presently being achieved by only a select few.

Do You Have the Courage to Look into Your Own Heart?

If you are not among the select few who have achieved **intimacy**, even though you think you are a wonderful husband, **please humor me** by reading on. If you are unsure as to whether your relationship is intimate, I suggest that you read the Notes to Chapter Fourteen.

The story of Scrooge demonstrates that the first step on anyone's path to a great relationship is the admission or acceptance of all that is revealed by the search into his or her own heart. As his "own keeper," not his "brother's" (or his wife's) keeper, a man cannot safely ignore or hide **anything**, especially those failings and weaknesses that will keep him from being vain or thoughtless. Humility is the great virtue of being able to accept one's own **truth. Acceptance of self**, that is, the willingness to freely expose and share what he (or she) has, and what he is, despite the consequences to himself, is the key that leads him (or her) to connection, and ultimately to love. If he is unwilling to expose himself honestly because he is afraid no one would accept him as he is, he will surely make many or all of the mistakes in relating to others that were made by Brian, Johnny, Ned, Beth, Dottie, Wanda, Toby, and the fifty-or-so other heroes and heroines mentioned in this book. Having made his **acceptance by others** his top priority, instead of humbly accepting himself as he is, and then proceeding to work on that "problem," he continues to live the lie that isolates him from a sound relationship with anyone.

Just as in AA, or any other 'twelve-step" group, a man (or woman) who wants to change his life, who is dissatisfied with his marriage, and who wants to make it better, must, before anything else, make a decision, a personal commitment. He must have **a change of heart**.

Those people who have difficulty understanding precisely what is meant by changing one's heart might use the **phrases changing priorities or changing what one most desires.** Few of us, unfortunately, give more than a smidgen of our attention or thought to our desires, even though our desires drive everything we do. Most of what we do in life as in marriage is done **half-heartedly** or reactively, or, is done out of frustration, impatience, or anger. Is it any wonder that most marriages are still in the conflicted stage?

Obviously, marriage is not the only battleground in our lives. The frustration, resentment, and bitterness manifested in marriage is merely the intensified version of the same conflicts of interest that we see every day on the highways, in waiting rooms, or in waiting lines. Ask yourself: do any of these angry people (or you) hold themselves in warm regard, love, or reverence? If they (or if you) have no gripes or discomforts about themselves and where they are in their lives and in their personal relationships, then why are they so obviously angry? How could they possibly respect themselves and still evidence so much **free-floating anger**, that is, anger they will unload on complete strangers after just a few seconds contact? You might also wonder where most of the people in our country think they are in their life, what are their priorities or their most important needs. When a man or woman has his/her life in order would he always be in a hurry, running **to** or running **from** someone or something.

I think we are forever **doing** because we are afraid to face ourselves. By our frenzied activity, we allow no time for our minds to see **what we are** or even **what we want**. First, by forever doing something, we allow insufficient time to reflect on our desires and priorities in a way that would be most appropriate for us and in accord with our long term best interests. Even though such **focused** reflection would allow us to manage our actions, thought, and feelings more intelligently and more freely, we rarely take the time. Rather than slow down enough to make each choice a free, considered, deliberate decision which we could then embrace **wholeheartedly,** we persist in pursuing fuzzy goals in a fashion best-described as hectic, hap-hazard, or hit-or-miss. The saddest result of our frenzied activity might well-be that we never experience the grandeur of just "**being**" . . . content, happy, peaceful, contemplative, grateful, prayerful, thoughtful.

❖   Some of you read this, shrug your shoulders and perhaps even yawn. "S__, man! So what if everyone **does** move so fast and work so hard? We'll get into that contemplation, love and respect nonsense later, or some day. So, I don't get someone to love me, whatever that means. That stuff is over-rated, anyhow. Who has time to contemplate? You some kind of religious fanatic?

"Don't try to tell me, doc, your priorities were not money, a big house and car, and all the rest. That's the way to get respect. **You proved it.** Am I right, doctor, or not?"

My answers to his questions: "I did work much too hard. In fact, I even managed to get two heart attacks twenty years younger than my father, aunts, uncles or anyone else in the family ever did.

"I made love for my work my first priority. I judged that I had to. Thank God, I'm also the first person in my family to survive a heart attack. Like most men, I fear dying without love. Now however, I see quite clearly that serving others in order to be loved and affirmed, while quite logical and totally human, is not enough for me. Rather, service to others **for their sake** is infinitely more rewarding. Mother Teresa proved that a million times over.

"It is never too late to get wise, and change your focus, unless you're out in the cemetery. I definitely do not want my epitaph to read 'Here lies a very successful man, who took great pains to do all things well, and gave a lot of those pains to his family.'[2] As a result of my (belated) change of heart, even though my career has always demanded dedicated service, my **first priority** is no longer my work. My first priority is to be a good husband and father. **That is my vocation"**

Summarizing . . .

Intimacy is possible for anyone having a **well-developed sense of self,** that is, anyone who has looked honestly at who or what he (or she) is, without trying to deny or disguise **anything.** Before a person can open his or her heart to another, he must have made his decision that whatever is there is O.K. He must look into his heart on a regular basis, and continue to accept what he sees, if he hopes to maintain a close connection to anyone. For couples enmeshed in conflict, a commitment by both of them to search within and acknowledge honestly what each finds should precede any trip to the marriage counselor. Otherwise, he/she will only **dissemble** before the therapist and use that individual, however skilled he or she might be, to **collude** in the avoidance of personal awareness and responsibility.

Each person who would be a lover must find out first who he is and where's he's pointed, before he can act. Even then, he must **walk** (carefully, making one small decision at a time) before he can **run** with any major change in his life. In the next chapter, you will see that opening our hearts and changing our priorities can have consequences well beyond our families.

26

Healing Our Families as a Solution to Violence

> *". . . [T]he true measure of success [in a relationship, or climbing a mountain] is the distance traversed, how far you have come. [It is] not how high up you are."*
> —(Rabbi) Shmuley Boteach

It's Not the Old-Fashioned *Family Values* That Produce the Violence

Since we live in a **consumer-society** (translation: we endlessly acquire "things" we hope will provide us with joy and happiness), why shouldn't we expect that getting a neat spouse will make us happy, too? In fact, the one-hundred-eleven million Americans in 1998 who were legally living together as man and wife expected that marriage would improve their lives. They also provide proof that marriage is **not** about to become an **icon** of the past. Men and women still expect marriage to reduce or solve their problems of isolation and loneliness, not create more.

One hundred eleven million Americans demonstrate the continued popularity of marriage in America (as opposed to Sweden, for example, where only one in five co-habitating couples are married). Yet, the **breakdown of the American family** is increasingly offered as the reason our society is so violent. The attribution of the social evils in which America leads the world to the breakdown of the family prompts the immediate question: If our homes are fostering the violence that permeates our society, what has changed within the family to bring about such results? We no longer blame all the traffic deaths on the breakdown of our automobiles. Marriage should be dealt with in the same fashion. Instead of faulting the institution, let's check the persons who are signing the marriage contracts, and see if their problems can be corrected.

That violence in America is pervasive is indisputable. Every person is affected in some way. Plainly, the increase in the specific immorality we call violence is simply one result of an overall decline in morality or moral values. If our families and our schools are producing more and more violent and abusive children, the logical next question is: **what is the cause of the increasing moral indifference in our homes and in our schools?** Certainly, the bulk of the blame must be laid at the feet of the parents and teachers, themselves. That more and more of our children consider morality a "relative value,"—impractical, regressive, confusing, controlling—is undeniably the result of what has been modeled and taught. To put it in the gentlest of terms: "God" in the traditional sense of that word, doesn't get as much press as He/She used to. In the final part of the book, we will see all the "evils" resulting from the rejection of a transcendent, but "involved," and loving Creator, who put into our minds a sense of "the common good", and into our wills a hunger for freedom. Love will be seen as possible only because human beings have free will, and can choose to love. But freedom of choice allows one to choose to hate, or to become violent, as his or her substitute for loving actions.

Admittedly, Americans pay the highest price of any civilized country for the violent behavior of its citizens. But, placing the blame for this deplorable state of affairs on the best alternative society has for producing good citizens, namely, a contractually committed man and woman—is **patently absurd.** Blaming America's violent society on the family also means completely ignoring the horrible state of the **family relationships** that exist in virtually **every other society** on this planet. No demographic on the family that you can measure will explain our level of violence. In many countries the rate of divorce matches or exceeds ours and the number of single parents is as high or higher, the number of women working equals or exceeds our rate, women's rights are nowhere as good, and the number of churchgoers is lower in most of the industrialized countries. Obviously, we shouldn't use any of the preceding sociological factors as the explanation for our shameful statistics. Rather, just as there are too many automobile accidents because there are too many irresponsible people behind the wheel, so there are so many family breakdowns (and the consequences that follow from those breakdowns, such as violent and abusive children) because there are **too many irresponsible married people. Men and women are simply not getting marriage right!** Why is it so difficult, when examining the records of broken marriages, to see how ridiculous and futile it is to expect success in a relationship in which two people try to **"use"** each other to provide their own personal happiness, and, as a consequence, evidence little or **no love or reverence** for each other.

As a consequence of our failure to accord our highest priority and attention to nurturing love and connection, rather than to seeking success or wealth, America now has within its borders more lonely, isolated, unloved persons, than any other nation on earth. Mother Teresa's admonition, that "our love of things have replaced our love of one another," was precisely to the point.

Exchanging Unconditional Love in Marriage: An Antidote to Social Violence

Instead of making the family the scapegoat, as if it were a distinct entity apart from the individuals who comprise it, why don't we acknowledge that love of things can never be an adequate substitute for love of people? When love for people is not present, violence becomes inevitable. When there is no love present in a person's life, including even self-regard, whether that person is young or not-so-young, married or not-married, the sense of sin is lost, too. Why is that true? A sense that one is doing something to hurt another, or is not doing something that he should be doing for another—a sense of sin—requires that one **care** about the consequences to others, or to oneself. A person who lacks any reason to be "moral" will follow the easy path of "immorality or violence," at least until he or she can see a reason to care, or to love.

Undeniably, the most effective way to fall to the level of "not caring" is to never look! Maintaining the measure of self-awareness needed to prevent regression into levels of uncaring that are quite common—from simple insensitivity or thoughtlessness to unpleasantness and outright rudeness—requires regular self check-ups or self-appraisals. "Self-care" is never selfish. In marriage, it's a matter of personal survival. Husbands will not handle wisely the constant array of daily choices presented by spouse and children, unless they care. That caring can only come from an accurate assessment of how they are relating, and how they could relate better. Husbands and wives who blindly follow their feelings, or who simply react to the feelings or actions of their partners, are on the path to an unhappy marriage, if they are not already there.

Before anyone can become the person they want to be, he (or she) must spend a lot of private time evaluating his day-to-day performances. He must look especially for anger, impatience, rudeness, avoidance, and the like—those feelings and emotions that affect others adversely—if he wishes an accurate picture of who he is now. This self-examination will also reveal the paths he must follow to become the better person that he, himself, would like to be with in a relationship. While each spouse can provide (and would do it gladly) a long list of changes that would make his or her partner a better person, and a better husband or wife, the system just doesn't work that way. Criticism, or "report cards" are invariably counter-productive; except for the two exceptions noted in Chapter Eighteen. Each partner must **report** to himself (or herself) about his own performance.

27

A New Understanding of Intimacy

"The beginning of love is to let those we love be perfectly themselves,
and not to twist them to fit our own image. Otherwise we love
only the reflection of ourselves we find in them."
—Thomas Merton

Equality: the Foundation of Marital Intimacy

Before proceeding to **Part Four** and an exhortation and justification for **changing the attitudes** of married people, most **especially the priorities of men**, one final review, limited to the most obvious points, might be helpful.

The restrictions on women's freedom have **not** been entirely eliminated. Although most of this discrimination has been removed by new laws, the **unwritten rules** that are still very much a part of our culture pose real obstacles to women. American women are still not allowed, at least always and everywhere, to **seek all the same goals** as men. Marriage, of course, should not hinder a woman's freedom, but rather enhance it. Making **marriage an equal-opportunity job** is probably organized feminism's highest priority right now, even above equal pay for equal work. As Cokie Roberts expressed in her book, *We Are Our Mother's Daughters,* "a woman's place is anywhere she wants it to be." That includes married women, too.

It is an injustice to limit any woman to the "role" of wife/mother especially if part of the job description is "servant." (Chesterton, though, has a point when he says that automatically giving "victim" status to a wife because she has no other career is comparable to feeling sorry for a **king** whose only job is to rule.) It is also wrong to make a mother **solely** responsible for the character of her children, though, in most cases, she should be the one whose opinions regarding their care should carry the greatest weight. It is also an injustice to charge women with the preservation of community standards, or, to subject women to gender norms that began with the industrial revolution, and which were basically intended to keep women "in their place." And **violence toward women**—which has united women as much as any other issue—is still of tremendous importance.

All of the above actual or potential tyrannies, however, even when added to the facts showing that women initiate many more divorces than men, that as many as one-third of wives are unfaithful to their husbands, and that most wives give their husbands poor grades on performance, **do not support** an assertion that men are primarily responsible for the sad state of American marriages. Only ignorance, or foolishness, supports a denial that, in virtually *every* case, when a marriage fails, both partners are guilty.

Accepting Equal Responsibility for a Failed Marriage

Three chapters of my previous book were given over to documenting how, with rare exceptions (a forced marriage or a marriage entirely motivated by a desire for social or financial gain), you choose a mate who is at a nearly identical level of maturity. There, and in several chapters of this book, the point was emphasized that even the women who marries the **misogynist**, that is, the women hater, is getting the mate she "wanted, the husband who would control her."[1]

Clearly, in considering the dynamics of our own or anyone else's marriage, it is **foolish and fruitless** to try to find which partner is the "patient," when the marriage gets "sick." A more appropriate question: "why is neither partner giving first priority to him/herself, not in the selfish sense of indulging his or her desires, but in the extremely demanding sense of examining assets and liabilities, and doing something about them?" Only after each person looks into his own heart and mind, can the sometimes arduous task begin of "accentuating the positives, [the attributes] and eliminating the negatives, [the faults]."[2] Include with the negatives all the obstacles to intimacy that have been set forth throughout this book: the unrealistic expectations, the misguided goals, all the leaning, blaming and shaming, the criticism, the failure to control our anger or accept differences, the selfishness, the laziness, and the repeated using of another person that creates the deadly dependencies and generates so much resentment. Add to the positives the most vital truth of all: **that marriage is the most efficient and most practical school for developing our talent for loving and being loved.** Isn't that what our lives should be all about?

Equal, but Quite Different

With the demise of political and social systems that forced men and women to remain under one roof despite compelling reasons why they should not, we need a new and clear understanding of **gender differences,** preferably before the marriage commitment is made so that the marriage can get started on the right foot. To suggest that such differences should be squashed is not only arrogant, but also foolish. If marriages are to prosper, the most important change needed is the acceptance of women as equals in every sense of the word. Some major changes in education are needed from the earliest levels so that **gender equality** becomes something that our sons and daughters **live** not only at home but also in school.

The problem of violence remains America's biggest problem. Because violence generally begets a violent response of some sort, the focus must be kept on ways to prevent it. It is entirely possible that we may be unable to stop the decline in moral values before our own civilization is destroyed. (Some French literati already claim that the United States is the only country ever to go from a primitive society to decadence without going through a civilized phase.) How could anyone dispute that **our highest national priority** should be to stop our social decline by providing, affirming and supporting **a**

clear set of values for those responsible for preparing children to be responsible adults. Whatever it takes should be done to keep our homes and schools from being the breeding grounds for violence.

Marriage must provide the means **to remove**, not add to, the social crimes that manifest a man or woman's denial and escape from anger, pain, sadness, fear, shame, or guilt. Unless the individuals in the partnership attend to a process of self-care, so that each can live up to his or her responsibilities, and not "use," "exploit," or otherwise "dump on" the spouse, violence of one form or another becomes possible. The **reason for this book is the belief that our marriages can supply the best solution to the escalating violence.** By providing the best environment to challenge, inspire, and force husbands, wives, and children to work, learn, adapt, and grow, the traditional family unit provides the best vehicle for turning our shamefully violent society around. Adopting the approach to marriage dynamics presented in this book—that fit the present realities—would be a step in the right direction, even more so if we could teach and model that approach to our children. The approach has been characterized as **simple, but not easy**: each married man and woman must take personal responsibility for who they are now and for what they are doing, hiding nothing from themselves, and, avoiding any dishonesty or deceit with the one with whom they are sharing their life. Both must be motivated by the reality of our **universal human dignity**. We are all lovable; we are each unique.

Until these changes are made, which will end the mutual exploitation that so often describes our dealings with others, marriage will continue to be the "crap-shoot" it has become. Money or good intentions won't keep a marriage from sinking, but there are any number of virtues that will, and we all know them. **Reverence is the father and mother of them all. When we start doing marriage right, we can start solving our social problems**.

Celibate Love Involves Different Dynamics

Hopefully, each prospective bride and groom would recognize that marriage is uniquely different from a religious vocation that involves **celibacy**. If you want the perfect vehicle for developing and exercising your abilities to relate intimately with another human being, marriage is it. The religious life isn't. If either partner enters marriage in a **spirit of self-sacrifice** typically demanded of celibate religious, his or her spouse may be only too thrilled to accept the gift of service. Regrettably, the one who sacrifices his/her energies in such service, can reasonably expect the attention, the reverence, and the wages of a servant.

We must replace our view that marriage requires total selflessness and heroic sacrifice—a view that is high-minded and certainly challenging, but which fails with alarming frequency, and never leads to intimacy—with the **new understanding of human relationships, love, and intimacy** that this book has already set forth, and which will be re-presented in a somewhat-different manner in **Part Four.**

Part 4
A Legacy of Love

*"Don't you know [success] is all about being able to extend love
to people? Not in a big, capital letter sense but in the everyday.
Little by little, task by task, gesture by gesture, word by word."*
—Ralph Fiennes (*The English Patient*)

28

Putting the Realities of Love Together

I, (bride or groom), realizing that my love for you, however sincere and total it is now, is only a shadow of what it can become, do pledge today, to you and to those present, that I will try, until death do us part, for my sake and for yours, to become the best person I can be.

I promise not to give you any evaluations, unless you specifically request my evaluation of you, but to evaluate myself as often as I can on my progress in making myself as good and as accomplished and as loving a person as God intended for me to be.

I also promise to give first priority to my quest for intimacy with you in the fond hope that, one day, I may always wish your happiness as much as I wish my own.

All the Heroes Have Not Gone

A successful marriage is one filled with love **and reverence**. The love in fairy tales and most of the greatest literature was believable because the lovers reverenced, or "valued," each other. They were, after all, royal, brave, courageous, handsome, and beautiful men and women with high principles. You could believe that they cared about each other because you cared about them. Certainly, all these heroes and heroines were people worth our concern, our caring.

Earlier, I wrote that any love story is believable only as long as, and to the extent that the love that is presented to us, is mutual and unconditional. I added that when one or the other unilaterally presents conditions for his/her love, the element for pathos or tragedy is introduced. Though there were more kings, queens, and other nobles "once upon a time," we still hold the same ideals. You can only love or care about someone to the extent that you see value somewhere in your decision, and in them. You judge that they are worthy of your caring, of your reverence. In the same way, your hope to be loved becomes stronger and more reasonable to the extent that you see yourself as worthy of love.

We Are All Lovable

Parts One, Two, and Three said much about why we should value or reverence ourselves, and a lot about why we don't. Admittedly, none of us can provide the ultimate justification for our self-regard for the simple reason that we owe our gifts to an entity or a being outside ourselves. Our life must have a meaning beyond the few short years we spend on earth, otherwise might is right and "survival of the fittest" applies to our lives, too.

Our "value" is present in both the "I'm O.K., You're O.K. perception of reality and the Judeo-Christian doctrine of the uniqueness of each individual as a result of each person's special creation. (Chapter Twelve and Notes.) It is surely consoling to me to believe that my unique "worth" as a human being, is dependent, not on consensus, but on the existence of the same God that guarantees my right to life, liberty, and the pursuit of happiness. But then, men and women in every age and nation have judged it reasonable to believe in the existence of an objective guarantor of their intrinsic worth and dignity.

While Aristotle, among many other philosophers, has provided compelling proofs for a **transcendent** Creator, it is the oral Traditions and written Canons of the major religions of the world that provide the basis for a reasonable belief in an **immanent and personal** Creator. A God who is involved, or interested in his creatures is also the only absolute guarantor that might cannot determine what is right, and that each individual has inalienable rights which are independent of the will of the majority.

Implicit in the foregoing faith is a hope that the guarantor knows what is happening to us, and if we are "good," as each sees the good, we will be accorded a reward in this or some other life. That those who are unjust, dishonest, or destructive will not be rewarded, is an equally important part of that faith, which sustains most of human-kind .

Having or not having self-regard is the vital determinant of the quality of all our relationships. The Canons of religion tell us that the highest love of which we are capable is the love that we have and demonstrate for our God **and for ourselves**. The love a man or a woman has for his **neighbor** should equal the love each has for him/herself. Therefore, whether our view of men and women is a human-ist or religious one, to achieve any level of intimacy we must value ourselves first, so that we can eventually love someone else.

It is a fact of history that many persons, in every era, have chosen to give their lives in defense of their belief in God. But, it is also undeniable that many others have used their belief in God to justify causes and programs that seem now to have been misguided. Harris writes with much justification, that the "non-adult, or I'm O.K but you're not O.K." transmission of Christ's message has been the main reason the message has not been more universally accepted.[1]

For the purpose of our treatise on the path to deeper marital closeness and fulfillment, it will be enough to accept that in rever-encing each other in marriage we are acting in accord with all that is right and true about who and what we are. As the Buddhists so rightly observe, ". . . [I]n forgetting about yourself, being absorbed in desiring the happiness of another, that's when you have the highest happiness."[2]

We are also, by our mutual regard, or reverence, making pos-sible the love that sustains and nourishes our deepest yearnings. These yearnings, evidence of our common humanity—brothers and sisters all—are written in our hearts, and expressed in our fables, legends, folklore, poetry, prose, language, and religions.

29

Becoming Heroes, Again

> *"Fable is more historical than fact, because fact tells us about one man and fable tells us about a million men. . . . It is far easier to believe in a million fairy tales than to believe in one man who does not like fairy tales."*
> —G. K. Chesterton

The Essence of Knighthood: Service

Perceval, a Knight of the Roundtable, after a life-long search for the Holy Grail, finally discovers that satisfaction and fulfillment comes not from the acquisition of anything—even the Holy Grail. Rather, the highest or **noblest quest, is serving the highest values.**

Viktor Frankl, the famous psychiatrist, who survived a Nazi concentration camp, saved the lives of many inmates of the camp, and many patients afterward, by his insight that men and women do much better when they have **something to which they can devote themselves**.[1] Ultimately, most of us reach the conclusion that the noblest quest to which we can devote ourselves should be in accord with **who we are and why we are here,** that is, subjects of a God who commanded us to love and serve. Frankl also proved, as have millions of people before and since, that "If there is a **why** [we should make love and service our highest priority], then we can [always] find a "**how**."[2]

We define ourselves by our priorities, making our ideals the best predictors of our final legacy. Even though our life experiences teach us to value love more and more, most men fail to ever give the search for love the highest priority, or give that search the status of a quest. Ironically, the present crisis in "masculinity," that has given rise to so many male movements (referred to in **Part One**), has been the result of the failure of American men to find a "worthy cause," for which they could unite and bond, and to which they could dedicate their lives. Recognition of this void has prompted one important **consensus** among those determined to improve the situation, namely, "that service is the central organizing force of mature manhood, and . . . [A man] needs to be actively engaged in something other than his own success and happiness."[3]

Perceval was an old man before he acquired the wisdom that changed his life. I have confessed to devoting most of my life to a "heart-attack-producing" pursuit of **status**, although my highest priority was the **economic preservation** of my wife and six children. In Chapters Five and Nine, I admitted my failure to make the day-to-day "events" of the family my first priority. My **third** sin was also not of commission but of neglect—that is, of reserving little energy to a quest for an intimate relationship with my wife. (Although such a pursuit was always in the back of my mind.)

All husbands, consciously or unconsciously (probably mostly the latter) decide, before the marriage, or early in the marriage, the part that their family is going to play in their lives, and they **never change their priorities** after that. The amount of energy and effort available during our free time, that is spent in direct connection or company with wife and/or children—the visible and tangible evidence in the family's minds of a husband's and father's caring—pretty much depends on those priority decisions. Many American men abandon entirely the quest for intimacy. A rare few embrace the quest totally. Those of us who are left include every level of effort between the two extremes.

The typical man of the twentieth century has endured whatever was necessary to provide for his family. If he didn't succeed, neither did his family. The level of his success determined, for the most part, the style of living for the family. In return for his effort, which often called forth all the manly virtues possible to a person who was essentially desperate and powerless, he generally insisted upon, or expected, his wife's total compliance in anything that he felt was necessary for his own survival, including a modicum—or a lot, in some cases—of personal affirmation and personal services. Now, because the game has been gradually changing, his wife is now his equal—if not in fact, then at least in theory, and in the law.

In times past, by a process dictated by social, political, and economic realities, described in earlier chapters, man the breadwinner was forced to forsake bonding or affiliation with other males, and instead forced to compete with them for status or for survival. In the process, he often had to remove himself for all practical purposes from a warm and close relationship to his family. Equally tragic, the husband had to be steadfast, brave, persevering, and **stoic**, that is, deny any weakness, any personal feelings or emotions which might diminish his ability to "win" his livelihood.

We Are Not Learning from Our Past Mistakes

But, if the game and rules have changed, and both players are now on the same level, the socialization process that "molds a boy into a man," has remained the same. The pre-eminent ideal of manhood remains the isolated, stoic, and fiercely independent hero. That ideal remains the problem.

To "produce" such heroes, boys must be trained virtually from birth to become insensitive and unfeeling, setting the stage for trouble at any time. Adolescent boys, especially, if not continuously and scrupulously mentored or supervised can very easily be seriously wounded or scarred emotionally and psychologically by the bullies among them. These wounds from mockery and scorn can evoke patterns of revenge and retribution now so common that instances of mass violence don't always get "featured status" anymore on the front pages of our newspapers or on the evening news.

Describing the socialization process for boy/men accounted for a large part of the first five chapters. Despite the increasing magnitude of the problem with successive generations of boys/men/husbands, those who most influence our society stubbornly refuse to embrace in any significant way the idea that love and caring and emotional honesty and vulnerability are to be modeled and praised at home, at school, in our sports and games, and in the media. Perhaps, only when preventing crime and handling criminals has become our number one industry (that day may, in fact, be here), will those with the power and influence to effect change take notice.

Tragically, the biggest obstacles to change come from our men, themselves. Husbands and fathers seem determined to be as emotionally inexpressive as ever; and it remains a rare husband who gives priority to spending his quality time with his wife. [4] Many fathers devote themselves to their sons, but their devotion does not seem to involve modeling love or caring or helping those less talented or fortunate. The message is most likely to be: "do whatever it takes to win, even if pain and sacrifice is needed, (and even if mom doesn't understand or approve)." Have you ever wondered why the nearly invariable response of a young athlete when he sees that the TV cameras are focused on him is "hi mom?" (Once he has proved his mettle, isn't that his way to narrow his culturally- and/or self-imposed separation?) Unfortunately, the practices built around a few hundred years of "rugged individualism" cannot be easily reversed.

If men would only realize what they miss!

30

Giving Your Wife What She Wants[1]

*"When you help others, you also help yourself. Seen from **that** perspective, helping others—being unselfish—is the most selfish of all activities, for that is what helps to free us from our loneliness and isolation and suffering."*
—Dean Ornish

The Secret to Success

This book is about **possibilities.** The continuing tragedy for American men is all the **benefits** to themselves that they miss by their attitude toward their wives and families. Whether or not that attitude is explainable or inevitable in the light of their nurturing is totally beside the point.

John Gray focuses on the main point, "a loving relationship allows us to stay in touch with our day-to-day feelings of what is going on. . . . Without love, these feelings can't come out. . . . It is being in touch with our feelings and feeling loved, that we are able to heal ourselves."[2]

What attitude would American women like to see?

I would like to share some of my patients' answers to the contentious question "What do women want?"

(**Note:** the questionnaires were answered anonymously)

"A gentle man." "Kindness, cooperation, respect, and companionship." "Love, kindness, warmth, attention, thoughtfulness, tenderness, above all—caring." "More help with the children . . . him to be a rock I can lean on." "To be heard and know that you and your opinions are valued. That you and the kids come first, before work and his mother." "Affection, understanding." "Faithfulness, understanding and communication." "Commitment is #1. Understanding, protection, care." "Kindness." "Love and friendship." "Love and security." "I'm the only one who doesn't get time off! Help with the kids." "To be seen, heard, touched, revered—to be special."

What **these women** want is **plain and simple.** All the angst about "why are you asking the question" or the snickers that "only a man could ask such a stupid question," or, "a man wouldn't understand the answers," are ignoring the obvious truths of the situation.

In several chapters, I made the claim that most men *understand* well enough what their wives want. And women sense (at least) that their husbands know, which is why they get so angry. Men **withhold** affection, care, communication, and the other fifteen gifts just listed, which are easily within their power to give, as their way of returning **the normal marital sadism** to which I have also already referred. One very common example: he will withhold signs of affection and caring until she is more receptive to his overtures in the bedroom. She will be more receptive to his advances in the bedroom if he gives her more attention and caring.

Again, the tragedy is that both are shooting themselves in the foot. However, there **is** an important difference. **He** is using a rifle. A man's willful refusal to love his wife in the way she wants to be loved, costs him more than he will ever realize, in terms of peace, joy, and self-regard, because it is his wife (and the children) who are the only ones to whom he will ever matter. Any meanness, sadism, or indifference merits him a miserable family atmosphere, filled with loneliness and resentment, all of which is deserved. Without question, time spent "tending to the well-being of wife and family is a very rewarding exercise of mature self-care and self-interested sacrifice. Devotion to family brings with it abundant self-esteem, not to mention a happy, joyful home."[3]

The "Men's Movement," which has as its goal, reconnecting men with each other in community, instead of in ruthless competition, depends for its success on each man's commitment to reconnect first to his deepest thoughts, emotions, and feelings, and then to reconnect to his family.[4] For example, the same process of reconnection the "Promise-Keepers" propose, conforms precisely to the principle presented in this book, namely, that the path to intimacy, to relationship, to love, always begins with a search into one's own heart!

The Story of Joe and Mary

❖ The dog's barking awakened Joe from a very deep sleep. His arm was still under his sleeping wife's back and shoulder, so he took care not to move too suddenly and startle her.

He thought happily of their laughing and talking and hugging and kissing of the night before, but couldn't remember who had fallen asleep first.

On the eve of the days that he didn't have to leave for work before dawn, Joe and his wife, Mary, would usually retire early to the bedroom and catch up on each other's lives. If both were in the mood, which was most of the time, they would make love.

As he put on his walking clothes, Joe smiled fondly toward the "sixty-something" lady still soundly sleeping on his side of the bed, a bed they had shared for over forty years.

A few minutes later, as their Alaskan Husky begins pulling him on what will be a two-and-a-half mile, thirty-five minute hike, Joe allows his memories to go back twenty years, to a time when his wife and even his children gave him more aggravation than consolation. . . .

In those days, hardly a week would go by without a re-enactment of "the fight" that had been repeated so many times that they could change roles and still probably get all the lines right. The curses, shouts, and vicious personal insults simply seemed to be delivered at higher and higher volume as one miserable year followed another. Mary screamed that he was always criticizing her while he felt that her explicitly-expressed "disgust" for twenty or thirty of the things he did on a routine basis was the ultimate criticism. Their three sons were evidence that they had sex, but that had become rare.

Mary especially "despised" (her word) his total lack of response to concerns, grievances, and feelings that she would try to share with him on a fairly-regular basis, at least in the early years of their marriage. For his part, Joe would usually be so upset, angered, or confused by his wife's insinuations, complaints, or feelings that his response would be totally suppressed, lest he expose his own fears, anger, pain, weakness, doubts or anxieties. They should have gone to counseling, but they had reached a point where it didn't seem to matter anymore. Thinking about those awful days, Joe could not keep back some tears.

Finally, Joe's thoughts move to the events that changed his life. . . .

It all began with Joe's near-fatal "accident" at the shore. Like his father, Joe liked to swim in the ocean before breakfast. Unlike his father, however, who had a regular exercise program to stay fit, Joe rarely had time to exercise for strength and endurance, and should never have ventured out for his swim on that beautiful and fateful September morning. Although the sky was cloudless and the water as warm as it would get that year, a distant hurricane had churned the waters and created a dangerous undertow that took Joe out to sea.

It was miraculous that within minutes of passing out in the ocean from sheer exhaustion, Joe was rescued by a small Coast-Guard patrol boat that was rushing back to shore.

A helicopter whisked a comatose body requiring life support equipment to the University Hospital 100 miles away. It was two weeks to the day before Joe emerged briefly from his coma for the first time. In the weeks that followed he started to slowly but steadily improve. By Christmas Eve, Joe was able to go home.

During the 142 days that Joe spent in the hospital, Mary and/or one or all of the boys were always at his side, except for those minutes when the nurse or doctor requested they step outside the room.

It was thirteen more months before Joe regained full health and was able to return to the engineering position that had been the most important thing in his life until the accident.

By the half-way point in his walk with the dog, Joe had already been stopped four times by neighborhood friends who would have chatted with Joe if he had so-desired. But Joe was so alone inside with his thoughts that he allowed the husky to pull him away each time.

Joe and Mary's relationship would never be the same. Each member of the family seemed to place the cares and concerns of the others above their own. Joe's gratitude to his wife and sons became as boundless as their love and concern had been for him.

Experts might say that Joe and Mary had achieved intimacy, but as far as this happy couple was concerned, they were simply each other's best **friend.** As he turned the corner for the final quarter-mile, Joe' s mental noting of friendship evoked a little knowing look on his face as he realized what had probably prompted this morning's trip down memory lane. The priest's talk on Sunday had been a very stirring discussion of friendship.

Two insights on **friendship** had been introduced in the priest's remarks which had moved Joe to tears. Mary inquired three times during services if anything was wrong. The speaker noted that the Bible claims that there is no greater love possible to man than that expressed by laying down his life for a *friend.* It does not say laying down his life for a spouse, a child, a king, or a lover. The priest also went on to point out that the traditional marriage promises end at death, since the words are clear: "until death do us part." Thus if your mate is not also your friend any relationship between you might be lost when you both are dead. The New Testament supports this view when Jesus informs the Sadducees that there is no marriage or giving of marriage in Heaven.

After Joe had finished tying up his dog, "Giant," and had given him a few squeezes, he went over to the garden to pick a bouquet of late-blooming day-lilies to present to his "lover" and "friend."

Can't Everyone Recognize By Now That God Doesn't Make *Junk*

When a man can wholeheartedly put the welfare and desires of his wife and family first, he is truly **free—because his self-worth is no longer defined by his resume, but rather by what he can share and what he can forego.**

Whatever else that search into one's heart reveals, there is one reality that underlies the searcher's opinion of his own worth, and the ultimate justification for his heroic effort on re-creating his family connections. That reality is: each and every person ever born is infinitely valuable, and worthy of love. But there are many people who do not believe it, who do not see any worth or value in themselves, and see no value in anyone else's life, either. As a consequence, they choose not to love. Their decision not only effects them, but all of us, in one way or another.

31

In the Absence of Love . . .

> "Life is not lost by dying; life is lost minute by minute,
> day by dragging day, in all the thousand small uncaring ways."
> —Stephen Vincent Benet

Missing the Mark by Failing Life's Noblest Challenge

Consider the effects on ourselves, our family, and on society of our failure to do the **good** things that are personally possible for us to do, not to mention the **bad** things that we are free to choose. I am referring, of course, to what is most often referred to as **sin. Unconditional love can never be anything more in our lives than an abstraction, if we fail to grasp the significance of sin.**

Certainly, the undeniable existence of evil, of the kind that makes us afraid to go out alone, or even together at night, that causes us to lock our doors, and to spent vast sums for the court system, security systems, police forces, jails, and prisons—while emphasizing the enormous significance of free will—challenges us to make the quest for love in our own lives, and in the lives of our families, our highest priority.

Any person who has ever glimpsed into the face of evil, especially of the violent kind, will rush to find a safe haven, and to experience at least a measure of love. A man (or woman) who has

212

ever experienced the only love worthy of the name, that is, unconditional love, will also know, at least intuitively or in his deepest heart, the evil of sin, which is, in essence, a rejection of the wonderful possibilities of love.

As a corollary of that truth, we know with confidence that no matter what else ever happens in the life of one who has been blessed by love—even if he (or she) falls to the lowest depths of depravity—his reconnection to society remains possible. As Rachel Naomi Remen writes: "Once you have the experience that you matter, that you are seen—you have that strength forever. It is an "all-or-non phenomenon. Perhaps that is why good parenting is so important."[1] On the other hand, one who has **never** known love finds it exceedingly difficult to ever find the path to positive human connections. His or her journey, made in personal isolation without love and guidance, is almost always a violent one.

The Dream of a More Civilized Society Is Not an Impossible Dream

I have provided statistics on violence and social evils of which we can all be frightened and ashamed, but which should no longer be surprising to us. If you haven't experienced violence and abuse in your own family, or neighborhood, or schools, you are a part of a small and fortunate minority. The upward spiral of violence seems not to be slowing even though the overwhelming majority of our fellow citizens, husbands and wives desperately want happier and more secure lives, **and more joyous homes**, and, express the reasonable hope for improvement.

If for no other reason than for the sake of the next generation, the situation in **our homes, and in our schools**, has to improve! The sign on every school entrance should read "No Violence (Hate, Irreverence, Tyranny) allowed." Each school should have a place set aside for those who feel oppressed, or for those who have been angered by mockery, so that students can share vulnerabilities and learn how to empathize or to affirm each other. No child can be totally protected from derision and it would be foolish for anyone to suggest otherwise. But there must be a mechanism in place, apart from the parents, where no records are kept, adult wisdom is available, and love and hugs are freely exchanged. These adolescent wounds can, and must be healed. [2]

Equally important, **creating good marriages is the key to reversing the steady increase of violence and immorality** (or however you label the actions of people hurting themselves and/or others). The initial inspiration for this book was to help the husbands of the women in my practice find a way to know what their wives wanted. As I have just demonstrated, the task of **telling** men what women want could be accomplished in about twenty words, but that doesn't mean that women will ever get those gifts which they desperately need and deserve. Therefore, once the research and writing began, and the book took on a life of its own, a larger purpose for my book was envisioned: to provide **not just an explanation**, but also, more importantly, to provide an **exhortation** on the wonderful possibilities inherent in the institution of marriage, especially for the millions of macho husbands who hadn't a clue to the happiness and joy that they were tossing away.

Amazingly, my two extra years of research for this book ultimately led me to the identical solution to violence that had already been clearly summarized in two sentences of *It's Your Life: a Gynecologist Challenges You to Take Control:*

"For marriage to be the secret weapon that could bring our country back to civilization from a condition of decadence, _men_ must first choose to begin the process of reconnecting with their deepest feelings.

"At the same time, their wives would have to be willing to help, guide, and encourage their mates in the launching of a "**dialogue of love**."[3]

One Final *How-to-Do-It*: Share Feelings Freely, but Thoughts Thoughtfully

Specifically, each couple commits to communication of honest **feelings**, which will automatically bring about emotional equality and keep each partner vulnerable and lovable and **present to each other** in all the moments they choose to share. The exchange of

thoughts will be done with scrupulous care, so that judgments and criticism can be avoided. (Exception: when not to criticize would make one partner an "enabler" of the spouse's foolishness. For example, when accepting or ignoring his or her addiction sends the message that you don't care.)

Each spouse performs regular "examens" of consciousness (what have been referred to throughout this book as "searching one's own heart"), for the purpose of self-work on the feelings, deficiencies, and **possibilities** that the examination reveals. Infinite possibilities exist. If a man (or woman) 's awareness and intention can be focused, he will soon find the helps and resources, the **how**, that is, the ways to love and serve that have been missed up to that point in the marriage. The commitment to regular "soul-searching" can "bring forces into play that are part of life's mystery."[4]

Maintaining commitments is more important than techniques. Keeping your own heart open to yourself will help to keep it open to your spouse, and keep the path to love and intimacy clearly marked. If your self-exam leads you to the realization that a sense of self, or self-worth is lacking, then you have to begin the job, that is often painful, of constructing a sense of self-worth, as your first contribution to a better marriage.

This safe and sound approach to a great and intimate relationship, added to the insights carefully explained in the previous chapters could bring you peace and joy of which you may have never dreamed. It has provided peace and joy to me!

The **quest** that I propose is indeed worthy of each person's finest efforts.

I WISH EVERY HUSBAND AND WIFE SUCCESS!

Appendix

SAMPLE OF PATIENT QUESTIONNAIRE

NO NAMES PLEASE. THIS MUST BE ANONYMOUS.

Do you want to help me write my book for husbands?
If you do, please answer some or all of the following questions:
Use as many sheets of paper as you want

What do you like/dislike about your husband?

What do you need/miss most from your husband?

Have you any hope your marriage will improve? Do you want it to improve? Would you be willing to pay for counseling?

Has your husband ever struck you? Been verbally abusive?

Did you marry for romance? How long did your romantic period last? Do you think you could go to that level again?

How would you describe your sexual relationship?
What do you think women want most from men?

Optional: age?　　　How long married?
No. of children?　　Married before?

"The First and Greatest Commandment"

Who could argue with the answer Jesus gave to the ill-intentioned lawyer in Matthew *22:34-40*, [who asked], "Teacher, which commandment in the law is the greatest?" If we do not argue, or at least question, the answer Jesus gave, it may only show that we do not understand what Jesus was saying. To believe in God is to believe in a transcendent being, a being who is beyond space and time, a being totally other than ourselves, a being without a physical body and therefore without gender. And we are to love this being with our whole heart, soul, and mind. Really now, isn't that a bit much?

It is far easier to fulfill the second commandment, the one that says we are to love our neighbors as ourselves. Here the object of our love is a person we can see, we can know, we can touch, we can help. Little wonder that some theologians have tried to collapse the first great commandment into the second. It is in loving our neighbor, they claim, that we show our love for God. Some would go so far as to say loving our neighbor suffices. This is a nice way to fill the world with anonymous Christians. It could also eliminate the distinction between a Christian and an atheist. Heeding the call to be men and women for others, some contemporary Christians subscribe to the second commandment but not to the first.

Did Jesus intend to put both commandments on an equal footing? In fulfilling the second commandment, do we fulfill the first? Jesus once told us that as often as we fed or clothed our neighbor, as often as we cared for our neighbor in time of sickness, or visited our neighbor in prison, we were actually doing all those things to Him. Surely our love of neighbor can mirror our love of God. But to do so, the love of God must come first. This brings us back to the need for arguing with, or at least questioning the answer Jesus gave to the lawyer.

How can we love a God who is transcendent, totally other than ourselves, and having no physical features? To believe in God? Yes. To hope in God? Yes. To trust in God? Yes. But to love God? If we cannot love God, neither the prophets of Israel nor God's Word incarnated in Jesus Christ could have commanded us to do so. There must be a way.

As much as we like to think of ourselves as great lovers, in this instance we need to accept ourselves as the beloved. Only when we recognize the loving goodness of God touching our lives can we then love God as Jesus commanded us to do. Every day our lives are touched by God's goodness from the first glittering rays of the rising sun to the after glow of the setting sun. As the earth yields once more an abundant harvest our lives are touched by God's loving goodness. Not only in the vigor of our youth, but even in the sufferings of old age, we are tenderly embraced by God's love. To be so totally loved by God, what choice do we have but to love God with our whole being in return?

(Homily by the **REV. JAMES W. MOORE, S.J.**,
at ST. MATTHIAS CHURCH
BALA CYNWYD, PA
on 10/24/99

A Man Who *Became the Husband…*

(The following copyrighted article by Bill Lyon about Payne Stewart appeared in *The Philadelphia Inquirer,* October 26, 1999. It is "Reprinted with permission from *The Philadelphia Inquirer, October 26, 1999.)*

Stewart Won the Biggest Battle of All, the Personal Battle with Himself

He was a fierce competitor who so burned to win that for a time there was almost nothing he wouldn't do to achieve success.

So it was especially revealing, and memorable, that one of the very last things Payne Stewart did in public was to concede, to simply hand over certain victory.

In many ways, that act outshone every difficult putt he ever made, every championship he ever won, because it reflected his estimable growth not so much as a golfer but as a man.

Last month, on the 18th green on the final day of the Ryder Cup, on one of the most emotionally-charged days ever in sports, Payne Stewart was all but assured of joining the glorious American stampede to a most improbable comeback. The Yanks had overcome one of the more daunting deficits in any sport.

And now Stewart had come to the final hole even with his match-play opponent, the wonderfully skilled and combustible Scot, Colin Montgomerie. But Stewart, with true grit, seemed to have the hole won. Montgomerie needed to make a treacherous sliding 20-footer to avoid losing the hole and the match.

Montgomerie never got a chance to pull back his putter.

Payne Stewart conceded the putt.

Conceded the match.

Conceded ego and bravado, conceded self-indulgence and personal gain.

Montgomerie was stunned. And, correctly so, touched by such a magnanimous act.

It was a grand gesture, one of compassion and graciousness and sportsmanship. It was a reminder of why golf, maddening and humbling as it may be, is our most civilized sport.

And it was a crossroads in the admirable transformation of Payne Stewart from sometimes cocky and arrogant and self-absorbed semi-adolescent into an aware and mature and remarkably serene human.

In June, Payne Stewart won the U.S. Open for the second time.

In a burst of extraordinary candor, he said, "I'm the only player to win the Open as two different people—first as something of a jerk and then as a pretty good guy."

He was 42, and it struck you that Payne Stewart had indeed achieved the most rousing sort of success. At 42, most of us are beyond learning or changing, admitting or adjusting. But here was a man who had confronted himself and didn't like a lot of what he saw, and he set about to change it.

And did.

That is worth a standing ovation. Salvation always is.

Alas, now it will have to be a moment of mourning instead, of respectful silence in honor of his memory. Payne Stewart perished yesterday in a bizarre airplane crash.

The shame of it is that we are deprived of his fluid swing and his solid game. The consolation, slim though it may be, is his legacy not just as an athlete but as a redeemed soul.

After he had conceded that putt to Montgomerie, who is always an object of goading torment by the morons in the gallery, Payne Stewart explained, "We had won. He had gone through enough."

So, he conceded, even though the record books would forever show that Payne Stewart, who burned so much to win, had lost his match on the day almost every other American was winning his. In a time in sports when so many are obsessed with taunting and celebrating over a fallen opponent, this was a shining moment.

When he had won the 1999 Open, at storied Pinehurst No. 2, Payne made a 15-foot uphill, left-to-right-break putt over a mound, on the last hole. First he lossed a punch and then a primal shriek. And then he sought out Phil Mickelson, whom he had defeated by one stroke.

At a moment when he could have been forgiven for celebrating his triumph, Payne Stewart's thoughts instead were of the man he had defeated, a man who was due to become a first-time father at any second. And it was, ironically, Father's Day.

"He told me my time would come," said Mickelson. "And he told me I'd make a great father and to cherish that."

Payne Stewart was a father himself, twice-over. His children, he said, had helped him find a peace that had eluded him for a lifetime. They went to Sunday school together. His 10-year-old son, Aaron, had given Payne Stewart a special bracelet. When Stewart tried to speak of it, his voice broke and his eyes filled.

"I'm so much more at peace with myself," he said.

All of his golfing life, people had marveled at Payne Stewart's golf swing. It was silk on satin. He had made it himself, of course, fashioned its repeating perfection with hour upon hour of practice.

But it was the person Payne Stewart built that will endure.

In golf, it is always you against yourself.

Payne Stewart won that match.

Notes

Preface

1. (pg. x.) Long before I became a gynecologist, I had started searching for the reasons American housewives seemed so unhappy. See **Notes, Chapter Eighteen, #1,** for an explanation.

2. (pg. x.) **Part Two** also contrasts the purpose marriage play's in a **husband's** life with his mates view. Because men generally view marriage as but one chapter in the story of their life (while women see it as the whole story), her rush to "closeness" can often trigger his flight to "independence." Once a man has won his selection as "husband," he is inclined to switch the energies used in courting to other goals **outside** the home. This switch is more likely if his wife stops saying "thank you" for all the little things her husband does, or if she stops sending out clear signals of her desires. (See next **Note.**)

3. (pg. xi.) Single women live significantly longer than those who are married. In contrast, men who marry live quite a few more years than those who don't, probably because **women typically rush to please their men**, and men quite naturally encourage them to do **that job** well. Many feminists have the opinion, with which I somewhat agree, that the "nunneries" would be filled with women—of many different religious persuasions—if perspective brides realized how awful marriage can be for women. The emotional or psychological cost when their most important life venture fails is indescribable. Women who have never married, widows, and divorced women have one-third the incidence of depression as those presently-married. Since a second meaning of "depression" is "to devalue," the high rates in marriage are an almost inevitable response to being in a culture that deeply fears and devalues the "feminine,"—a social reality discussed in both **Part One and Part Two**. Marital inequities ultimately ruin marriage for **both parties**.

4. (pg. xii.) Whatever the new problems are destined to bring, the fact remains that we all yearn to **express ourselves in relationship!** In the Judeo-Christian story of creation, even the Almighty had to agree with Adam's assessment that being a soul-mate to a giraffe (or **any** of the other animals then present in the Garden) was not the answer to Adam's needs.

5. (pg. xii.) A talent for intimacy, which makes better and better sex **possible**, is what a permanent relationship is supposed to develop. "Great sex," or joyous sex, is rarely (if ever) taught from a how-to manual, but **can be** a major reward of developing the "skill" of intimacy. The fact that sexual liberation for women, or the abundance of graphic and explicit sexual information, has not resulted in "better" marriages clearly proves that genital sexuality plays a lesser role in the **development** of the skill of intimacy than the foolish propaganda of the last four decades would suggest.

6. (pg. xii.) Also, those wives who "submit," or sacrifice themselves, for their husbands, may be blissfully rewarded, in this life or the next. Many such wives may well view their marriage as a **success**. However, such a one-sided relationship is **not intimate**, in the sense this book uses that term. The possibility for intimacy in a "sacrificial" marriage can only exist if *both* partners sacrifice **on a regular basis** and do it **unconditionally**. (Two people suffering and sacrificing for each other as their primary way of relating might be an interesting story for the ages, but such a tale would certainly be a "painful read," especially if it described two people for whom you cared.) However, if the "sacrifice" is unilateral and "submissive," then, of course, a relationship of intimacy would be impossible.

Before Proceeding...

1. (pg. xiv.) Since conventional expectations about manhood and masculinity causes parents, teachers and mentors to treat **boys** as "little men," it should not be surprising when **boys hide their depression in the same way men do.** Thus, a boy could use a "flight" reaction: hiding or withdrawing as evidenced by lack of eating or by poor sleep patterns; or, disguising the depression by using drugs, alcohol, or excessive involvement with work or sports. The boy could also adopt a "fight" approach with violence or bullying, reckless driving or engaging in high risk sports or dares. Adults often do not recognize depression in boys when it is disguised in these ways or expressed as anger or agitation. Boys, like men, would be shamed by an admission of sadness, much less depression. Unlike girls, boys do not typically ask for help. **Pollack, pg. 318-337.**

2. (pg. xiv.) One of **Freud's** principles still very much accepted is the concept of **unconscious guilt**. We can feel guilty for feelings, desires, impulses that never have reached our conscious minds! In order to deal with the guilt effectively, **Freud** taught that the feelings, desires, or impulses must somehow be brought to awareness and "faced."

3. (pg. xiv.) Our land provides opportunities, unmatched anywhere else in the world, which make it reasonable for men to dream and work for the **great** success, wealth, or power that would prove that they are great persons. Traditional socialization of boys teaches them the notion that worth comes only after achievement, and that the only real esteem is that based on performance. Clearly evident in many American families, the sacrifices required in a quest for wealth and power typically interfere with the creation of a happy and relaxed family life. Tremendous anxiety often motivates super-achievers, who correctly sense that any performance-based esteem will vanish when the wealth or power declines, or the business successes cease. When their fortunes do change for the worse, such husbands see themselves as worthless and incompetent, and often become the most pitiable and most selfish of men. See **Notes, Chapter Eleven, # 1,** for ways that a wife might best communicate with a depressed man. **Abraham J. Twerski,** a specialist for many years in the treatment of addiction, has provided clinical examples of how "super people," or "super-achievers" are prone to "super-denial." Those the world sees as successful who come for treatment consistently confess that "they have been phonies for as long as they can remember, and that despite their great success, "inside they are weak and frightened failures." "No matter the level of fame, a negative self-image is a rather constant finding among chemically-dependent people." **Twerski** stresses over and over that unless the negative self-image can be changed to a positive one, the addict will relapse. **Twerski, Chapter Twenty-Seven.**

4. (pg. xiv.) The prevalence of "a depression serious enough to interfere with [a person's] ability to function is twenty percent." The foregoing means that one of every five persons in our society at any given time is depressed. That figure *does not include* anyone who has a "clear external cause" for a depression. If we counted those with a known reason to be depressed, for example, loss of job, serious illness, loss of a loved one, the figure would be even higher. **O' Connor, Page 41.** Those who are "unhappily married" are twenty-five times more likely to have a depressive episode that those whose marriages are reported as "not unhappy." Quoted by **Donovan, (ed), pg. 23.** Women are **diagnosed** with depression two-and-a-half times more often than men because two-thirds of the depressed men are **covertly, not overtly depressed,** that is, the depres-

sion is **hidden** behind a personality disorder or an addiction. The consensus is that the incidence is equal in both sexes and that the lifetime incidence is nearly fifty percent. **Real, pg. 84.**

5. (pg. xv.) "The more whole I feel within myself, the greater capacity I have for intimacy with someone else." **Ornish, pg. 87. N**o one can share what he or she doesn't have!

6. (pg. xv.) A man (or woman) who is depressed, just like a man who is addicted, has a **negative self-image.** Unless that self-image can be turned into a **positive** one, the man will never escape for very long from his depression or from his addiction. A man in AA, after twenty-five years as a recovering alcoholic, put this truth very well: "The man I *was* drank, and the man I *was* will drink again." **Twerski, pg. 187.**

Understanding the Message...

1. (pg xix.) A man (or woman) has to have at least a few **defenses** to which he can run when faced with threatening or powerful feelings from others. TV can constitute his (or her) **safe house,** a refuge where he can be himself, where he "belongs," and where he will not be judged or criticized, or assailed with needs. TV can **thus** represent an attempt to hide or withdraw from the threatening atmosphere of the home. Unfortunately, now the average man has only one-half as much leisure time as his father had (only seventeen hours). Using up five hours on Sunday and three hours on Monday night watching the NFL can really kick the week off on the wrong foot. Who would deny that how he spends his leisure time reveals his **values** better than anything he might claim?

2. (pg. xix.) Unfortunately, it is the norm in our culture for a man to work frantically to make himself **special** so as to become loved. Setting yourself apart from people as a special, important, or worthy person is **not proposed** in this book as an ideal. Rather, the ideal proposed is that "wholeness"—becoming real, authentic, vulnerable, or mature—should be sought first so that the exchange of love becomes possible.

3. (pg. xx.) Taking personal responsibility means each spouse must seek to be an "**owner,**" that is, one who, having first made himself aware of his or her own thoughts, feelings, actions and needs, now accepts full responsibility for them. The only other alternative is to be a "**blamer.**" Blamers do not do well in marriage, especially when their mates become the favorite targets. A person who has made himself accountable does not lean on his or her mate. "**Leaners,**" that is, those who let other people do their work for them, don't do well in long-term relationships, either. (Allowing others to do for us what we could do for ourselves prevents intimacy. If a person is not leaning on anybody, then he or she can stand

on his/her own two feet and can maintain the proper distance to clearly see and appreciate the other person's thoughts, feelings, and needs. A love song from a few years ago wisely had one lover suggest to his beloved that their difficulties might be due to his "standing up too close or back too far". By looking into our loved one's eyes from the proper focus we should see more clearly what's going on in his/her heart. "Blamers go through life setting up and knocking down 'straw men.' Blamers suffer a kind of human exhaustion in their avoidance of responsibility. They seriously limit their potential self-knowledge, they never get to know themselves." **John Powell,** quoted by **Padovani, Foreword.**

4. (pg. xx.) **Pollack, pg. 391.**

5. (pg. xx.) Sociologist **David Popenoe**, quoted by **Ibid, pg. 201.**There are many economic, social, and political reasons why the real father is now more easily separated from his family, then a century ago. But our present concern is the part that male disconnection or isolation plays in marital discord and failure and what can be done about it. Ninety percent of custodial single parents are women.

6. (pg. xx.) Having someone to love and to love you has been documented as effective in prolonging life and decreasing the incidence of disease. **Ornish,** *Chapter Two and Three.*

PART ONE: THE PERILOUS PATH TO MANHOOD

1. What Can You Expect from "Snakes and Snails and Puppydog Tails…?"

1. (pg. 4.) **Vitz** mentions **Carl Rogers** twenty-eight different times, seldom favorably. See especially **pg. 146-150** to get an appraisal of Rogers' finished educational handiwork

2. (pg. 4.) **Nancy Chodorow** describes the **masculinization process:** dependency on mother, attachment to her, and identification with her represent that which is not masculine: a boy must reject dependency, deny attachment and identification." A boy is also trained to reject and devalue women themselves and also to devalue and reject whatever he considers feminine in the social world. Quoted by **Real, pg. 354.**

3. (pg. 6.) Researchers like **Tavris, Offir, Will, Self, Datan, and Florisha** provide clear evidence that **all** parents have a different response pattern for boys than for girls, and that even "toddlers have an intuitive grasp of their parents' preferences." Quoted by **Ibid, pg. 353.**

4. (pg. 7.) Obviously, delineating the connections between a child's relationship to his primary caregiver/s and subsequent marriage prob-

lems is beyond the scope of this book. However, from a practical point of view, several generalizations can be safely made: Each adult's **style of relating** to other people, including his (or her) spouse, while directly gender related in many ways, is primarily determined by that person's relationship in infancy to his or her primary caregiver. If that relationship was consistently good and supporting, one could reasonably expect the child to be capable of intimacy or closeness in adult life. If that infant relationship was inconsistent the tendency is for the individual to have excessive needs for support and affection as an adult. If the infant-primary caregiver bond is very unsatisfactory or virtually non-existent the relational techniques most likely to be seen in the adult are those of "avoidance," that is, the individual flees or avoids intimacy, seeing it as unnecessary and a source of emotional distress.

5. (pg. 7.) **John Gottman**, quoted by **Ibid, page 309.**

6. (pg. 7.) Ironically, people have read the story of Narcissus, and have concluded "what a selfish boy!" This **mistaken** judgment reflects the fact that the whole point of the myth has been missed. Narcissis was **not** selfish, self-centered, or self-aggrandizing, at all! Rather, he lacked even a "sense" of self. Narcissus never "faced" who he was, that is, he never experienced or "owned" himself—he was numb, dead, lifeless in terms of awareness of self-in-relationship. Therefore, he was unable to recognize his own image in the water. The term **grandiose** is probably a more apt term than **narcissistic** to describe a person who performs solely for his own self-aggrandizement, that is, without any charitable motives.

7. (pg. 8.) **Padovani, pg. 30.**

8. (pg. 8.) Boys are twice as likely to be autistic, four times more likely to be emotionally disturbed, six times more often hyperactive, much more likely to be retarded or have birth defects, 25% more likely to die in infancy, twice as likely to be learning disabled or physically abused (usually by the mother) and twice as likely to die from that abuse, four times more likely to commit suicide, and three times more likely to be a victim of violence (even when high school violence is included). Ref. **Gurian, pg.xvii**. Over seven-hundred thousand boys in this country are taking drugs for their "hyperactivity," (which is undoubtedly not always the condition ADHD, or "Attention Deficit Hyperactive Disorder, but rather a normal boy acting out stress or anxiety). In other countries, England, for example, the same problem is treated equally well according to some experts, with dietary supplements of essential fatty acids or their derivatives. Things don't get any better when boys grow up physically: A 1994 Department of Justice study showed that sixty-three percent more men than women are victimized by violence and three and-a-half times more men are murdered. Men, who represent fifty-five

percent of the work force, suffer ninety-three percent of all the job-related deaths. Four times more men than women commit suicide. Twice as many Vietnam veterans (100, 000) have committed suicide than were killed in that war. The rate of suicide in men is fives times more after age sixty-five. The problem of homelessness is primarily a problem of single male adults. Six million American men have only visiting rights to their children. **Kimbrell,** especially **Chapters One and Fifteen.**

9. (pg. 9.) When I speak of "normal male aggression," I am referring only to American culture. Anthropologists from the beginning have provided ample evidence from other cultures that men have often been the direct opposites of the competitive, self-centered, autonomous, power-driven, work-obsessed males, that we find now in America. Much present day research can also be found to refute the biologic determinism of writers like **George Will** and researchers like **Anne Moir** and **David Jessel,** who say that male aggression and **violence** is virtually inevitable because these actions are built right into male anatomy and physiology. **Ibid,** especially **Chapter Two.** See next **Note.**

10. (pg. 9.) However, when such biologic findings are used unscientifi-cally to explain female behavior, the feminists react with similar anger, since the assumptions are often used to justify discrimination against women. **Ibid, Chapter Two.** There is no one single hormone of aggres-sion and no one seat of aggression in the brain. "A recent text on neuropsychiatry by Jeffrey L. Saver and his colleagues links thirty-eight different parts of the brain to various behaviors that can be called aggres-sive." **Tangier, Chapter 14.** ". . . [Y]oung children are physically aggres-sive, and . . . before the age of three, there are no significant differences between girl aggression and boy aggression." **Kaj Bjorkqvist,** quoted in **Ibid, pg. 264.** For the lack of connection of testosterone with aggression, see **Ibid, pg 34-35,** and also the paper, **"Male testosterone linked to high social dominance but low physical aggression in early adolescence."** J Am Acad Child Adolesc Psychiatry. 35: 1322-1330. (1996.)

11. (pg. 10.) **Weingarten.** A book about mothers who let themselves be silenced, and what mothers should do about it.

12. (pg. 10.) The "Boy Code" is enforced by everybody, including moth-ers, from birth. This complete system of do-or-die rules, or injunctions, which boys, from earliest childhood seem to fear breaking, lest they experience shame, has been divided into four basic male "ideals," or models of behavior, by Professors **Deborah David and Robert Brown:** a. The "sturdy oak." Men should be stoic, stable, and independent. They should never show pain or grieve openly. They do not even ask for help in a confusing or frightening situation. (A lot of energy is required to maintain this false personna and a lot of acting ability.) b. The "Give 'em

hell" role. Like James Bond or Dirty Harry, nothing should be too daring, too risky, or too violent. c. The "big wheel." Men should achieve as much status, dominance, and power as they can. Or, they should wear the mask of "coolness," that is, avoid shame at all costs and act as though everything is all right and under control, even if it isn't. d. "No sissy stuff." This refers to the literal gender "straitjacket" that prohibits boys from expressing feelings or urges seen (mistakenly) as feminine—dependency, warmth, and empathy. Cruelly enforced by virtually everyone, a boy is shamed so quickly and forcefully when he acts "like a girl" or shows any "feminine" feelings that he tries never to repeat his mistake ever again. Showing fear is forbidden. Boys must toughen up or tough it out. The sanction for enforcing the Boy Code is shame. Thus, the same punishment that is used to silence the voices of adolescent girls is used in boys from earliest childhood. If girls become shame-*sensitive*, boys become shame-*phobic*. Girls can express, or admit their shame, and thus be helped and comforted, but boys risk their "manhood," as they see it drawn out for them, if they would confess their shame. Quoted by **Pollack, 276-77.**

13. (pg. 11.) **Shalit, pg. 12, 163-170.**

14. (pg. 11.) From an anthropological perspective, three hundred persons seem to be the highest number a tribe can have " if everyone is to be "seen" and "heard." Persons beyond that number would be experienced as "strangers." **Joan Borysenko**, quoted by **Ornish, pg. 194. Patricia Hersch's** documentary on present-day adolescent society reports that adolescents are living their discretionary hours, which amount to 40% of their time, virtually unsupervised and unmentored. The result is that even the best of parents are ignorant of their children's values, temptations, bad habits, feelings, pain or confusion. **Hersch, pg. 21.** Teachers seemed not to have a clue as to the amount of intimidation, abuse, and violence that occurred on a daily basis right under their noses, but which the victims were afraid to report. **Ibid, pg. 39. In a tribe,** each person has a role to play, and is thereby "valued." "With the enlightenment and the notion that each person is "free," the bonds of community, or living for the tribe were gradually lost or obscured.... [W]e've gone from 'There is nothing but duty [to the group]' to 'There is nothing but self.' And there has to be a point in between." **James H. Billings**, quoted by **Ornish, pg 231.**

15. (pg. 11.) **Real, page 236. Real** also "states that fathers may or may not be necessary for the psychological adjustment of their sons, but that "fathering is definitely necessary for the father's own psychological adjustment!" **Page 323.** See also **Gurian,** who is a worthwhile guide for an understanding of boys (and husbands), and of both their priorities and their language.

16. (pg. 14.) The use of shame to control boys is pervasive. He is shame-hardened at home, at school, and at play. A taunt by a sibling, rebuke by a parent or teacher, or ostracism by classmates come quickly and force-fully. Feelings that violate the Code and produce shame include being troubled, lonely, sad, afraid, or desperate. Boys can seem cheerful and resilient and not even realize themselves that they are hiding their true feelings. **Pollack, pg. 13, 40-41. Pollack** provides eight suggestions for parents to stay connected or to reconnect with their sons: give your son your undivided attention at least once a day, encourage his expression of all of his emotions, avoid teasing or taunting no matter what emotions he expresses, look behind his anger, aggression, or rambunctiousness for the underlying cause, express your love and empathy openly and gener-ously, and let your boys know that they don't need to be "sturdy oaks." **Pg. 47-51.**

17. (pg. 15.) **Rachel Naomi Remen,** quoted by **Ornish, pg. 209.**

2. "No More Tears!" "Everything is Just Fine"

1. (pg. 16.) **Gurian, pg. 24**. See also **Notes, Ch. 1, #11.**

2. (pg. 17.) **ibid, pg. xx.**

3. (pg. 19.) The mocking of children by any adult is especially reprehen-sible! Yet parents, teachers, coaches, and mentors frequently use shame to discipline, to get silence, to get conformity, to toughen children up, to teach a lesson, or to motivate (?). **Nuala O'Faolain**, the best-selling Irish writer, recalling being mocked by her teacher as "Miss Notice-Box," asks "why do adults react so negatively when children try to be noticed? Why do they want the children to "disappear?" **O'Faolain, Pg. 179.**

4. (pg. 19.) The **act of forgiving** (a decision) can be an accomplished fact long before one can **feel forgiving.** We need to confront our "unforgiving feelings" and deal with them honestly. For example, we can work through them by changing our perceptions of what happened, and why the other person acted as they did, so that eventually the feelings will dissipate. **Forgetting** does not necessarily mean forgiving. If we simply repress or suppress our feelings, and don't deal with them, such **buried** unforgiving feelings will come out eventually in a negative, or destruc-tive way.

5. (pg. 21.) My three sons, fortunately, seem to have retained most of their emotional expressivity and empathic sensitivity. A slide that I have used in my talks to parents states that children learn a little from what you tell them; they learn more from watching what you do; but children **always** learn what you carry in your deepest heart. The book written by my

oldest son, **James Louis Schaller**, a psychiatrist with special training to treat children, as well as adolescents and adults, captured what I carry in my deepest heart better than I could ever express it, namely, that I see the loving Fatherhood of God as a model for the absolute necessity for a father's active presence in the nurturing of each human life. James' book has been re-released for the mass market, in English, Korean, Russian, and French.

3. Is Mom Really a Problem?

1. (pg. 22.) Feminist sociologist, Nancy Chodorow, states that being masculine is defined as avoiding the feminine, especially the close-touch world of mother, and warm tender feelings like vulnerability, empathy, and compassion. Quoted in **Pollack, pg. 29. Pollack** asks us to "imagine the sense of loss a boy must feel as he is prodded to separate from the most cherished, admired, and loved person in his life, the shame and embarrassment he often encounters when he's asked to 'act like a man' but doesn't feel equipped to do so, [and] the destructive feelings—self-hatred, inadequacy, loneliness—that become deeply imbedded within the definition he creates of his own nascent masculine identity." **Ibid, pg. 29. Pollack describes shame as the feeling state that accompanies emotional disconnection.** Fear of humiliation and embarrassment for violating the Boy Code makes a boy/man silent about his pain, thus further isolating him. Shame-*phobic* boys (see **Notes, Ch. One, #12**) are exquisitely and unconsciously attuned to any signal of 'loss of face' and will do just about whatever it takes to avoid shame—including avoidance of dependency, with the substitution of bravado, rage or violence. **Ibid, pg. 33.**

2. (pg. 23.) *It's Your Life*, **pg. 221**. In the legend of the Holy Grail, the mother of the boy Perceval hides him away after his father, a knight, is killed. When the boy, some years later, sees a group of knights going by, he is so taken by their appearance that he runs away and joins up with them. His mother then drops dead immediately. Some things never change. The fresh-faced tyke Anakin Skywalker in George Lucas' *Star Wars: Episode I—The Phantom Menace* must be taken from his mother, Shmi Skywalker, in order to begin the process of making him a **Jedi**. The fact that he grows up to become the villain, Darth Vader, should not surprise anyone.

3. (pg. 24.) Many wives express frustration that their husbands are not "more open." Couple-Therapists report that one of the most common reasons wives pursue therapy is their hope that the therapist will be able **to get their husbands to talk more.**

4. Man's Futile Search for Sports Glory

1. (pg. 27.) Sports can be a forum where boys learn how to deal openly with feelings of failure, shame, sadness, and the simple realities of human limitations. Sports can help boys break out from behind the mask of silence. **Pollack, pg. 275.**

2. (pg. 28.). One-third of all high school **football** players are injured, and one-half million high school boys are injured in **all sports** every year. *The Masculine Mystique,* **page 221.**

3. (pg. 28.) Buddha warned that **human desire** is the source of all suffering. **Anthony DeMello** clarifies that thought by saying suffering comes from attaching too much importance to the acquisition of some-one or something. If our "**attachment desire**" is for a person, that person becomes a thing as soon, and as long as, we cannot be happy without them. Quoted by **Schnarch,** *Passionate Marriage.* **Page 425.**

5. Coping with Inadequacy in a Boy/Man's Way

1.(pg. 31.) In **Part Three,** "carried feelings"—the name applied to feelings that children assume or transfer to themselves from their parents out of pity or out of a need to keep their primary caregivers "intact" or function-ing—will be identified as one way in which children try "to parent their parents." Such carried feelings, when retained into adulthood, can have negative, or destructive, effects. See **Notes, Chapter Twenty-One, # 5.**

2. (pg. 31) It has been estimated that there are 1.6 million co-habitant couples, gays and lesbians, in the United States. And, approximately 2 million gay and lesbian parents (including children born in heterosexual unions before their parents "coming out," those born through adoption, through cooperative parenting arrangements, or those resulting from artificial insemination.) **Westheimer and Yagoda. Page 33.**

3. (pg. 32.) **Kimbrell, pg. 281.**

4. (pg. 32.) **Schaller,** *Its Your Life: a Gynecologist's Guide for Taking Control of It,* **pg. 179-181.**

5. (pg. 32.) "Impingement" (**Michael Gurian's** term), or "intergeneration-al violence," (**John Bradshaw or Maggie Scarf**) are terms used for this excessive dependence of parents on their children. In the case of a boy and his mother, this forced and premature assumption of adult emo-tions, or responsibility for an adult level of relating, can generate a son's deep resentment toward all women. Intergenerational violence can also surely be applied to active abuse, either physical or sexual, and passive

abuse (neglect) of those entrusted to parents and other care-givers or mentors.

6. (pg. 33.) Couple therapist **Mark A. Karpel** sees the presence of strong conflict in a relationship as a sign of *vitality*, that is, a hopeful sign. He borrows **Carol Anderson** and **Diane Holder's** phrase "marriages without weather" to describe relationships in which couples rarely argue, have little emotional reactivity, and almost invariably lack passion or intimacy. **Karpel, pg. 46, 87.**

7. (pg. 34.) See **Chapter 14, The Growing-Up Dividend,** for some reasons why "reconnection" to self and family is a better life goal.

8. (pg. 38.) **Ornish, pg. 83.**

PART TWO. THE NATURAL DIFFERENCE OF A WOMAN: FACT OR FICTION

6. When *"Sugar and Spice . . .* Becomes Something Else

1. (pg. 43.) **Schaller,** *Its Your Life: a Gynecologist Challenges You To Take Control.* See also **Chapter Thirty** of this book for a ten-line review.

2. (pg. 43.). **Ibid, pg. 184-200.**

3. (pg. 43.) If the women throughout the world used as few cosmetics and beauty aids as the girls and women of my town of origin (Lancaster, Pennsylvania) used at the time I lived there, some economies, especially America's, might soon collapse. The women of Lancaster generally wore only lipstick. Some did not even use that. The Amish and Mennonite women wore no make-up, and neither Amish men nor Amish women had pockets in their clothing, lest they be tempted to display or accumulate **things**. For the same reasons, they also did not wear trinkets or rings.

4. (pg. 44.) **Ibid, pg. 122-123.**

5. (pg. 44.) **Wolf. Introduction.**

6. (pg. 44.) **Shalit, pg. 182.**

7. (pg. 44.) Feminist **Sally Cline** now refers to the sexual revolution as the "Genital Appropriation Era."
  "What the Genital Appropriation Era actually permitted was more access to women's bodies by more men; what it actually achieved was not a great deal of liberation for women but a great deal of legitimacy for male promiscuity; what it actually passed on to women was the male fragmentation of emotion from body, and the easily internalized schism between genital sex and responsible loving." Quoted by **Shalit, page 192.**

8. (pg. 44.) "If female sexuality is muted compared to that of men, then why must men the world over go to extreme lengths to control and contain it?" **Tangier, pg. 335.** I agree with **Helen Fisher**, who quotes **Euripides** "Man's most valuable trait is a judicious sense of what not to believe," in order to make the point that using questionnaires to compare women's sexuality with men's is a foolish approach. She adds that "women's sex drive is . . . different, more subtle, more complex, and much more misunderstood." Amen! **Fisher** also quotes a Prodigy computer network survey of 14,070 men and women that reported that 74% believed women were more **sensual** than men. **Fisher, pg. 202.**

9. (pg. 45.) **Shalit, pg.147.**

10. (pg. 45.). **Ibid, pg. 39.**

11. (pg. 45.) **Ibid, pg. 46**

12. (pg. 45.) **Ibid, Chapter Nine. Wendy Shalit** makes many assertions with which I totally agree: "Modesty is prudery's true opposite, because it admits that one *can* be moved and issues a special invitation for one man to try. (emphasis author's) **Ibid, pg. 182.** "Without...support...for modesty, a woman who doesn't want to sleep with a man is insulting him." **Ibid, pg. 56.** "When modesty was given a sanction, woman not only had the right to say no to a man's advances, but her good opinion of him was revered." **Ibid, pg. 60.** "Modesty is a reflex, arising naturally to help a woman protect her hopes and guide their fulfillment—specifically, this hope for one man." **Ibid, pg 94.** ". . . [W]hat women will and will not permit does have a profound way of influencing the behavior of an entire society. . . . In a society that respected the power of female modesty, the men were motivated to do what the women wanted." **Ibid, pg. 98.** "Encouraged to act immodestly, a woman exposes her vulnerability and she then *becomes*, in fact, the weaker sex. (italics author's) **Ibid, pg. 108.** "The twin themes of modesty—of sexual vulnerability, and of what-is-about-to-be-revealed being more exciting than what is seen—are as old as humanity itself." **Ibid, pg. 125.** ". . . one of modesty's paradoxes . . . is that it is usually a reflection of self-worth, of having such a high opinion of yourself that you don't need to boast or put your body on display for all to see." **Ibid, pg. 132.**

13. (pg. 46.) *Sexual Personnae.* **Camille Paglia's** thesis, at least as summarized by **David Schnarch**, is that women's erotic development is more restricted than men's by contemporary society, but more evolved sociobiologically (that is, a woman is naturally more erotic). *Passionate Marriage,* **pg. 421.**

14. (pg. 46.) **Real, pg. 318.**

15. (pg. 47.) The relationship proposed is much like those of the heroes and heroines in the best romantic novels written by women. In these relationships of love, the hero and heroine are equally strong. One excellent example of strength, independence, and equality in a loving relationship: Jane Eyre and Edward Rochester in **Charlotte Bronte's** novel.

16. (pg, 48.) Most men welcome opportunities to please their wives. Thus, a wife is being foolish when she presumes that "a good husband should know what I want by now." It's often difficult for a man to separate needs from desires or which need has to be taken care of first. A smart wife will thus clearly separate in her own mind what she **must have** and what she **would like,** so that she can let her husband know her **desires.**

17. (pg. 48.) Quoted by **Valentis and Devane, pg. 96.**

18. (pg. 49.) Both **erotic** and **pornographic** literature is clearly based, by definition, on the fantasy of a woman (or a man) complying with another's sexual desires. One person is **using** another for his/her own pleasure and gratification. For that reason alone, many people—radical feminists especially—condemn them both. However, in women's romantic or erotic novels the compliance is voluntary. The male hero, if he is used at all, is used by the woman for her pleasure to virtually the same degree as she is used by him. The man is never one-up, always equal. In **pornography** the compliance is, by definition, involuntary. The woman (or rarely, a man) is objectified, dehumanized, or used against her wishes. The failure of the people who are most zealous in defending our First Amendment rights to make the **simple** distinction between pornography and what millions of normal women read without taking any offense, allows pornographic materials, that have the potential to influence young minds for life, to be easily available.

19. (pg. 49.) Consider these comments from **Carolyn Heilbrun**, who, in *Reinventing Womanhood,* writes: Woman has convinced herself that man, in whom society and the family invest all power, is mysteriously fragile. He is fragile not before other men, who may fight with him in the street, tackle him on the playing field, contend with him in battle; he is frail before women, and offers as the price of woman's selfhood his own intact sexuality…. Who can do justice to this riddle: man's superiority must not be challenged. It is a fact. At the same time, that superiority is so frail that woman must contrive with man to sustain it … because … sexually, women fear male impotence, fear any blow to the male sexual ego…. [I]n bed … [the male] … is seen in constant danger of intimidation. The penis may collapse, crushing the male ego and the marriage in its flaccidity. Quoted by **Heyn.** *Marriage Shock*, **pg. 173-74. Mae West's**

comment that "a good man is hard to find," would seem to apply here. She also said (neatly) "Too much of a good thing is wonderful." **Heyn** says that men impose all kinds of restrictions on women's use of their sexuality because they fear that allowing a woman to more freely express sexual desire would result in chaos in society. Too many women would abandon their families. On the contrary, she insists, the problem is that **"the denial of this desire really is causing the chaos and abandonment right now." (ibid, page 175.)** Mae West may have been more of a spokesperson for women than she was given credit for, at the time. Her oft-quoted "When I'm good, I'm good, and when I'm bad, I'm even better!" seems pertinent here, too. Both **West** and **Heyn** proclaim that women greatly desire a **sexual** relationship in which the man is "**man enough**" to bring out the best in his woman.

7. Keeping Women in Their Place

1. (pg. 50.) The methods men have devised in the last few centuries to control women's more passionate nature are detailed in **Heyn,** *Marriage Shock.*

2. (pg. 51.) A partial list of **conduct books** from the 18th and 19th centuries in given in **Ibid, pg. 205.**

3. (pg. 51.) **Harvey Green.**

4. (pg. 51.) James Barrie's depiction of the typical English husband in 1900 should be viewed in the context of a society in which the wife's only direct emotional connection to her spouse was as a "cheerleader" for his continuing success as the "breadwinner" in a very hostile and competitive world of men. Certainly, however, the centuries-in-the-making process of separating a man from the land he could call his own, and from his participation in the daily life of the family, should not be blamed on the man being separated! A woman's place in society at the end of the last century is lucidly and movingly presented by **Green.** But, to appreciate a man's emotional isolation from his wife and children, the serious reader has to supply *all* the elements at work at that time.

5. (pg. 51.) **Heyn,** *Marriage Shock,* provides a extensive list of sources for further documentation of women's anger, then and now.

6. (pg. 52.) *It's Your Life,* my previous book makes precisely the point, with considerable documentation, that male control is the source of women's anger. "[Marriage] is an institution, and I can't think of a single institution . . . that has ever truly welcomed women's voices. The culture's cherished belief that marriage is where women flourish, then, is

simply at odds with the reality of women's distress, disorientation, and, yes, depression in it." **Heyn,** *Marriage Shock,* **pg. xiii.**

7. (pg. 52.) Precise statistics vary quite a bit from one reference to another. Census Bureau figures released for the year 1998 revealed that fifty-six percent of all American adults are legally married and living with their spouse. However, more than three times as many divorced adults have not remarried than a generation ago—approximately ten versus three percent— or now nearly twenty million.

8. Oppressor and Oppressed: Is It Still a Core Marriage Dynamic?

1. (pg. 53.) **Scarf's** *Intimate Partners,* **Chapter Eight,** provides a frightening description of the psychological weapons and intimidating power used on a wife and family by a "very successful" bread-winner. **Everyone** in the family was "one-down."

2. (pg. 54.) Before we fault the Judeo-Christian Canons for denying women priestly powers, let's have a few women Presidents to show that we fully accept this concept of equality on a **human** level.

PART THREE: GETTING MARRIAGE RIGHT

9. Brides and Grooms Rarely Get What They Expect

1. (pg. 61.) **Tangier, pg.** *307.*

2. (pg. 61.) Quoted in **Marlin et al, pg 367.**

3. (pg. 62.) The psychology of mate selection was discussed in my previous book, *It's Your Life. Ch. 10-13.*

4. (pg. 64.) **Carter and Sokol, pg. 226.**

5. (pg. 64.) See **Chapter Eleven** for some practical reasons why a woman (usually, but sometimes a man) should clearly distinguish in her own mind between **needs,** that is, essential goods and services she must have, and **wants, or desires,** those goods and services that she would like to have.

6. (pg. 67.) Again, "she" thinks "he's" a prince, but, alas, she discovers that he's only a frog. But, then, he already knew that. He had expected that her love would transform him into a prince. Both are soon disappointed and start the "shame and blame" game.

10. Fall from Grace? "My Fair Lady""The Little Mrs. "My Old Lady"

1. (pg. 69.) I am not asserting that all wives experience "shock" when they realize what marriage demands, just most of them.

11. The Woman *Beside* Every Successful Man

1. (pg. 73.) A wife should never underestimate the good that she can accomplish, with professional help, in dealing with a depressed or addicted husband. **Laura Epstein Rosen and Xavier Francisco Amador** suggest five effective ways to communicate to a depressed man. They advise that you should expect him to avoid any discussion of it, but to let him know you are there for him whenever he wants to talk and that you are concerned. Also the husband's concern with his competency and independent must be honored when you say, for example, "I know how hard things are for you now. If there is anything I can do, let me know." Give your husband multiple choices to describe how he feels, for example, "Are you angry, sad, or worried right now." Share your experiences, but remain watchful of his reactions. Ask him about what actions he could suggest to solve his problems, while showing sympathy and understanding that finding answers may be difficult. **Pg. 130-131.**

2. (pg. 76.) The word **patriarchy** also refers to a social, economic, and political system that has, over the last 500 years, affected the way men relate to each other and to their families: 100's of millions of men have been conscripted (one hundred million in the twentieth century alone) to risk their lives in the military; the system has taken the ownership or use of the land away from individual men or collectives and placed that ownership into the hands of a few owners who did little or no work; and, as a consequence of this institutionalization of power, men had to forsake, for the most part, fellowship with each other; and, finally, these changes forced them to replace their previously affirming relationships with their neighbors with a brutal competition for an always-limited number of monotonous, tedious, onerous, often-dangerous, and demeaning jobs. If they were to fulfill their mandated and primary function of being the family's breadwinner, they had no other recourse.

12. The Core of the Marriage Challenge: Staying Free and Equal

1. (pg. 78.) Obviously, a discussion of "Secular Humanism"—the "common faith" planted in our public schools by **John Dewey** and his follow-

ers—is beyond the scope of this book. The story of the erosion of traditional morality and its replacement in Western societies by humanism's devotion to self, and to "humanity," is lucidly traced by **Vitz**, who also quotes **Donald Campbell's** 1972 address as President of the American Psychological Society: ". . . in psychology . . . the assumption that the human impulses provided by biological evolution are right and optimal . . . and repressive and inhibitory moral traditions are wrong . . . may now be regarded as scientifically wrong. . . . [Moral] traditions may be extremely valuable social-evolutionary inhibitory systems." (**Page 46.**) It is certainly no accident that the sexual revolution of the past forty years is nearly precisely co-existent with the "selfist" theories popularized, or wholesaled to the masses, since the beginning of the 1960's. The relentlessly "anti-family" or "anti-marriage" content of both the sexual liberation and the movement of **selfism** (the latter **Abraham Maslow** gathered into his theory of "self-actualization"), certainly had much to do with the divorce boom of recent decades. Our schools still teach **Maslow's** theories that children are good by nature, and creative, and that the child's priorities should begin with satisfying his/her physiological and "safety" needs. **Maslow** also insisted that caring about anyone else, or even one's own character development, were extraneous considerations. However, **Maslow** himself had come to explicitly repudiate many of his own ideas by 1970, the year in which he died. Although there are no longer courses in the public schools labeled "values clarification," the courses that have been substituted all teach **moral relativism**, that is, the courses stress the processes of "deciding," 'choosing," "decision-making", and avoid any emphasis on content. Strategies are still used that strongly encourage the student to understand "morality" as self-gratification. (**Page 72.**) Regardless of your personal view of modern psychological theories, the belief that psychological techniques can make you happy has been totally rejected.

2. (pg. 79.) **Berne** developed the concept of 'Transactional Analysis" in the late 1950's. The system was then defined and popularized by men like **Harris.**

3. (pg. 79.) **Jean Piaget** stated that a child's first recognition of the first position is the beginning of rational thought. **Harris, page 65-67**.

4. (pg. 80.) *Games People Play* by **Eric Berne**, published first in 1964. This book quickly sold three million copies. In the words of Paul Vitz, "the goal of [Berne's] therapy is to help people become autonomous adults characterized by spontaneity, unbiased awareness of reality, and candid intimacy with others." Quoted by **Vitz, pg. 25**. Obviously, candid intimacy with more than a very few others is not possible, if one uses the correct definition of intimacy. I believe **Berne** was describing closeness, not intimacy.

5. (pg. 81.) When I first learned about TA almost forty years ago, I was not the only one struck by the concept of **the parent.** This psychological reality, this **tape recorder** in our mind, contained all the "truths and principles" those responsible for our care thought we should know and live by. When a child reached five years of age, the parent tapes that were in his mind were said to be **filled. Voltaire,** several centuries ago, postulated much the same idea, saying that once a child has been indoctrinated in a system of beliefs, it became extremely difficult, if not impossible, to change his beliefs. One's parent **tapes** can start playing at any time, including those times when a person was engaged in conversation. In fact, soon after TA became popular, people began deliberately trying to "hook the parent" of their friends or enemies in an effort to find and to expose their biases. In TA, one could only reach an **adult** position by separating the veritable information on those tapes from the false and incorrect data, which was then to be erased so that correct data could replace it. Ever after my learning of this idea that pre-recorded tapes could direct a person's behavior, I have tended in conversation to be sensitive to the appearance of "the parent" into the conversation. When I am able to discern that a person's parent tapes are in "play" position, I try to end the conversation as quickly as I can. Anyone who isn't motivated to shut off the tape player when in conversation, will not benefit from anything they hear from me. **Chapters Ten through Fourteen** of *It's Your Life: a Gynecologist Challenges You to Take Control* could be considered a short course on "creating love," Those pages emphasized that **awareness** of one's true self is key to **beginning** on the path to becoming a better person. This self-awareness is the first step on that path. Total **acceptance** and responsibility for both the good and the bad things one finds in himself (or herself) as a result of the search within, is the **first step to any personal relationship.**

13. *Self-Awareness*—the First Requirement for Reaching Maturity

1. (pg. 89.) As interpreted by **Terence Real,** *I Don't Want to Talk About It, pg 234-6)*

2. (pg. 89.) The urgent need to find the courage to **look within** is taken up again in **Chapter Twenty-Five.**

3. (pg. 90.) **Terence Real** writes "contrary to the overwrought concerns about 'family values', research clearly indicates that boys raised in healthy, loving families without fathers do not reveal appreciable signs of psychological ill health.../[W]hat fathers bequeath to their children is their own unacknowledged pain, and, in instances of violence, an entitle-

ment to inflict it on others." **Ibid, pg. 235.** My point on this subject was expressed in **Chapter Two.** Achieving a more commendable level of maturity should be easier if the father is part of the family, since parenting is a full time task, demanding the best efforts of a male and female role model. In adolescence especially, but even before and after, a father's guidance and protection from our culture's misguided ideals—for both son and daughter—can be critical. Father's can also help to protect their sons and daughters from intimidation and violence, modeling a caring, involved, reverent approach to others, while shielding his daughters from those obscenely destructive aspects of sexual liberation that would rob her of her womanhood. (For more on that last thought, see **Chapter Six, including Notes.**

4. (pg. 90.) Although the figure is variously reported anywhere between thirty-five and fifty percent, probably at least forty percent of our population, at sometime in their lives, would qualify as mentally ill—counting depression, anxiety disorders, substance abuse, and anti-social personality disorders. Men are more than twice as likely to be alcoholics, and four times more likely to have antisocial personality disorders. Ninety-three percent of the prison population are men, although the number of women is increasing. As Adam blamed Eve, and Eve blamed the devil, we often blame all our social ills on the primary caregivers who actively (physical or sexual) or passively (neglect) abuse children. Undeniably, the reaction patterns nurtured in our home, our family of origin, can influence our thoughts, feelings, and actions throughout our lives. Tragically, "children develop pathological attachments to those who abuse and neglect them, attachments that they will strive to maintain even at the sacrifice of their own welfare, their own reality, their own lives." Trauma expert, **Judith Herman**, quoted by **Real, page 205.** See also **Notes, Chapter Five, # 5;** and **Chapter Twenty-One, # 5.** Since children see the parent as necessary for their own survival, they will "take on" any parental problem as their own, in order that the parent can be kept functioning. Viewing themselves with contempt for the parental shame and guilt that they have transferred to themselves, abused and neglected children bring to adult life these "carried feelings," and continue to abuse and neglect themselves. Such children can carry into their adult lives **both aspects of a sado-masochistic parent-child relationship**. Thus, they can become sadistic abusers, instead of victims. The physical or sexual abuse, or the neglect we experienced in our own family of origin, cannot be changed now. But, the environment that we provide our own children *can* be changed. In fact, it is vital to our common future that we educate ourselves on the **gender-specific requirements** for raising our children—protecting both our sons and our daughters from narrow and dangerous ideals, that have been spotlighted in **Part One** (for boys) and

Part Two (for girls), and shielding both from the violence that assails each sex, although in nearly-totally different forms. Obviously, despite what has been said in **this note** and the one preceding, if I believed your past **determined** your future, this book would have never been written.

5. (pg. 90.) **Konrad Lorenz, Niki Tinbergen, Rene Dubois, Ludwig von Bertalanffy, and Scott Peck** are just a few of the experts who postulate aggression, a **sin,** as a **basic** human tendency. **Vitz, page 37.)**

14. Some "Growing-Up" Dividends

1. (pg. 93.) Like the theories of Secular Humanism, the theories of **psycho-sexual** development are beyond the scope of this book. Obviously, we are always free to be biased (or use our parent tapes) when dealing with fundamental principles that could change our way of thinking or our life choices. There is always the possibility that we will see, understand, or remember only what we like or agree with—ideas that agree or reinforce our biases. Since **Carl Jung** and his concept of self-realization, a steady stream of theories of human development have been promulgated which promised that **full** psycho-sexual development would free a person from most of his anxieties or fears. These theories propose that such full development would be marked by the absence of most negative feelings and emotions. The hope was offered that belief in yourself and your abilities would lead you to "salvation" in this life, that is, to success. You could "create" your own happiness. At least, that was the theory of "selfism," which has dominated 20th century thought in both psychology and in religion. Obviously, as a follower of a Judeo-Christian Tradition, my judgment is that the "self" is the problem, not the solution. Throughout this book, **the exhortation to accept yourself always includes the acknowledgment that the guilt and sinfulness which we find within us is of our own making."** Maturity, or "differentiation," like "perfection" is a goal, a quest, or an ideal, which no one ever achieves. That humbling fact does not prevent the goal from providing a beacon of light pointing out the path to intimacy and to a good measure of joy and satisfaction (if we work at it). Despite the clarity of the path, we can still choose, at any given moment, to be greedy, proud, or selfish. The foolishness of making "psychological development" an end in itself, as if that would make you happy, even if no one else in your life benefited, eventually made millions lose heart and lose faith in themselves. As **Vitz** says so rightly, "psychologically creating your own worth is like printing your own currency—it leads to false prosperity; inflation followed by depression." **Pg. 131.** As a result of selfish principles, the men and women of our society, like Narcissis of Greek mythology, are starving to death for lack of "real" connections. Unfortunately, once people came to realize

that psychology was not religion, many also lost confidence in the benefits of becoming more mature. This book is about "psychological development," that is, becoming mature, for the sake of ourselves **and** others. Even those who are "religious" must add to knowing, loving, and serving God the goal of being "nice"—being good neighbors, spouses, parents, and, "kind" in their relationships. The "mature" people that we propose as a worthwhile ideal, live these qualities. They are also people that you would love to have as friends. *Vitz' wide-ranging and scholarly discussion of the most influential minds in the area of psychology, and of the part religion has played in influencing psychological thought (or vice-versa) over the past two centuries, might help to spare you from the tragic consequences of making any psychology your religion.*

2. (pg. 93.) The **initial versions** of **Anne Frank's Diary** (published circa 1951) contained few passages describing her pubertal sexual awakenings (presumably because the "world" at that time was not ready for it). This first diary did contain many angry or unflattering comments about her mother.

The **B version**, that is, the diary that was rewritten by Anne herself at the age of fourteen (and released in print in 1991) had many sexual references but retained few of the critical remarks about her mother.

The recent disclosure on the *Internet* of the contents of **the five pages on the "B" version that Anne's father withheld** goes a long way in explaining why Anne's judgment of her mother changed. Those hidden pages revealed Anne's new understanding of her mother's **lot** in marriage, that is, to have a husband who didn't love her in the way she wanted and needed to be loved. Having been rejected as a suitor by the wealthy family to which his first love belonged, he chose Anne's mother as a "suitable" or convenient candidate for providing him with children.

3. (pg. 94.) "Both **Fromm** and **Moustakas** assert that the ability to be alone is a crucial precondition to the ability to love." Quoted by **Schnarch,** *Constructing The Sexual Crucible,* **pg. 108.**

4. (pg. 94.) **Marlin et al, pg. 357.**

5. (pg. 94.) **David Schnarch** outlines what differentiation implies: "the ability to maintain one's sense of separate self in close proximity to a partner; non-reactivity to other's people's reactivity; self-regulation of emotionality so that judgment can be used; [and] the ability to tolerate pain for growth." *Constructing the Sexual Crucible,* **page 114.**

6. (pg. 95.) **Schnarch** devotes sixty pages to the definition of intimacy, beginning with an emphasis on what intimacy is **not**. Rejecting the idea that **other-validated intimacy** is intimacy at all, he presents a "rare as hen's teeth" clinical model of **self-validated intimacy** as the **highest ideal** to be sought. **Disclosure reciprocity** (translation: you tell me your secrets

and I will tell you mine) is definitely **not part of the intimacy ideal** which **Schnarch** describes. An alliance between yourself and the most important other in your life, built on the mutual trust that the other will accept your deep, secret, and private self, and then respond by disclosing for your acceptance an equivalent depth of her secret self, is an attempt to build **other-validated intimacy,** which is not intimacy at all, because it is not unconditional. Quoting **Malone and Malone**: (on **page 92**) "There are many words used to attempt to describe the functional (useful) human relationship . . . love, openness, commitment, genuine closeness, supportiveness, affirming awareness, mature relationship. We speak of being yourself with others, of honestly relating. . . . [Though] . . . these terms . . . are subtly different . . . [and] . . . each describe some particular aspect of relationship. . . . [W]e use them . . . interchangeably: to be open is to be aware; to be aware is to be mature, honest, and committed in relationship; to be all of these is to be genuinely close. This is not true. . . . Many . . . of these different aspects of relationship . . . are not at all what we mean by the term *intimate."* **Schnarch** rejects any connection between intimacy, on the one hand, and, the revealing of our true, authentic, or "core self" to another as a means to obtain their acceptance, or their validation of our worth. Seeking someone to reassure us that we are worth loving, or "seeking a reflected sense of self", is other-validated intimacy, and is **not** the highest ideal he proposes for the "select few" willing to fully grow up. It is **entirely wrong** to say that intimacy must involve trust, caring, acceptance, commitment or tenderness, since **any conditions** or needs can impede intimacy. This is not to deny, however, that these virtues make intimacy possible or more likely. The intimacy **David Schnarch** proposes is definitely not for everyone, nor for anyone all the time. Those individuals whose attachment to their primary caregivers was problematic can experience intense anxiety and resort to extreme avoidance when invited to be intimate. Intimacy can bring disquiet, turbulence, discomfort, and painful challenges for more growth to anyone, especially to those for whom honest disclosures are hurtful. A fear of being hurt can lead lovers to set limits on the level of intimacy, but in doing that they risk losing their skill of connecting intimately. In fact, expecting never to be challenged by our partner, or refusing to be, is a direct **impediment to intimacy**. Taking care not to "hurt" someone by our self-disclosures may be loving, but it is not intimate. "Caretaking is a necessary affirming and sustaining part of a relationship; it maintains the status quo. Intimacy facilitates change, but not necessarily short-term stability." **(Ibid, page 104.)**

7. (pg. 96.) Quoting **Masters, Johnson, and Kolodny**: ". . . Intimate partners usually reach an early understanding about the boundaries of their closeness, permitting their relationship to continue under a mutually agreeable set of expectations." **(ibid, page 100.) Schnarch** lets **Malone**

and **Malone** describe the subjective experience of intimacy as quite distinct from closeness: Few of us could sit in a closet with another person for any length of time without learning a great deal about that person. In the closet our own awareness is focused on the other while we are close. But in some rare moments, in that shared space of our closet and in the presence of the other, we may experience ourselves in some new, different, and more profound way. This is *intimacy*. When I am close, I know you; when I am intimate, I know myself. When I am close, I know you in your presence; when I am intimate I know myself in your presence. Intimacy is a remarkable experience. Usually I know myself only in my aloneness, my dreams, my personal space. But to feel and know myself in the presence of another is enlivening, enlightening, joyful, and most of all, freeing. I can be who I am freely and fully in the presence of another. It is the only true freedom we have as human beings. . . . (*quoted* **Ibid, pg. 123.**)

8. (pg. 96.) Few married people, or the professionals who counsel them, realize that developing these abilities could not only save the marriage but enhance their tolerance for intense intimacy, including sexual intimacy. "Aversion" to sexual intimacy is a matter of degree—what a person's emotional comfort zone is—and not a matter for most of us of being **functional or dysfunctional**. The general public, and the experts, fail to recognize that although almost all "normal" people flee from intense intimacy, sexual or otherwise, and clearly do not want to risk it, they are nevertheless capable of vastly increased intimacy tolerance, again by working to differentiate.

9. (pg. 97.) Our reluctance to hold out a **common ideal for both genders** is reinforced by the national belief that achieving "independence" in our lives, always touted as a male ideal, is more praiseworthy than the feminine talent for getting along with people. Nevertheless, the skill of acting intimately or exchanging highly satisfying and fulfilling acts of love are possible even for a man who cannot develop many of those qualities we ascribe primarily to women. A woman's attempts to get her husband to share his secret feelings, and confess to fear, weakness, doubt, or sadness, is usually perceived by the husband as criticism, specifically for his "not being more like a woman" **Chapters Two and Three** provide reasons why sending your husband the message that "he should be more like a woman" might backfire.

15. Simple Recipes for Marital Disaster

1. (pg. 99.) I use the word *giving* to each other, in referring to loving acts, because that is the word that is always used when one is describing what lover's do. When thinking about love and intimacy, however, always

substitute the word *sharing.* In using the skill of intimacy in loving, you do not lose anything or give anything away, but rather *share as much of yourself as you can—totally, deeply, and without any reservations.* You can, of course, always give something of yourself away if you choose, but that is not going to enhance your skill in being intimate, and, in fact, is a dangerous decision for lovers. See **Notes, Chapter Fourteen,** and **Notes, Chapter Sixteen, # 5.. Giving in** is what some wives (or husbands) do early and often in their marriages and then wonder why they come to feel used, and are resentful. (See the case of Ned and Beth, **Chapter Twenty-One.**)

2. (pg. 107.) *It's Your Life: a Gynecologist's Guide for Taking Control of It,* Schaller, pg. xvii-xix.

3. (pg. 107.) The excessive need for "closeness," referred to as "separation anxiety," is a destructive force in millions of marriages. Due to the pressures to think and feel alike, there is little individual growth, as too much of the energy and vitality is needed to maintain closeness and avoid differences and disagreements. Such couples, despite feeling bored, distressed or smothered by the sameness, consider closeness essential for maintaining the relationship.

4. (pg. 110.) Dean Ornish presents the scientific basis for the healing power of love. **Chapter Two.** See **Notes, Understanding the Message… #4.**

5. (pg. 113.) **Schaller,** *It's Your Life,* **Chapters Ten and Eleven** describe how to become the person you want to be.

6. (pg. 114.) See **Ibid, pg. 171-72,** for **Daphne Rose Kingma's** twenty-five ways a wife can guide her husband to **reconnection.**

16. Re-Searching What You Want From Marriage

1. (pg. 120.) The assertion that only one of twenty married couples get past the angry, or conflicted phase (there need not be any **apparent** anger) is found consistently in the literature on marriage counseling. **(Hendrix, pg. 81-82.)**

2. (pg. 121.) Focus groups committed to solving the problems of emotional isolation try to encourage members to identify their feelings and eventually disclose them. Then, each member is to learn how to listen to, and care about, the feelings of others in the group. Eventually, the members should develop the motivation, and the ability to exchange feelings with someone in their life who is outside the (safety of) the group. Unfortunately, keeping the group focused on the commitments just outlined requires a considerable degree of discipline, as breeches of

confidence, advice giving or problem-solving, impatience, and intolerance, as well as serious personality disorders within the membership,
can totally subvert the process of exchanging personal feelings.

3. (pg. 123.) Three chapters of my previous book *It's* <u>*Your*</u> *Life* were
devoted to ways to develop communication skills. (**Chapters 10-13.**) My
point in this chapter is that it is desirable to begin by developing personal
integrity, especially accepting one's own feelings so that the heart can be
keep "open." The only choices in communicating are to attack, to avoid,
or to confide or collaborate. Only the final two choices are desirable, but
they require an open heart. Communicating with a closed heart is a
weapon of destruction in a long-term relationship. See especially **Donovan. (ed.)**

4. (pg. 124.) **Schnarch,** *Constructing the Sexual Crucible,* **pg. 128.**

5. (pg. 125.) See **Ibid, Chapters Four and Five,** for a clear distinction
between "closeness" and "intimacy."

6. (pg. 125.) "And what of marriage?
      "Let there be spaces in your togetherness. And let the winds of the
heavens dance between you. "Love one another, **but make not a bond of
love:** Let it rather be a moving sea between the shores of your souls. "Fill
each other's cup, but drink not from one cup. Give one another of your
bread, but eat not from the same loaf. "Sing and Dance together and be
joyous, but let each one of you be alone, Even as the strings of a harp are
alone though they quiver with the same music. "Give your hearts, **but
not into each other's keeping.** For only the hand of Life can contain your
hearts. "And stand together, yet not too near together: for the pillars of
the temple stand apart, and the oak tree and the cypress grow not in each
other's shadow." *The Prophet.* **Kahlil Gibran.** 1923/1982. **Pg. 16-17**.
Quoted by **Schnarch,** *Constructing the Sexual Crucible.* **Pg. 129-130.**
(emphases are **Schnarch's**)

17. Keeping Your Own Candle Burning

1. (pg. 127.) **Hendrix, pg. 60-61.**

2. (pg. 128.) For example, **Mark 12:23** and **Hosea 6:1-6.**

18. Why Do So Many Things Go Wrong for So Many Wonderful People

1. (pg. 138.) How, you ask, could a sixteen-year-old boy presume to write
papers criticizing the state of the American family? My initial interest in

the subject began at about age five, when the oldest of my nine sisters left home to get married. I wondered how she could give up all the fun we had together in our home and neighborhood to live where there were only going to be two people in the home and the neighbors would all be strangers. When I became an "altar boy" at age ten, one of my regular duties on Saturday mornings, was to serve at weddings. Usually, I was given the job of moving the bride's long train each time she and the groom went to the altar. I started making mental notes of who the brides were. I would remember them and look for them and their husbands at subsequent parish events. What struck me was the marked decline in the brides apparent "happiness level" after the first year or two of marriage. The vivacious and joyous bride often became the sad and tired house- wife who appeared not to care too much about anything. **Betty Friedan,** in 1963, captured the ennui of the American housewife and revitalized the feminist movement. **Nuala O' Faolain**, in her 1996 Irish bestseller, chronicled the 1940's to 1990's in Ireland, and presented more or less the same picture of enslaved, trapped, controlled, submissive, abused, and **silenced** women. **O' Faolain's** word for Irish wives was "entombed." Very early in my life, the history of marriage and family life became one of my fascinations. By the time I was sixteen I had read hundreds of books and articles. As with anything else, the more one knows about a subject the more interesting the subject becomes. One thing that seemed to come up whenever family problems were discussed was the tremen- dous benefit to the family cohesion and spirit brought about by eating together. The war initiated working patterns that often interfered with the dining schedules, and these changes (for example, shift work) be- came permanent. The switch to larger, centralized elementary and sec- ondary schools, and an assortment of after-school programs caused many students, especially in high school, to miss even the evening meal with the rest of the family. The trend toward fewer and fewer meals together continues to this day. As pointed out in the text, even if the father is home for meals, he is often so tired that his presence is a negative influence on conversation and sharing. As **O'Faolain** writes, in speaking of her father and the family of nine surviving children, "father dumbly refused the ordinary efforts of being a father" and that included ever being home for dinner. **Pg. 156.**

2. (pg. 139.) **E.C.Graff** supports the contention that "we have never gotten marriage right." In fact, one of her most noteworthy jibes points out that it took the power of the Church three hundred years, at the beginning of the second millenium, to make the wife's consent necessary for a valid marriage. **Pg. 242.**

19. *Who Can We Blame?*

1. (pg. 141.) **Chapters Ten-Twelve** of *It's Your Life* summarize how modern men and women select a mate, and how to make sure the process works to their benefit. These chapters contain advice for "handling past mistakes" in the selection process.

2. (pg. 142.) See **Chapter Twenty -Four** for more comments on "burying the past" and the problem of "carried feelings." See also **Notes, Chapter Twenty-One, # 5.**

3. (pg. 143.) In **Chapter Twenty-three, great sex** will be presented as one of the fruits of a **great marriage,** built on integrity or authenticity or honesty. **Great Sex is not a requirement for a great marriage.** Some men may need *Viagra* because of high blood pressure or diabetes, but many more need it for psychological reasons, especially their fear of failure. See **Chapters Twenty-One** through **Twenty-Three.**

20. The Communication Games Married People Play

1. (pg. 144.) **Karpel, pg. 40.** For the "focus" and "goals" of communication, **Ibid, pg. 40-44.**

2. (pg. 145.) **Ibid, pg. 43.**

3. (pg. 145.) See *Constructing the Sexual Crucible,* especially Chapters Nine and Ten for the problems and politics of "human desire." **Schnarch** refers to the commonplace marital switch from "playing with the spouse's genitals to playing with his or her mind."

4. (pg. 147.) "Touching" someone, as any good doctor knows, can be a powerful way to heal. Touching a mate often can be an effective way to relieve their sense of loneliness or isolation. Only British couples touch each other in public less than American couples do. French couples touch fifty-five times more. French parents and children also touch each other three times more frequently than in American families. **Ornish, pg. 7, 140.** How often do we see married couples hold hands, hug, or kiss in public?

5. (pg. 149.) See **J. A. Schaller, pg. 206, for several references.**

21. The Problem: *Foreplay* Includes Everything But ...

1. (pg. 150.) They see the question as evidence of men's exasperation at "women's ingratitude and excessive neediness." But the fashionable

feminist proclamation that men, even apart from anything sexual, "just don't understand what women want," is simply not correct. Men _know_ what women want, but most of them choose not to act on their knowledge, as part of the *normal marital sadism,* which will be featured in some examples in **Part Three. (See also Chapter 30.)**

2. (pg. 152.) *Mars and Venus on a Date page 88-91.* Men understand or attend to information received audibly much better if it comes in from their "hearing side"—that right or left hemisphere connected with their awareness. With women it rarely matters from which side the sound comes from—they **hear** it—that is, they note it or consider it equally well in both sides of the brain. *You Just Don't Understand: Men and Women in Conversation,* **Deborah Tannen**'s analysis of "cross-cultural" gender differences, especially the incredibly different use of language between the sexes launched two decades of books on the male/female differences. For example, she contrasts a woman's need for "rapport" talk with a man's aversion for "unfocused" discussion. "Report" talk, given "one-way" without interruptions and devoid of any subjectivity or personal feelings, is a man's decided preference. Another helpful work of **Deborah Tannen**: *That's Not What I Meant! How Conversational Style Makes or Breaks Your Relationship With Others.* A most common marital scenario resulting from ignorance of gender difference: It is a rare husband who will connect his wife's sexual responsiveness to his **seeing** her and to his **listening** and realize that his wife will open her heart to him if he looks and listens.

3. (pg. 153.) **Paul Tournier,** the noted Swiss psychiatrist and author, in his forty-eight page classic work on marriage, makes precisely this point when he writes that a man who claims he "understands his wife" has given up any attempt to deepen his relationship or to seek intimacy. **Victor Hugo,** an eminently successful lover by all accounts, advised, "when a woman is speaking to you, listen to what she says with her eyes." **Reagan and Phillips, pg. 196.**

4. (pg. 153.) When a spouse says "I feel **that** . . . you are wrong," or, "I feel **like** . . . you don't understand," he (or she) is expressing his thoughts, not his feelings. One of the most useful insights to come out of the marriage encounter movement, was this distinction between exchanging thoughts and exchanging feelings. Men generally will not react negatively when a wife shares her feelings but if she expresses a critical thought the result is usually unpleasant. It is not that men typically overtly fight or resist an adverse criticism. They simply withdraw into silence. See **Ornish, pg. 101-119** ("Words Matter."), for a list of fourteen common feelings, and more on the vital difference between sharing thoughts and sharing feelings.

5. (pg. 154.) The clinical equivalent of "carried feelings" is "projective identification." One person injects, puts into, or transfers to another person those aspects of himself that he cannot or will not accept or handle. For clinical examples, see **Real, pg. 206-208.** See also **Notes, Chapter Five #1, and Notes, Notes, Chapter Thirteen, # 4, and Notes, Chapter Twenty-One, #5.** Couples respond automatically or unconsciously to each other all the time as part of what has been referred to as the "unconscious matrix" of a marriage. **Karpel, Chapter One.** The style of relating that a couple manifests, especially in the intimacy they can tolerate, has been unconsciously pre-determined by their relationships with their primary caregivers in infancy. In fact, Murray Bowen's term "unconscious complementarity" refers to the way mates are selected, that is, the internalized early-life experiences of relating are "re-awakened" when the adult unconsciously spots a "match." **Ibid, pg. 12, 13, 53.**

22. Work, Sports, Sex—Do Husbands Ever Think of Anything Else?

1. (pg. 156.) A survey of "happily married couples" in 1978, by **Frank, Anderson, and Rubinstein** noted that 40% of men report erectile or ejaculatory dysfunction and 63% of women report arousal or orgasmic dysfunction. One sexual problem—performance anxiety—will be a topic in **Chapter Twenty-Three.** Performance anxiety most often affects the husband, since an erection is impossible to fake, while women confess to faking orgasm whenever it serves their purposes. Since impotence is clearly connected, whether by cause or effect, to a man's sense of adequacy, a solution that works to end the excessive anxiety that aborts his ability to achieve an erection (or his wife, an orgasm), should also be effective in solving some of the non-sexual marital "hang-ups," that result from a husband's judgment that he is "one-down" to his wife.

2. (pg. 157.) Twentieth Century Psychiatry and Psychology tended almost exclusively **to pathologize** every patient, that is, to diagnose them as having a mental abnormality. Thus, the rationale, or reason to treat, was to correct their deviations from a theoretical "normal." The last two decades has seen a decided shift to a "non-pathologic" approach in which no one, especially those who are seeking "couple-therapy," are ever blamed or faulted for anything,

3. (pg. 158.) This term postmodern **usually** translates as one word—now—an adjective, that comes after the noun. For example, if you read about "post-modern ethics, you are probably reading about ethics this year, not necessarily ten years ago. **Paul Vitz** says "to a substantial degree, the concept *postmodern* often means *anti-modern.* " **Pg. 166.** The

bottom line in all this is that couples **now** are just as confused as their grandparents were. The only difference is that now the consequences of the confusion are more tragic.

23. Some Couples Don't Just Get *Older,* They Also Get *Better*

1. (pg.162.) **Masters and Johnson:** *Human Sexual Response &. Human Sexual Inadequacy.*

2. (pg. 163.) The brilliant contributions of **Masters and Johnson** are not being denigrated here. As fearless pioneers in the effort to deal with a world of seemingly sexually-incompatible or sexually-dysfunctional people they attempted to define and address in a fairly rigorous approach the normal and abnormal human reproductive physiology and function. They never tried to include in their studies such abstractions as values, passion, intimacy, or eroticism.

3. (pg. 165.) In the first-half of the twentieth century, in a town near San Francisco, there lived a jazz pianist whose **success with women** made him a legend in his own time. When he was finally convinced that he should share the secret of his success, this erstwhile Casanova confessed "the body and soul of a woman is so beautiful to me, that I **always cry** when she reveals herself to me. "Once my tears touch her body, she can't stop trying to show her appreciation!"

4. (pg. 168.) *Constructing the Sexual Crucible,* **pg. 371**. (See also **Schnarch,** in **Acknowledgements** and **Recommended Reading**.)

5. (pg. 169.) Both of the books written by Schnarch provide plenty of clinical examples of couples substituting mind games for sex play.

6. (pg. 171.) See **Notes, Chapter Fourteen, # 5 and # 6.**

7. (pg. 173.) **Schnarch,** *Constructing the Sexual Crucible, pg. 371.* These suggestions will not work as well for those who subscribe to the "piece of flesh" school of sex. This adolescent and narrow-minded, reptilian-mammalian approach to sexuality *ignores* what "everybody" knows (sic), namely, that ninety-nine percent of the pleasure in sex is a consequence of what you have going on in your head! Another important point should be pertinent: If the wife comes into marriage with her "modesty" and "womanhood" still intact (as **Wendy Shalit** goes to great lengths to neatly explain), when she does reveal herself to "the one," there is definitely more eroticism or fun invoked, since modesty is really the opposite of prudery. **Chapter Ten**. See also the five quotes from the same book, found in the **Notes for Chapter Six** of this book.

8. (pg. 173.) Gender politics has not only corrupted the male physician-female patient dialogue, but it has also sabotaged the media's handling of each gender's points of view. Censorship and biased networking, especially in the publishing and promotion of books on gender issues and relationships, as well as any discussion of these issues on television, plays a major role in what has become a "big time" propaganda war. Susan Faludi's *Backlash: The Undeclared War Against American Women* and Warren Farrell's *Women Can't Hear What Men Don't Say* provide a disturbing picture of the ways the media can create its own version of the truth. Andrew Kimbrell's *The Masculine Mystique* and the fifteen essays assembled by editors Julia E. Hanigberg and Sara Riddick, *Mother Troubles: Rethinking Contemporary Maternal Dilemmas*, present more restrained points of view and supply plenty of information on each gender's *unique* problems.

24. Yes, We *Can* Turn Our Marriages Around

1. (pg. 175.) The concept of **carried feelings**, to which I refer is an extremely important idea to try to understand. See **Chapter Five, Notes, Chapter Five, # 1, #5, Chapter Twenty-Four, Notes, Chapter Twenty-One, # 5.** Most of us have sadness, anger, pain, anxiety or doubts that are inappropriate for us in that they are not being generated by anything that happened to us. They are "burdens" our parents shared or somehow gave to us or that we relieved them from carrying, lest they be damaged or hurt to the extent that they couldn't guarantee our safety.

2. (pg. 175.) **Real, Pg. 206-209**.

3. (pg. 176.) **Peggy Claude-Pierre's** book is recommended for anyone involved with persons who have eating disorders.

4. (pg. 177.) Challenging people to accept responsibility **for what they do** is not at all the same as telling them **what to do.** People of all ages typically resist **directives** of all kinds, rather than conform. Often, they resent them. On the other hand, simply showing someone **what he/she is doing** may work wonders in effecting change. See also **Donovan (ed.), pg. 139.**

25. Needed: An Open Mind and a Change of Heart

1. (pg. 181.) **Notes, *Understanding the Message*, #3.**

2. (pg. 185.) (paraphrase) **Alan Benner**, quoted in **Reagan and Phillips**. **Nancy Sinatra**, in the Introduction of her book about her late father, says "he [was] a little crazy…because 'the overly concerned and sincere drive

themselves crazy'." I do not think the "overly concerned and sincere" have to drive themselves, or anyone else, crazy, though, because of their priorities, they usually do.

27. Summarizing Our New Understanding of Relationships

1. (pg. 192.) **Chapters Eleven through Thirteen** in my book *It's Your Life: A Gynecologist Challenges You To Take Control* stressed that the amount of our core self we own or master—the extent of our character development—is invariably **matched** by the person we select for a long-standing intimate relationship. This does not mean that we marry people "like" us. In fact, the person we select often seems our opposite. Men seeking greater insights into the reasons they choose to marry the women they did, what life is like for many women, and what women expect from men, would profit from reading *It's Your Life* in its entirety. (Perhaps, pages twenty-six to ninety-six, and pages 122 to 140, which have to do more with physiology than anything else, could be skipped.) I believe that men are just as anxious as their wives to improve their relationships. In fact, the affirming phone calls from men who have read my previous book and liked it, have provided the final inspiration for this one.

2. (pg. 193.) I hope **Johnny Mercer** won't turn over in his grave when he reads how I've used the words of the song he put at the top of the long-running radio show of the 40's and 50's, "Your Hit Parade."

PART FOUR. A LEGACY OF LOVE

28. Putting the Realities of Love Together

1. (pg. 201.) Support for that assertion is very graphically presented by **Bawer.** References to some of the horrible atrocities committed by Christians, especially against each other, were included in my previous book, *It's Your Life,* **pg. 302.**

2. (pg. 201.) Quoted by **Robert A. F. Thurman** in **Ornish, pg. 212.**

29. Becoming Heroes, Again

1. (pg. 202.) *Man's Search for Meaning.* Quoted by **Padovani, pg. 16.** Several ideas should have become clear in the course of reading this book, tying pain and suffering, healing, love, and intimacy into one very interconnected basket. See **next Note.**

2. (pg. 202.) See **Chapter 31** of my text for more on the "how." **Rachel Naomi Remen** points out that pain and suffering should lead to wisdom primarily because it motivates us to search for **meaning.** "Meaning is a function of the heart. . . . [W]hen we can experience not only our own heart, but the hearts of other people, we feel safe. . . . The more meaning we find, the less stress we feel….We suffer, not because we're in pain. The real suffering is that we feel we are in pain <u>alone</u>. Once you have the experience that you *matter*, that you are *seen*, you have . . . strength [from that] forever." Quoted by **Ornish, pg. 204. Ornish** expresses this truth in a slightly different way: "When we love someone and feel loved by them, somehow along the way our suffering subsides, our deepest wounds begin healing, our hearts start to feel safe enough to be vulnerable and open a little wider. We begin experiencing our own emotions and the feelings of those around us." **Pg. 96.**

3. (pg. 203.) **Real, pg. 322.**

4. (pg. 205.) My three and a half years living and traveling in Europe lead me to conclude that French and Italian men are every bit as demanding and self-centered as American men can be. Two European families we knew well were "relieved" and "glad" when the father in the family died, because he was so controlling! The patients who were sexually and physically abused in ways that I chose not to report earlier in the chapter on abuse, because of the horrifying dimensions of that abuse, were not abused by American men.

30. Giving Your Wife What She Wants

1. (pg. 206.) Writer and researcher, **Mary Block Jones,** used the responses to her nationwide survey of wives to produce a book listing four-hundred things wives **don't want.** One example: a husband who blew his nose in his shorts before his morning shower, then left the shorts on the bathroom floor!

2. (pg. 206.) Quoted by **Ornish, pg. 219.**

3. (pg. 207.) **Real, pg. 307**

4. (pg. 208.) "The essence of [' husband'] is . . . obligation. . . . [A] bonding to both family and nature through a clear appreciation of the responsibility inherent in the role of provider, caretaker, and steward. As men have increasingly been wrenched from their families and the earth upon which they worked, they have lost the appreciation for what it meant to live the role of the steward of the land and caretaker of our resources. Over the generations there has been a considerable erosion in the sus-

taining identity of the role of husband." **Robert Mannis**, quoted by **Kimbrell, pg. 300.**

31. In the Absence of Love

1. (pg. 213.) Quoted in **Ornish, pg. 204.**

2. (pg. 214.) **William Pollack** explains how parents can help create schools where boys can 'keep their voices' and help prevent the school violence that has become a fact of life in America. "It doesn't take a lot of extra funding or personnel to set up effective peer support groups, "social centers," discussion groups. . . . I believe every school should ask itself: 'If a student in our school is unhappy about something in his or her life, school-related or otherwise, would that student have a place he or she would *want* to go to talk about that unhappiness?' If the answer to that question is 'no,' the school probably has not met its responsibilities." **Pg. 262-271.**

3. (pg. 214.) Quotation from **pages 171-2,** of *It's* Your *Life: a Gynecologist Challenges You to Take Control.*

4. (pg. 215.) **Ornish,** *pg. 99.* To support his assertion that once a man makes his decision to seek more love and intimacy he will quickly find unexpected helps and resources, **Ornish** quotes the Christian Bible: "Ask and you shall receive, seek and you shall find, knock and it shall be opened unto you." **(Matthew 7:7)**

Bibliography

Angier, Natalie. *Woman: An Intimate Geography*. Houghton Mifflin: Boston. (1999.)

Bawer, Bruce. *Stealing Jesus: How Fundamentalism Betrays Christianity*. Crown Publishers: New York. 1997.

Berne, Eric. *Games People Play*. Ballantine: New York. 1985.

Block, Peter. *The Empowered Manager*. Jossey Bass Inc.: San Francisco. 1986

Boteach, Shmuley. *Kosher Sex*. Doubleday: New York. 1999.

Bowen, Murray. *Family Therapy in Clinical Practice*. Aronson: New York. 1978

Bradshaw, John. *Creating Love: the Next Great Stage of Growth*. Bantam: New York. 1992.

Bryan, Mark. *The Prodigal Father: Reuniting Fathers and Their Children*. Crown: New York. (Potter) 1997.

Canfield, Jack, and Mark Victor Hansen. *The Aladdin Factor*. Berkley Books: New York. 1995.

Carter, Steven, Julia Sokol. *Men Like Women Who Like Themselves (And Other Secrets That Smartest Women Know*. Delacorte: New York. 1996.

Chodorow, Nancy. *The Reproduction of Mothering*. University of California Press: Berkeley, CA. 1978.

de Silva, Alvaro (ed.) *G.K. Chesterton on Men & Women, Sex, Divorce, Marriage & the Family*. Ignatius Press: San Francisco. 1990.

Donovan, James E. (ed.) *Short-term Couple Therapy*. Guilford: New York. 1999.

Faludi, Susan. *Backlash: The Undeclared War Against American Women*. Dell: New York. 1992.

Farrell, Warren. *Women Can't Hear What Men Don't Say: Destroying Myths, Creating Love.* Tarcher/Putnam: New York, 1999

Fisher, Helen. *The First Sex: The Natural Talents of Women and How They Are Changing the World.* Random House: New York. 1999.

Forward, Susan, and Joan Torres. *Men Who Hate Women & the Women Who Love Them.* Bantam: New York. 1986.

Frankl, Viktor. *Man's Search for Meaning: An Introduction to Logo-therapy.* Beacon: Boston. 1992.

Friday, Nancy. *My Mother, My Self: The Daughter's Search for Identity.* Dell: New York. 1987.

Friedan, Betty. *The Feminine Mystique.* Dell: New York. 1984.

Graff, E.J. *What Is Marriage For? The Strange Social History of Our Most Intimate Institution.* Beacon Press: Boston. 1999.

Gray, John. *Mars and Venus on a Date: A Guide for Navigating the 5 Stages of Dating to Create a Loving and Lasting Relationship.* Harper Paperbacks: New York. 1997.

_____. *Men, Women, and Relationships: Making Peace with the Opposite Sex.* Beyond Words Publishing: Hillsboro, OR. 1993. (Revised.)

_____. *Men Are from Mars, Women Are from Venus.* HarperCollins: New York. 1992.

Green, Harvey. *The Light of the Home: An Intimate View of the Lives of Women in Victorian America.* Pantheon: New York. 1983.

Gurian, Michael. *The Wonder of Boys: What Parents, Mentors and Educators Can Do to Shape Boys into Exceptional Men.* Putnam: New York. 1996.

Hanigsberg, Julia E. & Sara Ruddick (eds.). *Mother Troubles: Rethinking Contemporary Maternal Dilemmas.* Beacon Press: Boston, 1999.

Harris, Thomas A. *I'm O.K.—You're O.K.* Harper and Row: New York. 1973.

Hendrix, Harville. *Getting the Love You Want: A Guide for Couples.* Harper Perennial: New York. 1988.

Heyn, Dalma. *Marriage Shock: The Transformation of Women into Wives.* Villard: New York. 1997.

Jones, Merry Bloch. *I Love Him, But . . . the Things That Men Do That Drive Their Wives Crazy.* Workman: New York. 1995.

Karpel, Mark A. *Evaluating Couples: A Handbook for Practitioners.* Norton: New York. 1994.

Kramer, Peter D. *Should You Leave: A Psychiatrist Explores Intimacy and Autonomy—and the Nature of Advice.* Scribner: New York. 1997.

_____. *Listening To Prozac.* Viking Penguin: New York. 1993.

Kimbrell, Andrew. *The Masculine Mystique.* Ballantine: New York. 1995.

Marlin, George J., Richard P. Rabatin, and John L. Swan. (ed.) *The Quotable Chesterton: A Topical Compilation of the Wit, Wisdom, and Satire of G. K. Chesterton.* Doubleday: New York. 1987.

Masters, W.H., and V.E.Johnson. *Human Sexual Response.* Little, Brown: Boston. 1966.

_____. *Human Sexual Inadequacy.* Little, Brown: Boston. 1970.

_____ and Robert C. Kolodny. *Human Sexuality.* HarperCollins: New York. 1992. (4th ed.)

Moustakas, Clark E. *Loneliness and Love.* Prentice Hall: Englewood Cliffs, NJ. 1972.

O' Connor, Richard. *Undoing Depression: What Therapy Doesn't Teach You and Medication Can't Give You.* Little, Brown: Boston. 1997.

O'Faolain, Nuala. *Are You Somebody? The Accidental Memoir of a Dublin Woman.* Holt: New York. 1996.

Ornish, Dean. *Love & Survival; 8 Pathways to Intimacy and Health.* HarperCollins: New York. 1998.

Padovani, Martin H. *Healing Wounded Emotions: Overcoming Life's Hurts.* Twenty-Third Publications: Mystic, CT. 1987.

Paglia, Camille. *Sexual Personae: Art and Decadence from Nefertiti to Emily Dickinson.* Vintage: New York. 1991.

Peddy, Shirley. *The Art of Mentoring: Lead, Follow and Get Out of the Way.* Bullion Books: Houston, TX. 1998.

Peck, Scott. *Denial of the Soul.* Crown: New York. 1997.

_____. *The Road Less Traveled.* Simon and Schuster: New York. 1978. (Touchstone.)

Pollack, William. *Real Boys: Rescuing Our Sons from the Myths of Boyhood.* Henry Holt: New York. 1998.

Powell, John. *Happiness Is an Inside Job.* Tabor: Valencia, CA. 1989.

_____. *Why Am I Afraid to Love?* Argus: Niles, IL. 1972.

Reagan, Michael, and Bob Phillips. *All-American Quote Book.* Harvest House: Eugene, OR (1995.)

Real, Terence. *I Don't Want to Talk About It: Overcoming the Secret Legacy of Male Depression.* Simon & Schuster: New York. 1997.

Roberts, Cokie. *We Are Our Mother's Daughters.* Morrow: New York. 1998.

Rosen, Laura Epstein, and Xavier Francisco Amador. *When Someone You Love Is Depressed: How to Help Your Loved One Without Losing Yourself.* The Free Press: New York. 1996.

Scarf, Maggie. *Intimate Partners: Patterns in Love and Marriage.* Ballantine: New York. 1988.

Schaller, James A. *It's Your Life: A Gynecologist's Guide For Taking Control of It.* Blue Dolphin Press: Nevada City, CA. (1997.)

Schaller, James A. *It's Your Life: a Gynecologist Challenges You to Take Control.* Blue Dolphin Press: Nevada City, CA. (Revision, 1999.)

Schaller, James L. *In Search of Lost Fathering: Rebuilding Your Father Relationship.* Baker Books:Grand Rapids, MI (1995.)

Schnarch, David. *Passionate Marriage: Sex, Love, and Intimacy in Emotionally Committed Relationships.* Norton: New York. 1997.

_____. *Constructing the Sexual Crucible: An Integration of Sexual and Marital Therapy.* Norton: New York. 1991.

Sher, Barbara. *Live the Life You Love: In Ten Easy Step-By-Step Lessons.* Delacorte Press: New York. 1996.

Silverstein, Olga, and Barbara Rushbaum. *The Courage to Raise Good Men.* Viking: New York. 1994.

Sinatra, Nancy. *Frank Sinatra: An American Legend.* Reader's Digest Ass. Pleasantville: NY (1998-Special Edition.)

Tannen, Deborah. *You Just Don't Understand: Men and Women in Conversation.* Ballantine: New York. 1990.

_____. *That's Not What I Meant! How Conversational Style Makes or Breaks Your Relationship with Others.* Morrow: New York. 1990.

Tournier, Paul. *To Understand Each Other: Why Love Dies and How to Make It Live Again.* John Knox: Atlanta, GA. 1977.

Twerski, Abraham J. *Substance-Abusing High Achievers: Addiction As an Equal Opportunity Destroyer.* Jason Aronson: Northvale, NJ. 1998.

Valentis, Mary and Anne Devane. *Female Rage: Unlocking Its Secrets, Claiming Its Power.* Carol Southern Books: New York. 1994.

Vitz, Paul C. *Psychology As Religion: The Cult of Self-Worship.* Wm.B. Eerdmans: Grand Rapids MI. (1994. 2nd Edition.)

Wallerstein, Judith and Stephen Blakeslee. *The Good Marriage.* Houghton Mifflin: Boston. 1995.

Weingarten, Kathy. *The Mother's Voice: Strengthening Initmacy in Families.* Harcourt, Brace: New York. 1994.

Westheimer, Ruth and Ben Yagoda. *The Value of Family: A Blueprint for the 21th Century.* Warner; New York. 1996.

Wolf, Naomi. *Promiscuities: The Secret Struggle for Womanhood.* Random House: New York. 1997

Acknowledgments

This book would never have been attempted were it not for the principles championed by two Ph. D.s, John Gray and David Schnarch. The life work of both men has been helping men and women achieve their potential for fulfillment in marriage.

John Gray's insistence that the differences between men and women exist independently of nurture was in direct opposition to the "gender" or "sameness" feminists whose ideas were subverting the dialogue on male-female issues. His nearly three decades of treating patients and teaching, and his immensely-popular books, have brought into clear focus the unalterable gender differences that produce conflict and misunderstanding.

For example, Gray's pivotal insight that a man is pleased and happy when a woman provides him clear opportunities to fulfill her desires, and a women is most fulfilled when her desires are met, corrects the common, but mistaken, notion that a woman's eagerness to please a man will increase his interest in her. It might do that briefly, but more likely he will "help" her to focus on how she can please him.

Gray's works, including his nine bestsellers, are contributing not only to the improvement of communication between the sexes, and to their understanding of each other, but they are also providing men and women with deeper insights into **themselves.** It is for this last contribution, that those of us who take up the quest for intimacy should be most grateful.

David Schnarch, a sensitive and experienced clinician, has described and defined an interpersonal state of intimacy at a level of refinement never previously attained by anyone.

Schnarch's insights into "human sexuality" are so profound and inspiring, and so vastly different from prevailing theory, that a prime architect of the current treatment of sexual dysfunction, William Masters, has insisted that Schnarch's ideas should not only be understood, but also mastered, by all psychotherapists.

Starting with an encyclopedic identification and understanding of virtually all the theories applied in marital and sexual and family systems therapy, he has achieved—in his seminars, writing, and clinical practice—not only a meaningful integration of the best and most effective treatment, but he has also provided lucid guidelines for the ways to become one of the "select few," whose marriages live up to potential.

My ideas on "growing up" as an essential precondition for both "great sex" and "intimacy," are clearly modeled on Schnarch's.

Constructing the Sexual Crucible: An Integration of Sexual and Marital Therapy is out of print, but still available on the Internet and in some larger bookstores. This book is meant for therapists, but still worth finding and studying. *Passionate Marriage: Sex, Love, and Intimacy in Emotionally Committed Relationships* is intended for anyone seeking a better relationship.)

I take full credit for all the errors and inadequacies found in these pages.

For all the good things, much credit must be given to:

Paul Clemens, my publisher who has taken on the role of editor for this book, both because he believed in what I had to say and because I desperately needed his guidance to say it.

To Charles Mungan and Rev. Jerry Finnegan, S. J. What they didn't say after carefully reading an early manuscript sent me rushing back to the drawing board in search of a new approach.

To my pastor, Fr. Arthur E. Rodgers, whose Doctorate of Philosophy did not prevent him from cautioning me that certain things are better left unsaid.

To Roger Van Allen, Ph.D., whose eight suggestions were immediately incorporated into my book and cover.

To my oldest son, James Louis, whose nine months effort when I was starting my book pointed me in the best direction, and to my wife, Marianne Eugenia, whose five month effort at the end forced me to make clarity my main priority.

Index

Note:
- Page numbers followed by *m* indicate passing mentions.
- Page numbers followed by *n* or *nn* indicate one or more endnotes. Note numbers follow the *n*s, and chapter numbers in parentheses follow for clarification when necessary.
- Page numbers followed by *q* indicate quotations.
- Page numbers followed by *w* indicate works cited.

criticism (of others) *(continued)*:
  hurtful, 110, 134, 134–135
  husbands and, 73, 109, 133
  husbands' evaluations, 23
  hypersensitivity to, 135
  inadequacy and, 133
  in marriage, 71, 108–111, 133–135, 215
  scorn (mockery) of children, 19,
    231*n3*
  wives and, 23, 109, 133
  wives' judgments, 73
crying. *See* tears
cultural imperatives for girls, 10
cynicism in marriage, 110

D
Dante, 29*q*
dark side of man, 78–79, 90
  See also sin
Darth Vader, 232*n2*
daughters. *See* girls
David, Deborah, 229–230*n12*
demands: needs expressed as, 74
DeMello, Anthony, 233*n3(ch4)*
denial:
  of faults, 83, 90
  of women's sexuality, 237*n19(ch6)*
dependency (neediness), 148
  expressions of, 48, 109
  and intimacy, 47–48
  sharing and, 112, 128
  in women, 48
  See also co-dependency
depression, xiv–xv
  in boys, 224*n1*
  covert, 225–226*n4*
  distrust/hostility/cynicism and, 110
  euphemisms, xiii
  in men, xiii–xv, 72–73, 225–226*n4*
  prevalence, 225*n4*
  treating, 72–73
  in women, 51, 72, 223*n3*, 225*n4*, 237–
    238*n6*, 249*n1*
  See also addictions
desire(s):
  and suffering, 233*n3(ch4)*
  unawareness of, 183–184
  See also sexual desire(s)
destiny: personal responsibility for, 181
destructive behavior, 5
  and bad marriages, 23
  See also addictions; violence

destructive force of closeness, 99, 100–
    102, 114, 247*n3*
Devane, Anne, 236*n17*
devotion to family, 207
Dewar, James, 179
Dewey, John, 4, 239–240*n1(ch12)*
Diana (Princess of Wales), 61
Diary of Anne Frank, 244*n2*
Dickens, Charles: *A Christmas Carol*,
    181–182, 183
differentiation, 93–97, 244*n5*
  affiliation and, 94
  and closeness, 95, 96
  and interdependence, 94–95, 96
  and intimacy, 96–97
  and self-sacrifice, 94–95
  and sexual dysfunctions, 161–166
  theoretical disputes over, 94, 97
  See also growing up; maturity
directives: resistance to, 254*n4*
disclosure reciprocity, 244–245*n6*
disconnection (isolation), 3–4, 83, 113,
    232*n1*
  individualism as, 94
  Narcissus, 7, 34, 104, 228*n6*
  separation of sons from mothers, 1*q*,
    22, 34, 205, 232*n1*
  and violence, 5, 20, 35
  See also individuality (aloneness/
    separation)
disillusionment with marriage, 62, 110
disputes. *See* conflict (in personal
    relationships); marital conflicts
distrust between spouses, 110
divorce:
  remarriage rate, 238*n7*
  and women, 52
Donovan, James E., 225*n4*, 254*n4*
dreams of men, 65–66
dreams of women, 66–67
dress: simplicity of Amish, 234*n3*
Dubois, Rene, 243*n5*
dumping emotions, 116

E
eating disorders, 176
eating meals together (in families),
    249*n1*
education: humanist ideal, 78, 81
emasculating wives. *See* castrating
    wives
emotional immaturity, 120–121

men *(continued)*
  arrogance, 23, 56
  attitudes toward wives. *See under*
    husbands
  as boys, 65
  as breadwinners, 137–138, 153
  career focus, 56, 63, 75–76
  chivalry, 45
  communication with wives. *See under*
    husbands
  competence needs, 56, 74
  competitiveness, 152
    in sports, 27–28
  control issues, 30, 73, 77
  control of women, 30–34, 51–52, 53–
    54, 55, 237–238*n6*, 238*n1(ch8)*
  coping with inadequacy, 29–38
  criticism of, 18, 19, 73, 109, 133
  and crying, 16–17
  depression in, xiii–xv, 72–73, 225–
    226*n4*
  differences between women and. *See*
    gender differences
  dreams/fantasies, 65–66
  empowerment by women, 72–73,
    109–110, 113–114, 239*n1(ch11)*
  as endangered, 228–229*n8*
  equality/inequality of women. *See*
    gender equality
  fear: of dying without love, 185
  and feelings, x, xi, xiv, 7–8, 14–15, 24
    See also feelings
  feminine side, 97
  feminist approaches to, xvi–xvii, 17
  flight reaction, 18, 64, 109
  heroes, 3, 27
  heroes as models for, 202–203
  and housework, 55, 64–65, 74
  ideals. *See* femininity; manliness
  inferiority complexes, 56
  and intimacy, 97, 246*n9*
  as judged, 61–62
  life expectancy, 223*n3*
  listening by, 55, 151–152, 251*n2*
  marriage and, xi, 55, 56, 63, 76, 91,
    223*n2*
  misogynists, 32–33, 192
  nonromantic, 48
  as obstacles to change, 205
  priorities, 56, 150, 203
  and projects, 55, 74
  and quests, 65, 203

men *(continued)*
  relating style, 151–153
  sexual desires, 146, 147, 148
  sexual dysfunctions. *See* sexual
    dysfunctions
  stinginess, 55, 56
  stoicism, 3, 11–12, 26, 232*n1*
  superiority complexes, 56
  tragedy of, 206, 207
  twentieth century men and women,
    203–204
  violence against, 5, 228–229*n8*
  violence of, 4–5, 20, 35, 88–89, 229*n9*
  vulnerability, 14–15
    to women, 23, 46, 165
  wives' communication with. *See*
    under wives
  women's attitudes toward:
    misunderstandings, 73, 137–138,
      150–151, 153, 250–251*n1(ch21)*
    resentment, 73, 150, 207
    See also wives: attitudes toward
      husbands
  women's control of, 49, 146–147
  See also boys (sons); husbands;
    manhood; manliness
Men's Movement, 22–23, 25, 49, 208
Menchen, H. L., 85*q*
mental illness: in America, 242*n4*
mentors: as powerful, 13
Mercer, Johnny, 255*n2(ch27)*
Merton, Thomas, 191*q*
mind:
  heart and, 179
  and sex, 166, 168, 168–170
misogynists: as husbands, 32–33, 192
misunderstandings of men by women,
    73, 137–138, 150–151, 153, 250–
    251*n1(ch21)*
mockery (scorn): of children, 19, 231*n3*
modern psychology: view of man, 78
modesty: of women, 44–45, 235*nn9–12*,
    253*n7*
Moir, Anne, 229*n9*
mommy's boys, 34
money: men's stinginess with, 55
Moore, Rev. James W.: homily, 218–219
moral relativism, 188, 240*n1*
moral values:
  decline of: and violence in America,
    188–189
  fostering, 193–194

Perceval (Grail legend), 76*m*, 202, 203, 232*n*2
perfection, 112
performance adequacy (in sex), 47, 149, 171
performance anxiety (about sex), 161–166, 252*n*1
  overcoming, 162, 163–166
  self-regard and, 163, 170
  and sexual desire, 163–164, 165
personal relationships:
  acquisitions as substitutes for, 108
  conflict in, 127, 184, 234*n*6(*ch5*)
  displaced anger in, 118
  improving, 174–179
  See also growing up
  integrity in, 128, 143
  intimacy in. *See* intimacy
  loving, 206
  need for, 77, 224*n*4
  personal responsibility and, 90, 121, 241*n*5
  prerequisites, 93, 241*n*5
  self-acceptance and, 93, 183, 241*n*5
  self-awareness and, 241*n*5
  self-regard and, 201
  solution for troubled relationships, 36–37
  styles of relating, 226–227*n*3, 227–228*n*4, 252*n*5
    gender differences, 151–152, 251*n*3
  TA and inadequacy in, 79–82
  tragedy in, 112, 200
  TV and, xviii–xix
  understanding through TA, 83–84
  victory in, 83–84
  See also love affairs; marriage (marriages)
personal responsibility:
  challenging people to accept, 254*n*4
  closeness and, 116
  for destiny, 181
  for happiness, 180
  and intimacy, 93
  for marriage, 90, 136, 142, 180–181
    failed marriages, 192–193
  and personal relationships, 90, 121, 241*n*5
  self-acceptance and, 38
  self-regard and, 36–37, 141–142
  in TA, 82
Peter Pan (Barrie), 51, 237*n*4
Phillips, Bob, 251*n*3, 254*n*2(*ch25*)

physical abuse. *See* violence
Piaget, Jean, 240*n*3
placating spouses, 135
  See also compromise (in marital conflicts)
pleasure:
  hiding feelings of, 145–147
  of men in pleasing women, 48, 73–74, 236*n*16
  of sex, 168–169, 253*n*7
Pollack, William, 3*q*
  on connecting with sons, 231*n*16
  on depression in boys, 224*n*1
  on ideals for men, 227*nn*4,5, 229–230*n*12
  on school violence prevention, 257*n*2
  on separation of sons from mothers, 1*q*, 232*n*1
  on shame, 231*n*16
  on sports, 233*n*1(*ch4*)
Popenoe, David, 227*n*5
pornography:
  vs. erotic literature, 236*n*18
  substituting for spouses, 164
postmodern couples, 157–158, 252–253*n*3
Powell, John, 226–227*n*3
power-struggle phase in marriages, 70–71, 83–84, 132–136
  moving beyond, 136
preferred self, 131, 182
premature ejaculation, 170
  See also performance anxiety (about sex)
primary caregivers. *See* parents/primary caregivers
prime of life, 167–168
Prince Charming, 67, 238*n*6
priorities (of men), 56, 150, 203
  career focus, 56, 63, 75–76
  national leaders, 204–205
  Schaller (author), 75, 185, 203
procreative sex, 148–149
projective identification. *See* carried feelings
projects: men and, 55, 74
  See also quests
The Prophet (Gibran), 248*n*6
provokers, 70
psychiatry: rationale for, 78–79
psycho-sexual development theories, 243–244*n*1
psychology, modern: view of man, 78

About the Author

The first day of the new millennium marked the first day of a **new emphasis** in the career of James A. Schaller.

Dr. Schaller has arranged for another board-certified obstetrician-gynecologist to take over his office, limiting his role with patients to explaining their best health options. His purpose is to allow each patient, working in concert with her own physician, to choose the plan for health that best suits her own objectives and life-style.

Instead of one-on-one patient care, the author and his wife of forty years, Marianne, are traveling America to spread the message contained in the two books published this year: *"If you wish to maximize your chances for health and a happy relationship, you have to select a plan and give it your time and energy."*

Dr. Schaller is the scientific advisor for women's health for vitacost.com, the place to get quality nutritional supplements from many different companies at wholesale prices, and the place to get the latest information on all the most important health issues.

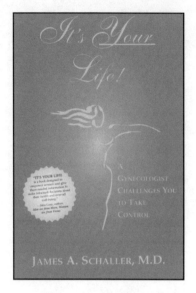

It's Your Life!

A Gynecologist Challenges You to Take Control

James A. Schaller, M.D.

ISBN: 1-57733-004-8, paperback, $16.95

Dr. Schaller believes a woman should make her *own* choices! *It's Your Life* provides answers to a woman's most important questions, giving her the information she needs to make choices wisely.

Written for the millions of girls and women who have questions about their bodies, their feelings and emotions, their relationships, even life's purpose, Dr. Schaller's warm and friendly book is brimming with useful information on a wide range of women's medical issues. Puberty, PMS, pregnancy, sexuality, menopause are just a few. In addition, he has written a completely engaging summary of information on women's issues, self-help, relationships, and family life.

Witnessing the body/mind connection again and again, he feels women must empower themselves in every aspect of their lives. Part of this is realizing that their own needs are just as important as all the people whom they nurture.

At the end of a medical appointment, he would at times ask his patient, "Now, what's really going on?" After thirty years of listening to women's intimate concerns, Dr. Schaller shares the way relationships and personal problems become reflected in medical symptoms and illness, and offers sensitive, intimate advice to every woman.